TEACHER'S STORIES, TEACHER'S LIVES

TEACHER'S STORIES, TEACHER'S LIVES

CAROLA CONLE

WITH

ROBIN HOFFMAN
MICHELE PINET
LOREEN TEOLI
JOSEPH TOTARO

Nova Science Publishers, Inc.
New York

Copyright © 2006 by Nova Science Publishers, Inc.

For permission to use material from this book please contact us:
Telephone 631-231-7269; Fax 631-231-8175
Web Site: http://www.novapublishers.com

NOTICE TO THE READER

LIBRARY OF CONGRESS CATALOGING-IN-PUBLICATION DATA
Teacher's stories, teacher's lives / Carola Conle (editor)
        p. cm.
Includes index.
ISBN 1-59454-472-7
1. Teachers--Training of--Canada--Case studies. 2. Education--Study and teaching (Higher)--Canada--Case studies. 3. Education--Biographical methods--Case studies. I. Conle, Carola.
LB2169.C2T43   2006
370.71'171--dc22 2005030350

Published by Nova Science Publishers, Inc. ✦*New York*

CONTENTS

INTRODUCTION

Carola Conle

"Tell me how to teach" is the urgent plea of many of my student teachers in our rushed preservice programs. Many instructors do their best to provide them with models and strategies. Typically, candidates are happy on occasions when something worked and blame themselves, the strategies, or the instructor, on occasions when something did not work. Technical solutions are paramount.

In this book we demonstrate a mode of teacher education that is practical in a non-technical sense and relies on Dewey's notion of curriculum as the reconstruction of experience. We present a curriculum that emerged through collaborative self-reflection and seeks to reconstruct personal histories of schooling. As four former preservice teachers and their instructor, we engaged in jointly constructed autobiographical inquiry in order to generate data on our own past and on our current histories of teaching and learning. We wanted to illuminate parts of our lives in schools that until now belonged to our 'normal' and taken-for-granted past. We did this in order to enjoy certain degrees of awareness and choice as to which of our living stories to reinforce and which to "let run out" in our classrooms today.

WHY NARRATIVE IN PRESERVICE TEACHER EDUCATION

I can only answer the question "What am I to do?" if I can answer the prior question "Of what story or stories do I find myself a part?" We enter human society, [...] with one or more imputed characters – roles into which we have been drafted – and we have to learn what they are in order to understand how others respond to us and how our responses to them are apt to be construed (MacIntyre, 1984, 216).

As teachers we make many decisions every minute of our teaching day. When we "think on our feet" (researchers such as Schön [1983] have called it reflection – in – action), deliberation is very quick, but decisions are nevertheless made. When more time for deliberation is available, perhaps we begin to worry, wonder, ponder and puzzle-out situations. What we write in this book is based on our agreement with MacIntyre, that in all of those moments of decision-making, we situate ourselves within story lines. In practice this means, we constantly think about who did what, where, when and why; we talk about who might do this or that, if... . We want to be such and such a person/character with this or that kind of qualities. We try to become clearer about the "roles into which we have been drafted"; we want to learn what they are in order to be able to understand how our students and their parents, how our colleagues and superiors, are apt to construe our actions.

Such desires are part of the moral dimension of our teaching lives. As moral agents we are characters in – and co-author of – enacted, experiential narratives. We tell our experiences to ourselves and to others to figure out what we are to do, in teaching, as well as in our everyday lives. During preservice, we appreciated the opportunity to initiate a mode of reflection that made us more aware of the stories of which we are a part. This is the motivation for our work in this book. In our view it has helped us act with greater self-confidence in our classroom and react to our students more tolerantly and appropriately. All five of us are convinced that because the narrative work has made us more conscious of the stories in our own lives and in the lives of those people with whom we share our educational settings, we are more prepared to take into account the personal situations of our students.

Narrative preservice work therefore seems to have started us, the instructor and her beginning teachers, on a road that seems commonsensical. It is also prompted by the need for teachers to understand student thinking. It was a way around the danger of seeing students as objects who need to meet performance and content standards.

Inquiry into "teacher thinking" has moved research onto a narrative path (Elbaz 1991). It is very likely that inquiry into "students thinking" will progress along the same path. We feel that our work is preparing a road to inquiry in that area.

In 1992, I as the instructor,[1] began to work with teaching candidates, basing the three courses I taught in the Foundational Studies Department on various forms of self-reflection. I soon found out from students that they had little use for all that reflection. The institution was in the midst of a renewal and I was part of a wave of newly hired faculty. The most prominent new orientations promoted classroom management techniques and co-operative learning techniques. These satisfied the students' all pervasive need for "how-to." Reflection did not seem a pressing need, survival was.

Only a few weeks after they arrive at our faculty, our institution sends candidates out into practicum sessions in the schools. They are evaluated by their associate teachers almost from day one of their arrival. In this setting, the candidates involved in this study wanted help, not only to survive this evaluation, but to do well in an extremely competitive market where 90 % of graduates were not being hired, except perhaps on one-year contracts or as temporary help in the schools[2].

I did not want to change my agenda because I appreciated the legitimacy of John Dewey's arguments against an early focus on teaching proficiency. How could I attend to the students' reality and still heed Dewey's warnings? In 1904, Dewey explained very carefully why teaching candidates needed to examine their own and their students' lives, rather than putting their initial efforts into classroom management and proficient teaching. He warned that "immediate skill may be got at the cost of power to go on growing" (1974, 320). Teacher preparation should be a process of "turning back upon one's own experiences, and turning them over to see how they were developed, what helped and hindered, the stimuli and the inhibitions both within and without" (324). This supports Socrates' dictum that the unexamined life is not worth living.

I decided that I was going to risk working against the flow that actually seemed to be an institutional tidal wave. I would try to convince my students that they would need to understand. Not only understand the subject matter that was the focus of their curriculum courses, but, especially in their foundational courses, they would need to understand themselves, their students, and their institutional contexts, in order to make educational decisions in their classrooms. Our task was to understand, not only to transmit. How could I prepare teachers for this task? Since I was in the Department of Foundational Studies, not in Curriculum and Instruction, I was not going to concentrate on understanding subject matter, but on the other three areas of understanding: self, student and milieu.

Essentially, both my students and I have to prepare ourselves to become competent interpreters of self and others and of our social environments. We have to establish habits that will continue throughout our teaching careers. To understand self, others and our milieu, we would, I decided, study our experiences, keeping in mind that the result would be not facts, but interpretive understandings. The interpretations would be made from particular vantage points and within particular horizons, created by particular socio-cultural histories. In other words, our understandings would be understandings within time and would be subject to change.

What was to be our method of inquiry? How could we stay closely connected to our practical experiences and be sensitive to temporal and physical contexts? The narrative inquiry that I had practiced and reflected on as a graduate student (Connelly and Clandinin 1988, Conle 1996, 1999, 2000) was a method of study that could potentially fulfill all those requirements. It had been a method of research for me. Could it become a method of inquiry for my students?

There was no well developed model, tried and tested, at least not in preservice education. I needed to explore and experiment, as well as understand and conceptualize, what I was doing as I proceeded. In the first four or five years I engaged in copious reflective projects, using student feedback, formal and informal self-study, and joint reflection with peers after mutual observation. Through the practical experience of teaching, the familiarity of certain concepts often shifted into a new focus; and it seemed as if I understood them for the first time. The professional development agenda I had in mind for my students, was also a narrative action research and learning agenda for me. In other words, I too was a student in a narrative curriculum.

Over the next few years I developed various key narrative activities that became the basis for the courses I taught. The narrative assignments fell into five categories:

1) Focusing on their immediate milieu, students, in pairs, studied a school of their choice and created a narrative *Portrait of a School.*

2) Focusing on understanding self and prior experiences in schools, each candidate wrote and told a *Personal Narrative of Teaching and Learning.* This was a major assignment, usually between 15 to 25 pages in length. Four of these in chapters 2-5.

3) Focusing on their racial, religious, class or ethnic background, each candidate wrote a *Personal Cultural Narrative.* Students were not to present themselves as good examples of sociological research, but were asked to narrate their experiences. Many of the narratives were at least partially shared with classmates. In this sharing the curricular focus shifted from understanding self to understanding others, especially those others that were different from self in major respects.

My classes are socio-culturally quite heterogeneous and students had to listen to stories that portrayed views and customs with which they were often uncomfortable. The sharing of personal narratives did not lead to arguments. How can we argue with someone's experience? Instead the process involved resonance (Conle 1996), that is to say, it involved "me too" or "not me" reactions leading to further stories by the listeners. Often one's own stories were retold because of the vicarious experience of listening to difference. In this way, candidates prepared themselves for teaching the culturally highly heterogeneous classes awaiting them in our country of immigrants.

4) Finally, I also had my students construct narrative versions of the techniques and strategies they encountered and used in their practicums. These stories of teaching practice made available to reflection the kind of action and knowledge that often get submerged in the hectic and tension-filled life of the student teacher.[3] As they listened to their colleagues narrative versions of "how-to" experiences, their own repertoire was enriched through the input of vicarious experience such narratives offered.

Another input consisted of the theoretical readings I assigned: articles about narrative inquiry, about multiculturalism, racism, gender in the curriculum, about a variety of school settings and educational philosophies. This theoretical input often became fodder for further narratives about self, others and educational settings. It also often changed the perspectives from which a candidate originally told a particular story. It could change the story itself, since the perspectives from which a story is told are always an integral part of the story itself.

In what way were these narrative activities particularly productive educationally? I have a large collection of reflective comments from students on the process as they saw it. Many mentioned a heightened sense of self-confidence, a sense of community, a better understanding of what students bring with them into their classroom, an awareness of their ability to choose the best from different cultural background, an increased ability to discuss "what influenced me," or "comfort to know that I'm not the only person to feel these tensions." However I have as yet no systematic study in this area, especially since only some of the roughly one thousand students we graduate every year were getting jobs in the no hiring environment at the time, and only some of these hired students have taken my courses. To my knowledge there is as yet no formal study about the effects of narrative curricula on candidates' teaching performance.

The basis of the narrative curricula as portrayed in this book is their connection to experience. Dewey argues against seeing education predominantly as the acquisition of information, against leaving aside its experiential and moral dimensions.

Already in 1904, Dewey noticed that education was often in danger of becoming a presentation of a "body of facts and truths ascertained by others" or a mere "record of knowledge [...] taken to *be* knowledge" (366). Knowledge was being identified with "propositions stating information" (366) because "the mind of man [was] taken captive by the spoils of its prior victories" (366).

The dangers Dewey began to notice in 1904 have become overwhelming problems in the schools of our day. Teachers are entreated to teach a confusing array of subject matter in an increasingly confused social context. The confusion entail lack of meaning. According to Postman (1995), old "gods" are discredited and new gods are either socially dysfunctional or non-existent. Postman's gods are providers of meaning. Students find little meaning in their education, he warns, other than perhaps job preparation. A teacher might ask in frustration: Are we to educate students for now largely non-existent communal life? Are we to transmit knowledge that will be, or is already, outdated? Where is the moral, social consensus from which, or toward which, we are to proceed? How are we to counter the early onslaught of violence on our students' imagination in a media-constituted and computerized environment? What do we do with the unexamined meanings derived from advertisements and commercials? Are we to pass on to children and teens our own postmodern skepticism and moral relativism? Are we to do all this when we as educators and researchers don't really know ourselves? Often we are "like instruments on which fashion and habit play their tunes, or like stage masks through which an actor's voice speaks" (Nussbaum 1997, 29). Confusion that comes about when education turns into a mere array of hopefully useful information, but nevertheless fails to help students make meaning of their actions, lives and contexts. It might begin to clear when students of all ages are afforded an education that uses their past life experiences and provides new experience. Dewey stresses the connection between three kinds of experience: the individual experience of the child, the cumulative experience represented in subject matter and the experience of a social community. Narrative curricula have the potential to do this; they work with, and on, student's past experiences and create new, in-class experiences (Conle 1996, Conle 1997).

There are voices advocating the usefulness of narrative and these voices all speak to the litany of ills I have just alluded to. They advocate narrative as a way of making meaning and of staying close to experience. It is seen as a feature of socialization that has the potential to reinstate, if not "gods," then some common values and purposes.

Noddings (1997, 13) perceives the cultivation of "narrative imagination as an essential preparation for moral interaction" (90) and Nussbaum (1997, 110) perceives it as a vehicle for multicultural world citizenship. Johnson (1993, 198) believes that "moral understanding is in large measure imaginatively structured" and that narrative can give voice to the contents of our moral imagination. "Tracing out over an extended time period the consequences of various moral deliberations is [...] crucial to our moral knowledge, and it is essential for moral education. It is through sustained life narrative—through the narratives we live out and construct, and through the fictional narratives we imaginatively inhabit— that we can perform these essential reflections and moral inquiries" (197). Furthermore, there is the conviction that narrative can give meaning to a world of education in which economic ends provide an inadequate reason for schooling and student achievement (Postman 1995). How could narrative accomplish all this? Narratives, both fictional and experiential, bestow meaning through specifying contexts, characters, plotlines, beginnings and endings and implicit imperatives. The fragmented bits of information often presented in schools need narrative connections.

For curriculum purposes, we need to remember that narratives do not need to be fictional, but classmates' experiential stories can have a very powerful impact on an audience (Conle et al, 2000). In my classes, narrative exchanges have two functions, one oriented toward the past, the other to the future. One I view as a way to greater self-knowledge and as a way of "damage control." The other I see as an offer of possible futures and a means of moral acculturation, critique and development.

When we construct an experiential narrative, we open our past to possible reflection and revision. After all, much of what we say and do in the present, we do not freely choose. Instead we act propelled by the sedimentations of our past. In Nussbaum's words, "All too often people's choices and statements are not their own. Words come out of their mouths and actions are performed by their bodies, but what their words and actions express may be the voice of tradition or convention, the words of parents, of friends, of fashion" (Nussbaum 1997, 28).

Those sedimentations of the past, I propose, are not necessarily fixed and invariable, but current experiences can have an influence. In a narrative reconstruction of experience, we inevitably bring current perspectives to bear on the past and thus change the past as it is for us—perhaps in major ways, perhaps only ever so slightly (Conle 1997). The same change process can take effect when we listen to the experiential reconstructions of others. Through resonance (Conle

1996), we respond to their stories with memories of our own; and these memories are tacitly reconstructed in the process, for they are affected by the current narrative context. Gerrig (1993) explained this phenomenon psychologically, suggesting that what is affected by an immersion into a narrative world is what a listener or reader bring to the encounter. It is therefore less a question of integrating into our psyche or into our curricular knowledge what we encounter narratively; rather it is a matter of exposing to modification whatever prior personal practical knowledge (Connelly and Clandinin, 1988) emerges in resonance with the contents of the narratives offered. This could indeed be a powerful change process for student teachers, but it likely happens primarily without our conscious knowledge, although we may keep track of some of its effects, at least to a certain extent, through ongoing, narrative self-study.

Narrative is not only important in order to reflect on our past, it is important for our future. The stories we hear create possibilities for us. *The* truth about someone's past may be less important than the service a story renders in presenting to listeners what might be, or what they may so far have never considered. Stories thus open possibilities to our imagination. The quality of those possibilities is vital to the quality of our future. A person without access to certain stories is a person without hope, a person without social vision. In Frye's words: "We choose in accordance with our vision of society. The essential thing is the power of choice" (1963, 63). This means that the narratives available to us delimit our areas of choice. What could be more important in education? It is our narrative understanding that helps us distinguish the world we live in from the world we want to live in.

All of these matters are often totally neglected in teacher preparation. Noddings (1997, 14) asks: "Why are teachers so poorly prepared to draw on stories in their disciplinary instruction?" She provides a possible reason: There may be a dangerous gap between the narrow expertise characteristic of today's liberal studies and the equally narrow expertise characteristic of professional schools. [...] Few professors in these disciplines address the questions that were once thought to be central to liberal studies: How should I live? What kind of life is worth living? How could I find meaning in life? Education schools and departments also fail to address these questions and concentrate on pedagogy, classroom management, school structure and related topics."

Our experiential narrative inquiry offers vicarious experience that might help students find answers to some of those questions. Narrative curricula in teacher education could help legitimize the use of narrative in academic settings and free those teachers who are comfortable with it to work with experiential narratives with students in the intermediate and even in upper grades, as well as in primary school where narratives find a place more readily. Furthermore, since the teaching candidates I meet only rarely have had any experience with self-study or inquiry into their cultural traditions, a narrative curriculum at this stage can be seen as providing remedy and damage control to lives overburdened and desiccated with technical know-how or abstract theories. They have the potential to meaningfully connect with a student's spirit, emotions, and everyday existence.

REFERENCES

Conle, C. (1996) Resonance in pre-service teacher inquiry. *American Educational Research Journal,* 33 (2), 297–325.

Conle, C. (1997) Images of change in narrative inquiry. *Teachers and Teaching: theory and practice.,* 3 (2): 205-219.

Conle, C. (1999) Why narrative? Which narrative? Struggling with time and place in life and research. *Curriculum Inquiry,* 29 (1), 7–33.

Connelly, M. and Clandinin, J. (1988) *Teachers as Curriculum Planners: Narratives of Experience* (New York: Teachers College Press).

Conle, C, Blanchard, D., Burton, K., Higgins, A., Kelly, M., Sullivan, L. and Tan, J. 2000. The asset of cultural pluralism: an account of cross-cultural learning in pre-service teacher education. *Teaching and Teacher Education* 16(3): 365-387

Dewey, J. (1974 [1904]) The relation of theory to practice in education. In R. D. Archambault (ed.), *John Dewey on Education: Selected writings.* Chicago: University of Chicago Press, pp. 313–338

Frye, N. (1963) *The educated imagination: Massey Lectures Series* (Toronto, ON: Canadian Broadcasting Company).

Johnson, M. 1993. *Moral imagination.* Chicago and London: The University of Chicago Press.

Noddings, N. 1997. Character education and community. In A. Molnar (Ed.) *The construction of children's character.* Ninety-sixth Yearbook of the National Society for the Study of Education, (pp. 1 -16). Chicago: University of Chicago Press.

Nussbaum, M. (1997) *Cultivating Humanity. A Classical Defense of Liberal Education.* Boston, MA: Harvard Educational Press.

Postman, N. 1995. *The End of Education: Redefining the Value of School.* New York: Knopf.

Schön, D. 1983. *The Reflective Practitioner.* New York: Basic Books.

ENDNOTES

[1]   This introduction was written by Carola Conle with help of the four co-authors.
[2]   This situation lasted for about six years and is only beginning to change this year.
[3]   At this point it is not our focus to tell these stories in order to contribute to the discovery of implicit moral ends in the practice of teaching, as MacIntyre might have wished us to do. I do not see this to be a task for teaching candidates alone, although theirs would be an important voice if the profession as a whole decided to make it a priority. Chapter 8 presents a reflection on this exercise.

In: Teacher's Stories, Teacher's Lives
Editor: Carola Conle, pp. 1-28

ISBN 1-59454-472-7
© 2006 Nova Science Publishers, Inc.

Chapter 1

WHEN NARRATIVES MEET: INTERACTIVE SELF-STUDY IN PRE-SERVICE TEACHER EDUCATION

Carola Conle

SELF-STUDY AND THE AUTOBIOGRAPHICAL TRADITION

Self-study as an impetus and direction for curriculum is a new field in pre-service teacher development.[1] It emerged out of areas of narrative teacher inquiry (Connelly and Clandinin 1990, Clandinin et al. 1993), autobiographical work (Hunt 1987, Grumet 1988) and teacher educators' self-study (Hamilton and 1998). In this volume we present the narratives of four pre-service teachers and their instructor to demonstrate a particular quality of inquiry into practical knowledge (Elbaz 1983) that self-study in a pre-service course makes possible.

Traditionally, autobiographical work was considered an accumulation of historical events in the life of a great person, usually male, whose social status was sanctioned sufficiently for him to be considered a model worth imitating (Watson 1993). Autobiography became a retrospective reflection on how this greatness was achieved. In traditional, male autobiography, conflicts tended to be intellectual or spiritual, the self being presented as the stage of a battle of opposing forces or the struggle of a misunderstood genius in a hostile intellectual environment (Verene 1991). Although our stories below are not stories of greatness, but of ordinary lives, they are at times stories of stuggle in seemingly hostile environments.

Autobiographical writing by women or persons of low social status constitute a different tradition. Women wrote "domestic memoirs" (Peterson 1993, 88) about everyday events, framing their self-representations through their relationship to others, as wives, daughters and mothers. This aim created would conflict with attempts by woman writers who were artists or actresses and wanted to combine what were considered *chroniques scandaleuses* — warning tales about what happens to socially "unprotected" women — with their roles as mothers or daughters (Peterson 1993, 92-97). Conflicted relationships to institutional or cultural "others" often defined identity struggles in ex-slave narratives or other non-canonical autobiographies (Barrett 1993). Relational writing, identity struggles and descriptions of everyday events also define self-study in teacher development.

The work we present here is relational in the sense that we see ourselves connected to others rather than as protagonists dramatizing our successes. There are struggles of identity and we acknowledge tensions with our environment in our roles as learners, often trying to understand personal and institutional histories that are not easily integrated into current philosophies and demands. In our work, tensions and struggles are converted into a very specific inquiry dynamic that propels our personal engagement with our own writing and our collaboration with our colleagues as they pursue similar aims.

The emphasis on inquiry rather than on literary qualities or reader appeal distinguishes what we do. We draw on elements in the male autobiographical tradition in that our narratives are not only — or not primarily — literary pursuits, but fall into a tradition grounded in the ancient philosophical project of the search for self-knowledge, a tradition that Verene links to the Italian thinker Giambattista Vico (1728, 1731) who believed that to "understand something is to discover its origin and to trace its genesis" (1991, 71). We too try to understand how our current practical knowledge came to be what it is today, but unlike Vico, we see such tracing in a less singular way. Our inquiry is a road of many possible paths toward multiple discoveries, most profitably pursued by several people jointly engaged in narrative inquiry. Our stories are constructed through dialogue, not only with ourselves, but with our colleagues. Autobiography as a philosophical idea lets us take up the task of self-knowledge (Verene1991, 89); autobiography as a relational enterprise lets us recognize our reality as developmental or historical, and lets the teaching self be apprehended in a relational mode formed through jointly constructed stories that can and do change.

We found interactive self-study useful in that it eventually afforded us some choice with regard to reenactments of prior learning. Our task below is to convey an understanding of the curriculum we constructed for ourselves and to characterize the particular forms of inquiry that it made possible. The documentation arose from our work in the first year the course was offered.

A SELF-STUDY CURRICULUM

In this paper we —Robin, Joe, Michele and Loreen as four beginning teachers— and Carola, our instructor, relate our experiences in our pre-service course, *Teachers' Stories, Teachers' Lives (TSTL)*. The course was introduced into the one-year pre-service program in the Foundations of Education Department at the Faculty of Education, University of Toronto[2] by Carola in 1993. She came to understand her work with her students as based on their capacities to reconstruct their experiences (Dewey 1938), on narrative change processes (Conle 1997b) and on the need for self-study.[3]

As the year progressed, Carola realized that we[4] were creating for ourselves a curriculum that was propelled for each of us by a very personal inquiry dynamic. Through that dynamic we became better acquainted with ourselves as learners "with a history;" we explored that history in us and now use it as a basis for the instructional choices we make in classrooms. We feel that our stories are what is most important and unique about our work. They are what stays with us most. They are our change agents. We also think that, ideally, it will be the stories that will stay with our audience. For this reason, we keep a narrative structure for most of this paper, rather than one of reasoned argument. We hope that we might encourage you, our audience, in your own narrative inquiry.[5] In this chapter, after a description of central facets of the course, we take a cut from our stories. The slice we choose, we entitle "The Walking Wounded." Seeing our selections with this title in mind allows us to speak of some of the practical consequences of our inquiry, for each of us not only came upon some hurt in our lives as learners, but also recognized these hurts as special sensitivities with which we meet our students. As a result we are now able to see our collection of stories as narrative resources that help us meet 'the walking wounded' among our students. Getting to know our practical knowledge in that way gave us a certain degree of choice, for each of us also recognized in our lives fragile stories of teaching and learning that we cherish and want to strengthen.

The delivery of the course, *Teachers Stories; Teachers Lives,*[6] is based on the need for teachers to gather narrative data on their teaching and learning experiences. We wrote experiential stories, first in journals, then in lengthy personal narratives. This work was accompanied by readings on narrative theory and by published autobiographical material written by teachers or students (e.g. , William 1994; Solnick 1992; Kotlowitz 1991; Kidder 1989; Rodriguez 1982; Angelou 1969; Ashton Warner 1964, 1958.) We formed a small study group at the end of the 1993 course to continue our "final" personal narratives and to talk about our professional lives. What follows are excerpts from the latter course assignment, as well as insights gained through many conversations since 1993. In this chapter, we went about clarifying in our own minds the processes that propelled our work and we link them to existing theoretical constructs. Although this was indeed an unusual project for us, in many respects we simply continued the inquiry orientation of our course.

TEACHER PREPARATION AS NARRATIVE DATA GATHERING AND RESPONSE TO DATA

In narrative research, as well as in courses that promote narrative inquiry, there is a seamless transition from data gathering/generation to final products to be shared among participants. Course assignments in our inquiry-oriented course became quasi-research texts and were gradually worked into our final assignment, our personal narrative. We illustrate this process below. Later, after the end of the course, texts were elaborated and reflected upon during approximately twenty, taped and untaped, three-to-four-hour meetings over the span of two years. Final products emerged during a two-day retreat.

Sharing Journals and Working at "Lost Questions" through "Resonance"

At the beginning of the course we needed to become comfortable with each other. We started to share journals. Carola told us that the journals would not be evaluated, but had to be done, and that they could be about anything and of any length.[7] We would not have to censor our writing, but focus on whatever seemed to be of some significance to us at the time. It has been Carola's experience that when students write journals in such a non-directed way, they often begin to "get on a road intellectually that they are traveling already experientially." In other words, they begin to work on their life histories piecemeal. By writing out things that are important to them at the time, they unintentionally begin to sound important themes in their lives and relate them to their ongoing teacher preparation work. They begin to construct a curriculum for themselves that is based on an urgency to get to know themselves better in order to be better teachers.

This inquiry curriculum has two important dimensions; one tacit and one concrete in the inquirer's awareness. As we tell a story, we explore something consciously by telling whatever we know or remember about it. It is the immediate object of inquiry as a narrative episode is written. But the choice of episode is motivated in some way. It is not determined by the instructor. It is somehow an answer to a "lost question" (Conle, 2000) that gets gradually recovered in greater fullness as many stories are told. Carola named this question our tacit or indirect object of inquiry.[8] Robin's journal will begin to illustrate these two dimensions of self-study. She wrote a reflective piece about something that had a great impact on her when she worked with an associate teacher in her practicum. This episode was her journal focus in what Bruner (1993, 45) might call a discourse of witness.

Sharing

> Associate teacher is probed about his son's death. They know somehow—these kids. Some say they heard it on the news but really it happened seven years ago—most of them would have been nine or ten. They pepper him with questions: Who did it? Where did they get the guns? How long did it take you and your wife to get over it? In Round Lake? You buried him *in* Round Lake? Did you want to get the kid who did it? Just pummel him? I would have wanted to just wrap him up!
>
> Finally the teacher goes and runs off a story from his computer. It's a wrenching account of his grief–a letter of sorts–to his son, who would have been nineteen by now. The class is silent–although preoccupied with who might be crying–Mr. Elliot[9] included. Finally at the end they ask more questions–amazing questions. What do you do on his birthday? Have you been back to the grave? Who do you blame? Do you every talk to the other boy? What happened to him? Sir? Did anything happen to him? Maybe you should talk to him.
>
> Turns out he brings a rosebush home every year and he and his wife plant it around the house. Wow.

Robin chose to write this in her journal. This student-teacher relationship implied here is a personal one, a trusting one. Only eventually, Robin came to realize that much of her writing and many of her conversations were motivated by a wish to keep her teacher-student roles flexible and free of labels. We might say, she tacitly selected the above piece as a signpost for a not-yet-named inquiry into a "lost question" about the issue of labelling and teacher-student relationships. More of this below.

Just as the teacher and his students in Robin's school, we in our course responded to each other; and Carola as our instructor noticed the bonding that happened through the sharing of experiential stories. Trust began to emerge, at least at the level of small groups of four or five people who frequently heard each other's stories. As Carola responded to journals each week, we began to feel more comfortable with her as well.

Carola had by then shared a journal of her own, one in which she inquired into events in her life that she linked to prejudice and stereotyping. Since all of us will very likely be working in multiethnic classrooms, we often ponder how we might deal with racism, prejudice and cultural identities. Carola also taught a course in Cross-Cultural Education and believed that in those matters we need to "start with ourselves" (Hidalgo 1993). She gave us a sense of this by sharing her journal with us. Just after writing it, she said she had a sense of tension, that there was something embarrassing or incriminating about it, but she nevertheless later passed the journal on to us. She gave it with the comment: "I think I was exploring my own prejudices here, something I feel I ought to do, if I want to explore multicultural education." Carola said that the journal had been significant for her in her earlier work, because it was an effort to "do something which is hard to do." She believes that we have strong inner barriers against seeing ourselves as prejudicial or racist individuals. Yet our histories — Carola's German history in particular, but also most cultural traditions we know — are filled with heavy racist and discriminatory practices. Some contend that whether we know it or not, whether we like it or not, this history is active within us (Mitscherlich 1993, Wolf 1976/1980).[10] After writing the journal, Carola said, she realized that perhaps her "lost question" had to do with her cultural history.

Through our stories we began to get some data that made us more aware of our personal educational histories. We needed this data, if we did not want to give free reign to our prejudgments, if we wanted to become aware of our own personal and cultural biography and its limiting traditions. What we subsequently do with what we have inherited is what really matters. This is probably as true of our cultural histories as it is of our educational ones. But often the inquiry into our lives and histories can only happen indirectly and by seemingly minute steps. A journal can be one of these steps.

A reader may wonder at the far-flung reach of the journals we present, at their stream-of-consciousness quality, their lack of structure and editing. If these journals are a means to gather data on ourselves, they have to be written in a manner that draws on a wide range of events and issues. After all, we do not know what that indirect, tacit object of inquiry — the "lost question" — of our data gathering will be. If we knew what we were looking for, we would not need to gather data or we would gather it in a more selective fashion.

Journals in this course are data-gathering devices for self-study, where indirectly — while we focus on a particular story — data emerges that will most likely become part of a larger account, or trigger data in someone else's inquiry. Getting to know our own makeup is difficult, and virtually impossible, if there are personal and social taboos or sanctions against certain behaviours and characteristics. When we let down our guard a little, as Carola did in her journal, we can at least begin to ask some questions. Some of these questions lead to further reading. For example, after asking herself questions about her personal past in post-war Germany, Carola decided to search for accounts of how other post-war Germans have dealt with their history. In their much noted German text, "*The Inability to Mourn; Fundamentals of Collective Behaviour,*" (1967) Alexander and Margarete Mitscherlich give evidence that second and third generations of post-war Germans may inherit the "sins of their fathers," unless the latter have been able to atone and mourn them. In order to mourn something, one has to recognize it first, and Carola feels she put herself on that path by writing this particular journal. She now includes sections on racism in her Cross-cultural Education course, focusing on practical and theoretical understanding of racism through self-study and a selection of current readings. She also structures all of her course in a way that facilitates student teacher efforts to recognize their own cultural histories through collaborative, narrative explorations of them. Carola's account of all of this to her students helps them to see a rationale for the activities of the course. The extent to which they will be able to adjust their practices will be evident much later, as their professional lives advance.

Many students wrote responses to Carola's journal. We also responded to each other's journals in our small "table groups." Sometimes Carola asked our permission to copy one of our journals for the whole class in order to slowly create a more public space for common reflection. Robin, who had been working in a group of four or five students at a table on the opposite side of the class from where Joe's group was working, wrote a response to Joe after we had all heard him read from his journal. Below we present excerpts from Joe's journal followed by Robin response. Joe's lost question or tacit object of inquiry was about to evolve through portrayals of respectful and humane interactions. These concerns began in his earliest journals through portrayals of situations when labels had a devastating effect on people. The concerns resounded in his conversations about interactions in schools two years later. By then they were also more consciously incorporated into instructional decisions and behaviours. Here we excerpt an early journal. It turned out that Joe's piece enabled Robin to do further work on her as yet unacknowledged theme of "labelling."

Joe's Journal

I don't know why the vulnerability of a gifted child is more readily apparent to me than the vulnerability of an average student, but it is. These gifted kids are completely centered on task accomplishment and "getting it right". When you correct a mistake on their worksheets, their look of remorse and terror is immediate. I find it difficult to ignore the shattered look in the eyes. It seems that for the average student, a mistake is a mistake is a mistake–"OK I'll get it right next time, if I remember." I learned quickly enough, however, that the shattered vulnerable look was preferable to the other standard response of the gifted kids, "Oh, this exercise is too dumb and too easy and too boring; I've done this stuff before." That response is as difficult to deal with as is the belligerent response of the budding "hood" in the classroom. They are linked, however, by the emotion of insecurity.

My own insecurity has been the axis of my thoughts for the past few days. I have spent untold hours at night gazing at French textbooks knowing I had to make a decision so I could BEGIN the lesson planning. I can't begin. Something keeps me riveted on the books and away from the decisions, the actions which will lead to a completed lesson plan and finally to bed.

I had forgotten about the sources of my deep insecurity concerning my intellectual ability, but as I walked around the school's middle class Italian and Greek neighborhood during this afternoon's lunch break, it all came flooding back to me. Of course, when I was younger I was forced to deal with this, and I did deal with it, but dealing with a ghost and putting the ghost firmly into perspective does not make the ghost go away. Once an addict always and addict; once an alcoholic always an alcoholic. In my case, no matter what I have accomplished, once labeled that label is always there in the deepest, farthest corner of my brain.

When I was in the sixth grade, the teacher asked me to take a large folded white paper down to the principal's office. Two days earlier, the class had been given an intelligence test. I knew the test scores were written on the paper I had in my hand. I can't remember when I decided to do it, but I whipped into the Boy's Room, went into a stall, closed the door, opened the paper, found my mane on the left had side of the paper and quickly followed with my eyes across the paper to the right side where the scores were recorded. I had an IQ of 90. I was almost certain the principal could not tell I was guilty of peeking as I handed the paper to him.

The full impact of my sneaking a peak at the paper Mrs. L. had asked me to take to the office smashed into my consciousness several months later. Up to that point, I though that the highest IQ score you could get was 100 so 90 was pretty good. It was in one of those Condensed Reader's Digest Magazines one often finds in Dentist's Offices that I read several months later (while waiting to get a cavity filled) that I was at the very, *very* bottom of the average group. According to the Reader's Digest article, one point less and I was well on the road to being an idiot. But I knew I was not that because my score was 90. 90 meant that I was less than average. My mother wondered why I had lost my appetite and appeared "a little sick" for the next few weeks. I was never able to tell my parents why I was "a little sick" because even at that point it had been made abundantly clear to me that I was going to get a university degree. Maybe even more than one. Maybe even one for each of the degrees my parents never had.

When I started seventh grade a few weeks later, I was still feeling "a little sick." But this seemed to disappear as time went by. In my high school, at the end of the seventh grade, you and the "school" made a choice about which "track" you were going to follow until graduation. If you wanted to follow the "academic track" in order to get into university, you had to study a foreign language because, at the time, you had to have studied a foreign language in order to meet entrance requirements for universities of distinction. Also, at the time, most universities required at least two years of university level foreign language study as part of the BA degree.

We were given a diagnostic linguistic test, and a week after the test, I was called into the Principal's Office. The results of the test showed that I was incapable of learning a foreign language, would not be able to pass the foreign language requirement for the high school diploma in the academic track, and therefore would not be able to get into a university. I should take this form home to my parents and decide which trade I wanted to learn, have them sign it, and I would be enrolled in the "general track." Even though I felt as if I was going to vomit as I left his office, it somehow seemed to make some kind of strange sense to me because I knew I only had a below average IQ. Nonetheless, I was not able to discuss this with my parents; I could not find the words. When my father was contacted by the school, because the "form" had not been returned, we were scheduled for a parents visit with the principal. My father insisted I was to be present at the meeting; I was the one who was going to have to do the work, after all was said and done. It was my first lesson on how to structure a meeting to achieve what you want no matter the agenda. I was well on the road to becoming an academic administrator before I was in high school.

Parental demand steamrolled the principal into submission, and I embarked on my first course of study in French knowing that I could not do it and that it was pretty amazing I could even read a book. I did five years of

French in high school, four at university, lived in a French speaking African country for two years, became completely fluent in French, and all the while, the ghost hovered, the ghost which said that no matter what I was actually doing, I should not be able to be doing it because I really was not capable of achieving what I had actually achieved!

The label still haunts me. Last night I had to peel it off one more time before I could begin thinking in French.

Joe had many stories to tell. As we listened to his stories, we eventually came to see an emphasis on episodes where he was treated without compassion, respect and civility. We saw stories where he struggled to introduce those very qualities into his students' lives. Joe, we told him, now seems to have an eye for recognizing potentially dehumanizing situations and fight them openly. He came to recognize this as an ongoing inquiry and he is now aware of his special sensitivities in school situations where similar issues arise. In other words, he is now consciously developing a once fragile story in his practical knowledge into a robust component of his teaching. The question mark became a quest. Joe later commented that the potential for learning is maximized when we "brush aside the baggage ... and attempt to get into contact with what is still percolating in [our] blood and breath and body and mind and soul" — an objective that sums up narrative inquiry for all of us and one that we are beginning to see as an objective in our teaching as well.

Coming back to the presentation of Joe's journal that day in class, the concrete images and concretely told situations in the journal presented many possibilities for response on the part of his colleagues. Different people responded to different aspects of his writing; everyone implicitly working at elaborations of his or her tacit inquiry while being helpful to a narrator's ongoing work. Responses to narrative work differ considerably from the usual academic discussion. They are experiential not argumentative.[11] Robin answered Joe in a flurry of reactions:

Dear Joe,

[...] on the day after my 28th birthday–I waited until now because I'm likely to be wiser or something–just kidding! I begin to read your story on the Bloor Subway–on the way to my literacy centre at 4:00 pm. I am so completely engrossed I miss my stop. I stop at a dingy little greasy spoon near the centre to have a coke and some noodles–might as well eat because there is no way I can go to the centre until I finish reading–now here I am on one of their computers–writing right away because I just *have* to.

First–I cried during the part about their letters–so honest so real. [...] I struggle with labels and slots of any kind and the way you weave the story of yourself as a child believing he had a 90 IQ was finely done–the story really brings me to the child sneaking a peek at the contents of the envelope...interesting because my first reaction as I was reading was, "Oh — I guess he was picked on because the kids found out he was brilliant."

Don't get me wrong, all labels have the potential to be equally damaging in one way or another but so many of the sharings I've been privy to are different from this one because they had the teachers on their side. Well maybe not on their side, but do you know what I mean? Pushed ahead can at least sometimes mean pushed into something better–well, no, I guess the word itself, pushed, underlines the external pressure rather than inspiration; yet, somehow being told that you just can't cut it is an entirely different piece of cake. If the expectation is that a learner just won't rise–it's really remarkable if and when a person can get out of such a trap.

Your example brings to mind one of the math teachers I work with. Her daughter is a little shy and generally a nice kid (I think she's eight). Her report card came home at the end of last year and Diane brought it in to show me. My response was the same as hers. Disbelief. The report was one page long and entirely anecdotal. In every single category including the additional comments section the child had been described as *average*, According to this report she was absolutely average in everything. It's interesting because when I discuss this with friends many can't see a thing wrong with it. "But don't you see," I say, "she must be good at something? She must have potential somewhere!"

I am told that I should relax. That maybe the kid is simply average. I feel like shouting "Have you people never heard of the self-fulfilling prophecy? Don't you think there must be *something* she's good at? Don't you think as teachers we have to look for strengths?" I am told that maybe there just aren't any. I'm sure it was my mother who told me that *everyone* is good at something. There is something unique and special about everybody.

I know I needed to read your piece for a reason. The spirit works in wonderful ways–lessons I need to learn surface again and again. Great now I sound like a new age flake and actually, as I say that, I'm smiling because I *am* kidding and I have vowed to be careful with labels–besides I have my special turquoise gem (that my mother gave me for its healing properties) in my pocket right at this moment — my mother would say this whole experience is a nudge. Maybe she's right.

Robin's piece is filled with resonance (Conle 1996) to Joe's writing. The story of the report card seems an obvious example. But most likely there was unacknowledged resonance as well; Robin said she cried; that she probably had to read Joe's piece for a reason; that the experience was a nudge. But she was not sure what the nudge actually consisted of. The lost question had not yet become apparent. As her teacher, Carola saw this journal as the beginning of an inquiry for Robin. She made a note to herself: "If Robin can now write more stories, she will be putting herself intellectually *on a road she is on already experientially.* Her curriculum will be guided by what Dewey (1934) calls *interest* and MacIntyre (1981/1984) calls being on a narrative *quest.*[12] Perhaps she and Joe will each gradually become aware of a tacit moral imperative, by that I mean a moral issue that is important for some reason and that is guiding decisions and actions." For Robin and Joe this issue indeed turned out to be one that had to do with the imperative "Don't label; respect the potential and humanity in each child."

Carola, in her comment, begins to describe what for her informs a curriculum in narrative self-study. Resonance is an important structuring principle in such a curriculum. It engages the emotions and connects intellect, imagination, feelings and moral attitudes. Getting, academically, onto the road on which we are already traveling in life is of paramount importance as well, because such a move counters alienation that can arise in academic settings, where the actual contents of lives are at a distance from intellectual endeavours. Dewey warns against this alienation in his *Child and the Curriculum* (1902) and tells us that sugar-coating will be necessary to get students to do work in those circumstances. Sugar-coating may be needed less in self-study, because the subject of the inquiry is inherently interesting and resonance is automatic and engaging.

The idea of "resonance" seemed to make immediate sense to us in class: Yes, we respond to each other's experiential stories through a "me too" or a "not me" reaction. Whether negative or positive, the reaction occurs through resonance. We do not argue with people's experience, but we respond with more stories. Carola asked us to read and comment on a draft of a related paper that she was about to send out for publication. We were not happy with all her philosophical references, but we generally agreed that when we respond to each other with stories, in a "that-reminds-me-of-when" reaction, the connection between trigger and response stories is not necessarily logical. However, it is also not arbitrary. Connections among such stories work at the writer's and the respondent's personal, practical knowledge, that is, the knowledge that tacitly shapes his or her actions and structures thoughts. Our excerpts illustrate the process: Joe's journal contained sets of images, or scenes, mini-narratives of sorts. Robin responded to one of them with another set of images, with a mini-narrative of her own. The connection between those two sets happened through metaphorical correspondance linking two sets of images. It also set in motion an inquiry into the respondent's practical knowledge.

Another teaching candidate, Loreen, eventually coined her own phrase for "resonance." Being a student of French literature and a teacher of French, she was reminded of Marcel Proust's book *The Remembrance of Things Past, [A la Recherche du Temps Perdu]* and how he told of remembering the exact taste of a certain pastry, a *madeleine,* given to him in his childhood. The taste in turn spawned further memories. Loreen's use of this term emerged in narratives about her previous experiences of teaching and learning. Her conscious intent and focal object of inquiry was initially nothing more than to track her process of becoming a teacher. Yet within the stories she tells, there are tacit question marks about a teacher's impact on students' lives.

Excerpts from *Shafts of light: Recollections of my Schooling*

I have spent much of this year remembering and looking back at myself in both the distant and recent past. Reminiscence, or reflection, has certainly been encouraged at the Faculty in many of my courses, but I believe that my mind's backward-looking activity has been aroused by the process of becoming a teacher in much the same way that Proust's was by the taste of a madeleine. Each time that I entered a classroom this year, as a teacher or as a student, I remembered a teacher from my past or an event from my past as a student. I believe that these memories are signs, or signposts, which are speaking to me and attempting to be understood with regard to the teacher that I am becoming.

***

In an ESL drama class, I introduced a game called "Life Raft." I had played it with my peers at the Faculty, and it had achieved both a freeing of inhibitions and group bonding. I placed five large pieces of paper on different parts of the floor in the drama room and told the students that these papers were life rafts. The water in which these rafts floated was shark-infested. The students were to move about the room quickly, pretending to swim, and when I yelled out "shark," they were all to find a space on one of the rafts as quickly as possible. I emphasized that everyone was to help everyone else stay on the rafts – the object of the game was co-operation, not competition. When the activity began, I noticed that Thanh, Viet, Judy and Donna were not engaged. They walked slowly around the outer edges of the classroom and only grudgingly found a raft on which to stand when I yelled "shark". As the game progressed, I removed some of the life rafts so that more and more students had to crowd together and really co-operate in order to all find space to stand or balance on the few pieces of paper. While some students were giddy with laughter, as I had been when I took part in this game, others appeared very uncomfortable, even frightened. When I spoke to my associate about this lesson later on, she apologized to me. She had known that this activity was part of my lesson plan, but had forgotten that a few of the students had escaped from their countries on small boats and that some of them had seen people eaten by sharks. I was devastated. How could I have been so insensitive? My goals had been to increase self-confidence and establish an atmosphere of trust and safety. For some of the students, the results were the complete opposite of what I had had in mind.

I tasted the madeleine again. [The above] teaching experience evoked a memory from grade two. I have only one school memory from that year. This is remarkable because I have such clear memories of earlier and later school years. My father died when I had almost completed grade two. Miss Clark was my teacher. My father had been ill for some time before his death, but I do not recall equating his illness with the knowledge that he would die.

I had not been allowed to attend my father's funeral, but I was kept home from school until my mother felt comfortable letting me return. Miss Clark was a "stickler" for notes explaining absences, and the adults at home had failed to provide me with one. When I tried to explain to Miss Clark the reason for my absence, she interrupted me quite abruptly and said again that she required a note. I waited until the class had begun quiet work and I approached Miss Clark at her desk. I bluntly said, "I was away from school because my father died." I remember that Miss Clark looked strange and that she said I would not need to bring in a note and then she left the room. I was quite pleased with my news and the effect that it had produced and I proceeded to tell all my classmates. (Twenty years later, when I read Agee's "Death in the Family", I was amazed to see some of myself in one of his characters).

Recently, my mother told me that the school phoned home that day. Miss Clark went home and was replaced by a substitute for two days. School staff and administration apparently watched me closely for signs of depression. They told my mother that I appeared well-adjusted and unaffected. But, I remember nothing else from that year. Except that Miss Clark looked like the Wicked Witch of the West from "The Wizard of Oz".

In hindsight, Miss Clark may have reminded me of the "wicked witch" from "The Wizard of Oz" because she persisted in seeing me only as a student inside of her classroom. The "wicked witch" only saw the ruby slippers on Dorothy's feet; Miss Clark only saw a student who had been absent from class for three days. Students and teachers have lives, whole histories, outside of and prior to their entrance into a classroom. Students are not "blank slates" onto which educators record facts. When we enter a classroom, we do not leave parts of ourselves outside.

Taking another look at the functioning of resonance, let us consider how it works within one and the same piece of writing. Looking at the metaphorical correspondance between various episodes in Loreen's stories, we can discern a link between sets of images: the image of a teacher trying to do her best, but unknowingly hurting a student. The hurt probably could have been avoided, if the two people knew each other better and had a caring, personal relationship. In journal writing about her experiences at our Faculty, Loreen recognized that caring and warmth seemed important to her: "If I sense that a teacher cares about me, if I understand that we have a relationship, then my learning accelerates."

After several further journals in which she described her need of caring relationships in educational settings, she asked herself, was her own caring too needy? At one point, she read and very much appreciated Nel Noddings' *The challenge to care in schools*. Finally, Loreen faced her important question: how, more specifically, was caring necessary to good teaching? Loreen's course work and her life started to merge. What are often considered as two separate paths became one road. After hesitating for months, she finally ventured into some difficult memories of her own schooling days. Not at all an easy task. As it turned out, the recollections clarified in her own mind those sections of her schooling history that were relevant to her current inquiry.

> No one must see me cry.
> The route to my school, along Finch Avenue, is a noisy one. I see dozens of other students walking together and singly. I watch them from lowered eyes for clues: is anyone as unhappy and nervous as I am? Are there any friends here for me? Who has money for clothing, accessories, make-up, movies? If anyone looks in my direction, I look away quickly; no one must see my need.
> (This is all so difficult to think and write about. I often pride myself on having left this part of my life behind, neatly compartmentalized and labeled "difficult youth" or "troubled childhood.")
> I enter the high school and spend an anxious few minutes locating my homeroom. In my continuing efforts to hide myself, I sit at the very back of the room and quickly slouch so that my hair hides my face. My homeroom is a shop class. There are mysterious tools and benches everywhere and the clean smell of sawdust. My teacher has a British accent and a bemused expression. He says very little to us before going up and down the rows to hand out papers that tell us our schedules, locker numbers, room locations, school rules. He pauses at my desk, looks down and tries to peer through my hairy camouflage. He says, "I'm sure that you're in there, somewhere." I respond with a grunt and a guttural expletive, but inwardly I am shaken. Somehow this teacher guessed that I am hiding, to him I am transparent.
> My subsequent encounters with teaching staff over the course of the week are similar. I am not left alone to wallow in my chosen cloak of invisibility and resentment. I continue to sit at the back of each classroom in brooding silence. When I am addressed or asked a question, I grunt or glare. I am not to be easily won over. I am not yet conscious of the rationale behind

my behaviour, but hindsight suggests I was testing these teachers: how much effort were they willing to put forth, how much of their time and energy would they invest in such a hopeless case? I looked for hope in their eyes — a dim reflection of myself.

My history teacher seemed always to be watching me. Whenever I glanced up from my post at the farthest recesses of the room, he was looking at me. He never failed to greet me when I entered his classroom and was never offended when I ignored him. I had an ally in this class, a young woman who was illiterate, and would now be labeled "behavioural," sat next to me. We exchanged dirty jokes and asides throughout the class. The teacher chose not to separate us, but to continue to give us joint assignments. One day he asked me to stay after class. I thought, with grim satisfaction, "Well, here it comes, the punishment which I so richly deserve." To my surprise, he thanked me for helping my "ally" and asked if I would be able to assist another student of his who was also experiencing language difficulties. My response was taciturn: "Okay — if you really want me to." He smiled and said, "Yes — I really want you to." I quickly left.

These are fragile stories in Loreen's life. But with the boost of narrative self-study, fragile stories can become strong and valuable components of teaching. The teacher cared; the student resisted the caring. Noddings (1992) insisted that the cared-for must be able to receive the caring. Almost a year after our course, Loreen, facing a group of teaching candidates to whom she had been asked to speak, took time to study them intently during the few moments left before the session began. In a flash, she came to a conclusion about her "caring and relationship" puzzle. Her need of close relationships with students had to do with a teacher's ability to 'read' her students in order to develop a caring approach to which students could respond and which will be the basis for her teaching decisions.

I had a small but meaningful revelation–I was studying this group of people so that I would have an idea as to how I should speak to them. Their physical attitudes, attire, expressions, even beverages, were clues which would help me to unravel the mystery of how to speak. This was the need of which I wrote and which I have been trying to clarify ever since I recorded it. I need the students to show me how to teach them.

Loreen's history is particularly interesting to us because we know that in our city's schools today there are many students just like the high school self she remembers. We want to find ways to reach such students. Loreen's story helps us find a way. For us who listened, Loreen's stories became exemplars, alive in our imagination, and seemingly waiting for resonance in action. The stories gradually became resource stories for us. They help us now in our efforts to meet needy students. This help is not technical. There are no specific guidelines and prescriptions. Rather the help comes to us through resonance. We wish for a storehouse of such narratives in our tacit memory to guide us!

FRAGILE STORIES GETTING STRONGER

Beattie and Conle (1996) describe how a beginning teacher had to strengthen a fragile story in her life to change her teaching approach and live more successfully with students in her classroom. One of us, Michele, also used self-study to puzzle out aspects of her history in schools and had the courage to deal with fragile stories in her life. She too came to understand more clearly her tacit inquiry into seemingly lost questions and now uses the results to guide her current teaching.

Excerpts from *The Challenge to Care — A Personal Narrative of Teaching and Learning*

I've come to a frightening conclusion that I am the decisive element in the classroom. It's my approach that creates the climate. It's my daily mood that makes the weather. As a teacher, I possess a tremendous power to make a child's life miserable or joyous. I can humiliate or humour, hurt or heal. In all situations, it is my response that decides whether a crisis will be escalated or de-escalated and a child humanized or de-humanized.

Michele begins the final version of her year-end assignment, her extensive personal narrative with this quote from Haim Ginott and then looks back on her narrative journey.

Feelings overwhelmed me as I thought about all that I have written and my experiences of having been a student and now a teacher and the path that has led me here.

Not so much as a child, but as a teenager I experienced the kind of 'abuse' a person in authority can exercise over a young person. I had to struggle through it and its consequences on my own. In those days, support systems where not so readily available.

[...] I am a teacher who still feels the student within me. That student is overwhelmed by the positive feedback and support that I now experience as a teacher.

If I didn't have them in the past, I have wonderful role models now in the professors that I had at the Faculty of Education; other teachers that I have met; the head of my department; and particularly the principal of the high school where I am presently employed.

It is a wonder at times that I survived and made it here, to where I am and that I am what I am. More than a survivor, more than someone who has broken free but someone who has used those experiences as a launching pad. I have taken flight.

In order to fully understand Michele's emotion, we would have to read her stories of the teenager she was, lacking confidence in her abilities and coping with low expectations. These are what she calls her demons. Early in her writing she worried:

Unfortunately, I still struggle on a daily basis with his legacy, a perception of myself that makes it difficult for me to believe that my successes are legitimate. I grapple with the discomfort of sudden support and positive feedback. I guess it's the same for my students. Telling someone they can and are doing something doesn't necessarily mean they will believe you or buy into it.

But this very history has given Michele a sensitivity that makes her particularly qualified to help students who do not come to academic success easily. She was one of the few graduates in the Faculty that year who got at least a contract job in a no-hiring environment. She was hired to work with multiply disabled children. In a subsequent year, she taught gifted children, but asked to be allowed to return to her troubled youngsters. Here are some of Michele's accounts of her life with them:

Me:	Sit down, please and get to work!
Students:	Are we getting to you, miss?
Me:	Ha ha. It would take more than you.
Students:	Oh, a challenge!
Me:	No, not a challenge - a simple statement.
	Don't you think that you could put your energy to better use?
Students:	But that's why we're here at Dumbvale, miss.
	We're *not suppose* to think!
Me:	Sorry, I don't buy it.
	I saw you thinking yesterday. Too bad.

You gave yourself away.
Now you're screwed , 'cause I know what you can do .
Oh well, them's the breaks!

They glare at me.
They are not amused.
They are dumb.
Everybody knows it.
What is wrong with this person!

Students:	But miss, we're basic.
	You're giving us *general level* stuff!
Me:	That's because, I think you can do it.
	I want to challenge you.
Students:	Geeze miss!

* * *

We are studying *Raisin in the Sun*...

Students:	*I hate this play! It's stupid! It's not real! Why do we have to study it?!*
Me:	*Let's see if we can figure that out together. What should Mama do with the insurance money?*
Students:	*Buy a house! Buy a liquor store! Go on a holiday!*
Me:	*What about the children's education?*
Students:	*Naw! No way! They should do something good with the money.*
Me:	*But education is an investment in their future and their children's future. It will break the family's cycle of poverty and ignorance.*
Students:	*Not education!*
Me:	Raisin in the Sun *is about dreams. Do you have dreams?*
Students:	*Yeah.*
Me:	*How are you going to get your dreams?*
Students:	*Well, I am going to college...etc., etc.*
Me:	*Do you need education for your dreams to come true?*
Students:	*Yeah.*
Me:	*If you had to choose between a nicer place to live and your education which would you choose?*
Students:	*Education.*
Me:	*I rest my case.*
Me:	*Let's have a vote. Like in court. Lawrence, please be the spokesperson for your group.*
Lawrence:	*No way! I don't want to be a nerd.*
Me:	*Lawrence, not a nerd, a leader.*

> *Take centre stage.*
> *Everyone respects you.*
> *No one would ever feel that way about you.*

Lawrence slowly gets to his feet and takes his place at the front of the class.

* * *

She looks at me with hard eyes as she hands me the paper.

Me: But you've only done half the assignment.

Her: I have nothing more to say. Besides, there isn't enough room on the paper.

Me: Well, you can turn the page over. There's a whole other side.

She glares at me.

I look at the sheet of vocabulary words that the students are to reflect on.

LIFE: When I think of LIFE, I remember my babies being born.

She is barely 17.

Me: You have babies? How wonderful! Giving birth must have been an incredible experience. You gave them 'life'. Now, I am sure they are your life. You must have more to say about them. I know you do.

Her eyes soften.

Her: Yeah, that's true.

The hard edges melt away. We speak quietly for a few more minutes. Our heads almost touching, like conspirators. Later she hands me her paper. I am touched by the feelings and experiences that she has chosen to share with me. Her hardness is the armour of a survivor. The next day, I hand back her paper. Without looking at it she grins.

Her: Aced it eh, Miss?

Me: Absolutely!

I think back to my own experiences as a student. Teachers seemed acutely aware of their power. They still are, according to many young people. These young people touch my heart. Many of them are abused and beaten down. Filled with low self-esteem. Not even trying, out of fear that they'll fail. Slowly in written reflections, they share their lives, their pain, sometimes even their joy and strength.

Like Joe, Robin, and Loreen, Michele found her way to describe to herself, and to us, how she links her life stories and her teaching. Working with troubled youth, many of whom are often labeled and face low expectations, she draws on many stories where she herself faced those conditions. But she also had to dig out fragile stories of success and build on those fragile strands to convince herself that "she could do it." Near the end of our work together, Michele says confidently: "My students and I will confront our inner demons together and we will succeed!"

By now it is probably evident to our readers that our stories interlink in many ways. We are each others' co-authors. Yet each of us has a very distinct story to tell, based on very specific life experiences.

STRUCTURES AND ISSUES IN A PRE-SERVICE CURRICULUM OF SELF-STUDY

Through our work we have caught glimpses of a curriculum that is not guided by specific outcomes or predetermined objectives other than the intention of self-study. It is a curriculum of inquiry where each inquirer is guided by the demands of his or her own history as it intersects with current settings. The steps of the inquiry are more often emotionally and imaginatively, rather than logically, constructed. They are propelled by the interests that emerge as each inquiry develops, but also by the long-term tacit interests that are firmly anchored in our lived practical knowledge.

The Indeterminate Objectives of Our Self-Study Curriculum

The richness of each life within its social and cultural contexts promises to be a potential source of myriads of inquiries. For each of us there was an inherent structure that propelled us along a certain path. It emerged from the "lost questions," the tensions and desires that permeated each of our lives. We have characterized the inquiry structure in various ways so far. Carola spoke of focal objects of inquiry that seem 'secretly' selected by the urgent subconscious question marks that are the tacit, 'indirect' objects of inquiry. Importantly, our pre-service work in this course was not just an academic enterprise, but merged with issues in our everyday existence. Our lives in and out of school came together as one road for us to travel in a special kind of inquiry.

An education for goodness and wisdom puts moral demands before demands of efficiency and clearly defined technical objectives. An open-ended searching for what is the right and good thing to do in our teaching is of paramount importance in the curriculum we describe. Not labeling, respecting someone's humanity, establishing caring connections, believing in our own potential and in that of others — these were goods we came to recognize in our lives and were also recognized as moral dimensions in our teaching. Through her journal Carola asked, "Are some of my reactions indicative of discriminatory behaviour?

Michele asked, "What if self-doubt and lack of self-esteem bedevil us? How do we exorcize the ingrained belief that we are dumb?" Narrative representation seemed to sharpen our ability to perceive those dilemmas in a very concrete, personalized way. We are still, continually, on the road to define, for ourselves and for each other, what the goods inherent in our history (MacIntyre 1981) may be in the long run; or what, on short notice, the right action might be. Unlike canonical male autobiographies, our self-studies will never be complete. And no one can do this work for us.

Narrative constructions in self-study present a new perspective on what John Dewey's believed to be the essence of education: the reconstruction of experience. Without a self-study curriculum where experiences of teaching and learning are reconstructed, valuable dimensions of teachers' practical knowledge may go unrecognized — dimensions that, although they seem sources of tension at first, once thematized, can become acknowledged sources of strength and bolster fragile stories in teachers' lives.

In our version of a self-study curriculum, a particular form of inquiry was essential. We worked on seemingly "lost questions" that pervaded our lives in and out of schools. These of course were not stated objectives. They could not be such, certainly not at the outset. Instead they propelled each inquiry and became more apparent as resonance did its work in the shared reconstruction of experience and as a moral sense of self helped us create the teaching "I" we wanted to create for our future work with students.

As a post-script, Carola wants to add comments from a later group of teacher candidates (with their permission) that express what we perhaps felt but did not say clearly— perhaps also it became more clearly into view as Carola was able to make the narrative processes more evident to her students. It concerns the bonding quality of narrative (Lyotard 1982) that makes our work particularly powerful and easy at the same time:

> I have found that by listening to people's stories, I can understand and learn to accept them just the way they are. This is not always an easy thing to do, but when you hear their story you *can* learn to love them (Alma Parker, Journal).
>
> It's funny. I feel most comfortable with people in my [...] class than in any of my other classes. Greg, Alf, Margarita and I go out for coffee after every class. Alma, Martha and Barb come and join us as much as they can. Once in a while, Janice, Laura and Vince drop by. We all get a cup of coffee and just talk. Most of the time, we discuss what was brought up in class. We express our ideas and share our related experiences. I find that we never argue. That's probably because when we discuss issues, we talk from an

experiential viewpoint. Because we all come from different backgrounds (ethnic, education, teaching experiences, etc.), I find that I am constantly learning new and exciting things. At the same time I find that I can relate to many of the stories told. I always catch myself saying, "I understand where you're coming from" or "That reminds me when ..." It's great.

All of us, at one point or another, have asked why we feel so comfortable with one another. I think it's because we trust one another. We are able to discuss our feelings and opinions about different topics and ideas brought up in our different courses. We are able to vent our frustrations and confusion. By doing this, I have been able to cope with my hectic schedule. I don't feel alone because I know that there are other people who feel the same way. We are sharing our experiential stories and by doing so, we are getting to know each other. We are learning and growing through resonance (Hatty Moon, Journal).

REFERENCES AND BIBLIOGRAPHY

Angelou, M. 1969. *I know why the caged bird sings.* New York: Random House Inc.

Ashton Warner, S. 1958. *Spinster.* London: Secker and Warburg.

Ashton-Warner, Sylvia. *Teacher.* New York: Bantam Books, 1964.

Barrett, L. 1993. Self-knowledge, law, and African American autobiography. In R. Folkenflik [Ed.], *The culture of autobiography. Constructions of self-representation.* Stanford, CA: Stanford University Press.

Beattie, M. 1995. Constructing professional knowledge in teaching: A narrative of change and development. Toronto and New York: OISE Press and Teachers College Press.

Beattie, M. and C. Conle. 1996. Teacher narrative, fragile stories and change. *Asia-Pacific Journal of Teacher Education* 24 (3) : 309-326.

Bell, J. 1991. Narrative self-study: The acquisition of literacy in a second language. Unpublished doctoral dissertation, University of Toronto.

Bruner, J. 1993. The autobiographical process. In R. Folkenflik [Ed.],*The culture of autobiography. Constructions of self-representation.* Stanford, CA: Stanford University Press.

Bullough, R. and D. Stokes. 1994. Analyzing personal teaching metaphors in pre-service teacher education as a means for encouraging professional development. *American Educational Research Journal,* 31(1): 197-224.

Clandinin, J., Davies, A., Hogan P., and B. Kennard. 1993. *Learning to teach, teaching to learn: Stories of Collaboration in Teacher Education.* New York: Teachers College Press.

Conle, C. 1993. Learning culture and embracing contraries: Narrative inquiry through stories of experience. Unpublished doctoral dissertation. University of Toronto.

Conle, C. 1996. Resonance in student teacher inquiry. *American Educational Research Journal* 33 (2): 297 - 325.

Conle, C. 1997a. Between fact and fiction: Dialogue within encounters of difference. *Educational Theory* 47(1): 181 - 201.

Conle, C. 1997b. Images of change in narrative inquiry. *Teachers and Teaching* 3(2): 205 -219.

Conle, C. 2000. Thesis as narrative. What is the inquiry in narrative inquiry? *Curriculum Inquiry* 30(2):189-214.

Conle, C. , Li, X. and J. Tan. 2002. Connecting vicarious experience to practice. *Curriculum Inquiry* 34 (4): 429-452.

Connelly, M. and D. Clandinin 1990. Stories of experience and narrative inquiry. *Educational Researcher* 14(5): 2-14.

Connelly, M. and D. Clandinin. 1994. Personal experience methods. In N. Denzin and Y. Lincoln (Eds.) *Handbook of qualitative research.* London: Sage Publications.

Connelly, M. and J. Clandinin. 1988. *Teachers as curriculum planners: Narratives of experience.* New York: Teachers College Press.

Crites, S. 1971.The narrative quality of experience. Journal *of the American Academy of Religion.* 39 (3): 391-411.

Davies, A.B., Sumara, D.T. & Kieren. 1996. Cognition, co-emergence, curriculum. *Jounal of Curriculum Studies* 28 (2) : 151-169.

de Man, P. 1984. Autobiography as de-facement. In *The rhetoric of romanticism,* pp.67 - 81. New York: Columbia University Press.

Delaney, L. A. 1891/1988. From the darkness cometh the light, or struggles for freedom. In W. L. Andrews (Ed.) *Six women's slave narratives.* New York: Oxford University Press.

Dewey, J. 1902. *The child and the curriculum.* Chicago: University of Chicago Press.

Dewey, J. 1934. *Art as experience.* New York: Capricorn Books.

Dewey, J. 1938. *Experience and education.* New York and London: Collier Macmillen Publishers.

Donmoyer, R. 1990. Generalizability and the single case study. In E. Eisner and A. Peshkin (Eds.) Qualitative inquiry in education. New York and London: Teachers College Press.

Elbaz, F. 1983. Teacher Thinking: A study of practical knowledge. London: Croom Helm.

Fenstermacher, G.D. 1994. The knower and the known: The nature of knowledge in research on teaching. In *Review of Research in Education* 20: 3-56.

Folkenflik, R. [Ed.]. 1993. *The culture of autobiography. Constructions of self-representation.* Stanford, CA: Stanford University Press.

Gadamer, H-G. 1975. *Truth and Method.* New York: Seabury Press. (German *Wahrheit und Methode* 1960)

Gallagher, S. 1992. Hermeneutics and education. New York: State University of New York Press.

Grumet, M.R. 1988. Bitter milk: Women and teaching. Amherst, MA: University of Massachusetts Press.

Hamilton, M.-L. [ed.] 1998. *Reconceptualizing Teacher Research as Self-Study.* London and New York: Falmer Press.

Hidalgo, N. 1993. Multicultural teacher introspection. In T. Perry and J. Fraser (Eds.) *Freedom's plow,* pp. 99 -106. New York : Routledge.

Hunt, D. 1987. Beginning with ourselves. Cambridge, Mass. and Toronto: Brookeline and OISE Press.

Kidder, T. 1989. *Among schoolchildren.* New York: Avon Books.

Knowles, G. and A. Cole. 1994. We're just like the beginning teachers we study: Letters and reflection on our first year as beginning professors. *Curriculum Inquiry* 24 (1) : 27 - 52

Knowles, G. and Holt-Reynolds. 1991. Shaping pedagogies through personal histories in pre-service teacher education. *Teachers College Record* 93 (1): 87- 113.

Kotlowitz, Alex. *There are no children here: The story of two boys growing up in the other America.* New York: Anchor Books, 1991.

Li, X. 1991. The moments of improvisation of my life experience. Unpublished Master's Thesis. Toronto: University of Toronto.

MacIntyre, A. 1984 [1981]. *After virtue: A study in moral theory.* Notre Dame, Indiana: University of Notre Dame Press.

Mitscherlich, A. and M. Mitscherlich. 1967. *Die Unfähigkeit zu trauern* [The inability to mourn]. Munich, Germany: Piper.

Mitscherlich, M. 1987. *Erinnerungsarbeit* (Memory work). Frankfurt am Main, Germany: Fischer Verlag GmbH.

Mullen, C. 1994. A narrative exploration of the self I dream. *Journal of Curriculum Studies* 26 (3): 253 -263.

Noddings, N. 1992. *The challenge to care in schools: An alternative approach to education.* New York: Teachers College Press.

Oser, F. 1994. Moral perspective on teaching. *Review of Research in Education.* 20 : 57 - 127.

Peterson, L. 1993. Institutionalizing women's' autobiography: Lucy A. Delaney's "From the darkness cometh the light. In R. Folkenflik [Ed.], *The culture of autobiography. Constructions of self-representation.* Stanford, CA: Stanford University Press.

Polkinghorne, D. 1988. *Narrative knowing and the human sciences.* New York: State University of New York Press.

Proust, M. 1934. *The remembrance of things past.* New York: Translation by C.K. Scott Moncrieff of *A la recherche du temps perdu.* Paris, France: Gallimard.

Ricci, Nino. 1993. *In A Glass House.* Toronto: McClelland & Stewart Inc.

Rodriguez, R. 1982. *Hunger of memory: The education of Richard Rodriguez.* New York: Bantam Books.

Russell, T. and F. Korthagen. 1995. *Teachers who teach teachers.* London, UK: Falmer Press.

Scheffler, Isreal. 1995. *Teachers of my youth: An American Jewish experience.* Boston : Kluwer Academic Publishers.

Schwab, J. 1970. The practical : A language for curriculum. Washington, D.C.:Natonal Education Association.

Solnicki, J. 1992. *The real me is gonna be a shock: A year in the life of a front-line teacher* Toronto: Lester Publishing Limited.

Tyler, R. 1984. Curriculum development and research. In P. Hosford [Ed.] *Using what we know about teaching,* pp. 29-41. Alexandria, Virginia: Association for Supervision and Curriculum Development.

Verene, D. 1991. The new art of autobiography. Oxford: Clarendon Press.

Vico, G. 1728 & 1731/ 1983. *The autobiography of Gambattista Vico.* Translation by M. Fisch and T. Bergin. Ithaca, NY: Cornell University Press.

Watson, J. 1993. Toward an anti-metaphysics of autobiography. In R. Folkenflik [Ed.],*The culture of autobiography. Constructions of self-representation.* Stanford, CA: Stanford University Press.

Williams, Donna. 1994. *Nobody Nowhere: The Extraordinary Autobiography of an Autistic.* Toronto: Doubleday Canada Limited.

Wolf, C. 1980. Patterns of childhood. New York: Farrar, Strauss and Giroux. German *Kindheitsmuster* 1976

ENDNOTES

[1] The growing Special Interest Group (SIG) in Self-Study at AERA held its first international conference at Herstmonceux Castle in England in August 1996.

[2] Pseudonym to be changed after the review process.

[3] In contrast to the related field of "action research," self-study does not require a problem to be remedied, nor is it necessarily undertaken within the frameworks of critical theory. The inquiry is therefore not explicitly guided by theories of emancipation. Rather, inquiry tends to emerge from a sense of ethical obligation and the conviction that increased self-knowledge is appropriate for teachers. MacIntyre's investigations (1981) and Gadamer's Hermeneutics (1960) provide the philosophical base for such work.

Striking advances in the field have been made through examples of self-study among professors of education (e.g., Russell and Korthagen 1995, Knowles and Cole 1995). At the graduate level, a series of autobiographical theses have pushed the boundaries of self-study in education (e.g., Bell 1991, Li 1991, Conle 1993, Mullen 1994). The contribution we intend to make through this paper regards pre-service teacher education. We are aware that journal writing and life history exercises are common practices in pre-service, but we do not know of documentation of courses where self-study is the explicit focus for pre-service teachers and their instructor.

[4]. Carola's voice carries this paper which is largely written by her. However, the paper is also the result of a three-year collaboration and contains large sections of writing by the other authors.

[5] Donmoyer (1990) explains how we might learn vicariously through narrative cases; Conle (1996, Conle, Li and Tan 2002) demonstrate a structuring principle for such narrative learning.

[6] This program leads to initial teacher certification which upon successful completion of two years of teaching can become permanent. However, for several years, there was almost no hiring of teachers in our area. In fact, in 1996, those who were lucky enough to have a job, were on short term contracts. By 1996, when our collaboration came to an end, it was not possible to track all four candidates as beginning secondary school teachers, although some related beginning teaching experiences during short-term contract positions since graduation.

[7] Carola had herself experienced this kind of work in her graduate studies with Michael Connelly at the Ontario Institute of Education and presented some of her own narratives to her pre-service students.

[8] Conle (2000) describes a similar process at the graduate level.

[9] All names mentioned in student teachers' accounts are pseudonyms. We at times fictionalized the circumstances sufficiently to safeguard the privacy of individuals concerned. Pseudonyms were used from the start so that our colleagues and the instructor usually did not know the real name of the school or the people involved.

[10] Carola often uses the theoretical frameworks of the German philosopher, Gadamer, who carefully worked out the notion of "effective history" or *Wirkungsgeschichte* (1960/1975) which proposes that we can never totally step out of our history into a state of functioning that is completely free of the baggage of the past.

[11] For an analysis of "narrative response" see Conle (1997a, 2001).

[12] Definitions and the connection between these terms (interest, eros, quest) are given below.

In: Teacher's Stories, Teacher's Lives
Editor: Carola Conle, pp. 29-66

ISBN 1-59454-472-7
© 2006 Nova Science Publishers, Inc.

Chapter 2

TEACHERS' STORIES; TEACHERS' LIVES: JOE'S STORY

Joseph Totaro

I don't know why the first image of my schooling experience which burst through nearly forty years of cobwebs was of the enormous cemetery which sprawled over rolling hills just in front of my high school. It could be that this cemetery divided the two key aspects of my early, that is to say, pre-university education. The elementary school I attended and disliked sat just across the street from the southern tip of the cemetery. At the northern end, atop a lovely hill, sat Upper Darby High School, the physical embodiment of a six year experience. Upper Darby is a wealthy and exclusive suburb of Philadelphia. We lived there not because we were wealthy or exclusive but because my father had purchased a home at a sheriffs auction for the unpaid property taxes. I went to the High School for six years because the community had grown so fast that there was not enough room at the Junior High School for all the students. About two hundred of us (those geographically closer to the high school) were mainstreamed into the life of the high school although we had a separate faculty. They were six very positive, supportive years filled with achievements which still resonate in my life So why did the cemetery come rushing to the forefront of memory? Why the cemetery and not the beautiful wooded glen which was behind the sports field and through which we ran after gym class rather than doing boring laps around a track?

For the past twenty-five years, my personal life and professional life (all too often one and the same life) have been dominated by my work in the theatre and an obsession with the use and power of language. The theatre, however, did not come bubbling to the top as the images began to percolate. It was Grade 12 English and Mr. Noel, a man whose last year in teaching corresponded with my last year in high school. Each Friday of the spring semester was set aside for the presentation of our "major report" and fifty percent of our final grade was the grade given for this report. Mr. Noel assigned each of us an author; we were required to read at least six of the author's works and incorporate our reactions to them in our report which alsohad to include the usual biographical information. I was assigned Joseph Conrad. I had never heard of Joseph Conrad. I began reading "The Heart of Darkness" and became terribly confused because for the first time in my reading life, I was caught up in the arrangement of words rather than the narrative meaning of words; I became aware of the evocative nature of words as powerful triggers to experience something emotionally and at a level deeper than merely story. I remember reading aloud passages which made me cry and which led me to explore for myself my own heart of darkness and the journey through it to the centre. It was an extremely powerful experience which I tried to share with my class in my report. They were utterly bored, glassy eyed, and yawned incessantly. I knew just enough about public presentation to know that you had "to keep your audience's attention". I had lost them, and I DID NOT CARE because I knew I could only share with them my real and true reactions to the material and share what I had discovered about myself. The procedure was that after each report, Mr. Noel would lead a class discussion and offer criticisms about how it might have been presented differently and then he would announce your grade. When I sat down, Mr. Noel came to the front of the class and said, "This is an A+ report; it is the first time in forty five years of teaching that I have had a student explain so clearly how a work of art had affected his life; his sharing of that experience has changed my life a little today." I noticed he was crying; I was stunned and pleased about the A+. I knew that as a result of my initial encounter with Conrad, the next time I was compelled to confront and explore the paths into my own heart of darkness, the journey would be less terrifying to begin. I knew that; I felt that; that was a prized piece of personal knowledge; I was secure in that understanding. What I found utterly bewildering were the negative reactions of my classmates expressed in derisive remarks about my performance. Their negative attitude towards me did not last long, though, maybe two weeks at the most. But the effects of my personal encounter with Joseph Conrad have endured, quite obviously, to this very moment.

* * *

The way I got to Columbia University is almost as bizarre as my arrival on that campus for the first time. I was living and teaching in the Ivory Coast in January 1966 and had already decided that the life there and the teaching of English as a Second Language at the Lycee Classique suited me very well. At least it suited me at the time since I was twenty-four and really had no other option for work or interest. But out of the blue came this extraordinary letter with an equally astonishing envelope.

Joseph Totaro
Somewhere in Africa
Peace Corps
Washington, DC

The letter got to me. It got to me in more ways than perhaps I shall ever be able to understand. The writer of the letter and the astonishing envelope was David Miller. David was my roommate during my senior year at university. We were both going to go into the Peace Corps, but in late April he received word that he had been awarded a FULL fellowship to do a PhD in Russian Language and Studies at Columbia University—at the time the preeminent American academic institution in the field of Russian Studies. I am talking about 1964 when the study of Russian was novel and, in some quarters, suspect. David went to Columbia and in December of 1965 happened to be in the Registrar's Office to pay a bill when someone tacked up on the bulletin board a poster advertising the formation of the new Professional Actor Training Program at Columbia University in the City of New York. David's note which he scrawled along the bottom edge said, "I immediately thought this was for you." He ripped down the poster, put it into the envelope, and not knowing my address, proceeded to write the envelope which in effect bullied the folks in Washington to find me. In September, 1966, the day before I began the training program at Columbia, David and his wife visited me in my apartment on the top floor of the brownstone which overlooked the Hudson River from 107th Street and from which I could look right up the river to the George Washington Bridge. They had joined the Peace Corps and were off to Afghanistan. That was the last time I saw them. I quickly became swallowed up in transforming my life; in the midst of discovering the theatre artist in me, I lacked the simple creativity to write an envelope with an address I did not know. I wish I knew where they are now. I would like them to read this and some of the other things which are brewing. David and his wife (her Christian name has forever faded from my memory) did hear the story of my arrival in New York, because I told it to them as a warning about the shock of coming back.

The chief criteria to get admitted to the new graduate MFA program at Columbia was an audition/interview. Sitting in the middle of the Ivory Coast in December, the idea of an audition in New York City many months down the road made little impact upon my sense of priorities. I did, however, notice an application deadline which was just one month away. With a real sense of the surreal, I managed to get together a letter which told them who I was, where I was living, and how difficult it was going to be for me to arrange for transcripts and letters of reference. Slowly, however, I did everything that was required to complete the application process. In a few months time, I received a letter telling me that based on my grades and letters of recommendation I was being provisionally admitted into the program pending the outcome of the audition which would be in New York City on the campus of Columbia University in Dodge Hall at 3:30 PM on July 25, 1966. If I was going to do this actor training thing that meant I had to be back in the United States at least by July 24 so that I could do the audition. Intellectually, I knew and understood precisely that the audition would be the single deciding factor in determining the future course of my life, the precipitating moment, the crucial element, but the urgency to do something about it simply did not impress itself on my mind. It was the last time I thought about the substance of the audition until the night before I was to leave for New York City. In between, I had to finish teaching my classes at the Lycee, see my students through the national exams, travel to Abidjan to be a part of the team recruited to correct the exams, say farewell to all the friends I had come to know during the past two years, go to the Army Hospital in Frankfurt for a two week treatment to have my blood sterilized for it seems I had acquired a rare tropical blood disease called Dingue Fever, get back to Abidjan, go through the two weeks of Peace Corps debriefing, say to colleagues some of the most painful goodbyes I had ever experienced up to that point in my life—or even since then. They were mostly silent farewells, looking into eyes, knowing that these were moments where words could not improve upon the eloquence of silence, allowing tears brimming, spilling, and streaming to be the only physical movement permitted in that moment. Then a long, firm hug, a few sobs that were released from depths unknown and not experienced up to that point, a relaxation, a turn, a parting, a walk into an airplane for him, her, them; a very silent taxi ride back into Abidjan for me, and some lonely walks through the frenetic streets. The audition had been pushed so far back into the recesses of my consciousness that it would not be recalled until the last possible moment when I would pull back from the edge of disaster, leap into the unknown, and soar—a pattern that repeats itself often in my life. For some time, I thought it indicated mere youthful callowness, but I have always had an innate sense of responsibility to myself, to others, and to the tasks that I undertake. I have slowly come to accept that my coming up to the edge of disaster is more a fascination with risk taking and the exhilaration of plunging into risks than a lack of responsibility. It also has to do with the essential nature of an actor's soul which is the ability and willingness to share selected private truths in a public way, a talent which cannot be taught or trained, a gift which sometimes needs releasing.

* * *

When it was my turn to leave Africa, I just left. I always avoided giving an answer to the question, "When are you going back?" The morning came and I taxied to the airport alone. It was as if I really wasn't leaving; I was going away for a little while. You leave someplace in order to go to someplace specific. Even though ostensibly I was headed towards Rome, I really did not know where I was going with my life. Rome. Milan. Paris. London. Toulouse. Marseille. Antibes. Venice. The Italian Lake District. Rome. These were all planned and achieved stops, and even though I managed to get one last trip to Beirut squeezed into all of it, all the trips were merely delaying the inevitable of "going back". I had a rather pressing need to get back, since the audition to get into Columbia had been scheduled for July 25. Knowing that, I had planned my trip through Europe so that I arrived in Philadelphia on July 23 in the evening. What amazes me even at this writing is that I began to think about what I was going to do at this audition on the plane trip from Rome to Philadelphia, and when I had arrived in Philadelphia I had decided to do "But soft what light through yonder window breaks" from ROMEO and a chunk of Jerry's huge monologue in Albee's ZOO STORY. But choosing material is a far cry from preparing material, and I solved that problem by memorizing the selections on the bus trip from Philadelphia to New York. My approach to the whole task was unreal. I understood that at the time but ignored it for I actually had not yet *returned* from Africa ... as I was to experience.

I stumbled off the bus at Port Authority and gripping the directions to the Columbia campus at 116th Street and Broadway, I started to look for the subway. I asked directions of several people, but they shrugged me off. New York City I thought. I asked a cop how to get to my destination, and he looked at me as if I were nuts. I asked again. He smiled weakly and gestured with his hands. Finally I showed him the letter I had gotten from Columbia with the directions and his face lite up with recognition. He *took* me to the subway platform and waited until the train came, told someone on the train to make sure I got off at 116th Street, and waved at me through the window as the subway car pulled out of the Port

Authority Station. I ran over my audition speeches one last time as the train rolled north up Manhatten Island. When I emerged from the station at 116th Street the great iron gates of the campus greeted me, but no one else did. I needed to ask directions to Dodge Hall which I did of several people passing by, but they all shrugged me off or made gestures of not knowing. I started to wander through the main part of the campus and finally stopped someone and asked again how to get to Dodge Hall. The response hit me as hard as if I had been punched in the face.

"Eh bien, tu prends le chemin a gauche. Ca ne vaut pas la peine de t'expliquer. Suis-moi. J'y vais toute de suite."

I followed him as he told me to do, but I kept thinking "Why is he speaking to me in French?" Finally I asked him outright. "Why are you speaking to me in French?" He looked me straight in the eye and said (in French) "Because, my friend, you are speaking to me in French! Here's Dodge Hall; good luck." And he walked off.

As I climbed the steps towards the third floor, the thought sank deeper and deeper into my consciousness that ever since arriving in New York I had been speaking in French, asking directions in French, and only through sheer luck had encountered a francophone on the Columbia campus. I remember thinking as I walked through the office door that I had gone crazy. The secretary looked up and said, "You must be Mr. Totaro." I took one step into the office and fainted. The following year when I was working with the same secretary as her "work-study" assistant, she told me that the first thing I asked when I had recovered was, "Please tell me what language am I speaking now?"

The person who was to audition me was Bernard Beckerman, the head of the program. He was coming in from his summer home on Long Island and had been delayed in traffic, so I had an hour to recover. I discovered that he was one of the world's foremost authorities on Shakespeare, had pioneered the research on the architectural aspects of the Globe Theatre, and was currently writing a massive book on the theory of dramatic analysis.

Bernard Beckerman had the face and demeanor of a fifty-five year old cherub. No matter how busy he was, and he was constantly busy, he always gave you the impression that when he was speaking with you, you were the only object of his attention. He knew how to look and to listen. The following year he hired me to type the last two drafts of his seminal work, "The Dynamics of Drama", and I had the opportunity to work with him for two hours a day five days a week. We never talked about what was happening in the studios; the entire faculty meet every Monday morning for three hours to review the past week and plan the coming week. Moreover, I knew I was not responding to the training; I was there; I worked extremely hard, but I was not able in any way to connect the outer technical aspects of the craft of acting with an inner core of emotion, my emotion, my feelings, my emotional centre of gravity. I could not-would not reveal the simple "me"; I could not-would not get to those private moments of truth and use them in a public way at the service of a text. There were fleeting moments of connection and display which flashed bright enough in the studio through an exercise to cause my teachers and me to continue to find a way to unlock things, but my grasp of the key—or keys—was tentative. I was as locked up inside myself as I had been imprisoned by fear on that audition day when my fear expressed itself through blocking out English and speaking in French. For an acting student, the denial of emotional release is as debilitating as denial of sleep and rest is to any person. Sometimes you need to crash. Sometimes you need a controlled push towards the crash. But crash (sleep) (release) must happen if any progress is to be made. We don't call them "crashes" in the profession; we refer to them as "breakthroughs".

My crash was precipitated through singing lessons. I had never sung in my life, but it was thought by the faculty that if I could hook into the physical process of singing, I might find the key to my soul. Was I a singer? It did not matter. What mattered was finding a way of using the power of breath and relaxation to allow a pure sound, a connected sound, a sound from the body to be released, to resonate, and to be coloured by the feelings at the moment of release. Luckily I had been born with the equipment necessary to achieve all this—large vocal folds, unusually large sinus cavities in the mask of the face, and supple ligaments which attached the base of the tongue to the larynx. But I also had a teacher who believed in my ability, or at least she believed totally in *her* ability to guide me to a personal understanding of the complex physical and psychological manipulations required to sing; for singing is not just sound, but the perfect union of physical vibrations infused with emotions and thought.

When Dr. Beckerman told me that the faculty had concerns about my growth in the program, about how well I was responding to the training, and that they wanted me to try singing as a path of exploration to unlock my emotional potential, he opened the door for me to share my own fears. I knew from my own musings that I had been learning a bunch of tools but I did not know how to make those tools my own. Perhaps I really did not have that special, unique ability to pick up a tool and use it in a way which distinguished me from everyone else in the world. "You mean, don't you," Dr. Beckerman said, "do I really have any talent? Well, *you* have to learn to accept your talent, Joe. We can only recognize it; only you can accept it. And you must know that Jenny [the master teacher of acting] and Margot [the singing teacher] are solidly in your corner. In fact, at this point they are the only members of the faculty who can recognize your talent, but their recognition is a powerful one."

"What about you?" the words shot out of my throat before I could censure myself. This conversation was taking place on his time as my employer and not as the teacher in charge of a program which was moulding me and my life, for in my mind I was still making a distinction between me as a person and me as a student. In fact, now that I look back on this time in my life, I realize that when I resolved that dichotomy, when I let go of that limiting self-view, I began to learn deeply from my teachers because I began to learn from within myself.

Dr. Beckerman smiled, laughed and said, "Well, I accepted you into this program, didn't I?, after you gave perhaps the most awful, ill prepared, ill advised, shallow, terrible audition I had ever seen in my whole life. It was also, by the way, one of the most arrogant. In fact, it was so arrogant—and coupled with such unspeakable badness—that I felt compelled to give you a second chance. I kept telling myself that he could not have come all the way from Africa to show me that. Do you remember what I did?"

I remember very well what he did; he cut me off, brushed aside the baggage I had brought, and attempted to get me into contact with what was still percolating in my blood and breath and body and mind and soul—the sights, sounds, rhythms, people, places and events of Africa. He asked me to tell him about someone I remembered. The image of the woman who sold oranges near the entrance to my apartment building mushroomed in my brain and the thoughts became so vivid, so powerful, so motivating that I became that woman. Through my second chance audition, I was learning one of the fundamental concepts of acting, the transforming power of a thought. When I began to teach acting, I had no clear approach to how I would teach it. I thought that it needed to be a slightly different approach for each student, but what was constant from the very beginning was the willingness to encourage starting all over again, going down as many paths as necessary in order to find the paths which would lead to self-discovery for my students.

* * *

I have come to this practice teaching session filled with the highest expectations. Not only does it represent the culmination of the year at the Faculty, but I am working with an associate whose reputation is solidly grounded in praise, respect, and awe from my colleagues who worked with her before me.[1] This is a teacher who really practices the drama in education method. A great part of the method rests on the ability of the teacher to react in situation, to have the ability to allow the decisions of the students during the course of exploring the drama to influence and indeed determine the next steps. While the teacher needs to know the beginning and end points of the exploration, the vast middle ground of the journey is etched out and built by the students. No amount of preparation will enable you to deal with that uncertainty; no amount of training will enable you to cope with the open ended lesson unless you as a teacher like it that way, are comfortable with thinking, culling, planning and directing ON YOUR FEET. It is teaching at risk.

But I have come to see that it is more than living in and through the moments of the drama with your students, it is also the ongoing process of learning and discovering along with your students; of realizing that what they may bring to the lesson will not only enrich the drama and the drama experience for the other students, but that their insights may profoundly affect the way you think and feel. It is the ultimate teaching at risk experience.

The first part of any drama course concerns itself with building group cohesion, trust, confidence, support, and acceptance. This is accomplished through the careful use of "games" or activities which are designed to place the students in a non-traditional learning situation where they learn about themselves and how they react and interact with others. The underlying glue of these activities is that they are fun and the aphorism "It is not who wins but how you play the game" truly applies.

I encountered this current class at _____ at the mid-semester point. They had been together for eight weeks, meeting for 78 minutes a day, five days a week. Not only were they a "good" class but they had formed some very strong group bonds. When I joined the class they had been working on a new unit for about four days. The theme was war. The class had been divided into groups of five; each group was given a large portfolio of photographic images relating to the Holocaust. They were assigned "roles" as curators of a public museum and were told to come up with an actual exhibit relating to the theme "This Must Never Happen Again". When they had completed their work, they were to present the exhibit to the class and justify their choices regarding arrangement of the images, how the images had been treated, and make a clear statement of what they intended to convey.

I arrived in class on a Monday when they were halfway through their role-playing exercise as curators. They were still working out the arrangement of images for their individual exhibits. I spent two days working with each of the groups asking questions about their work and trying to ease myself into their acceptance. It seemed to be going smoothly. On Wednesday, we began the second phase of the Museum Drama-Exhibit Presentation. For this, I went into role as the

Director of the Museum and welcomed them to the monthly Curators Meeting with the Director. I explained that due to budget cuts, unfortunately I would not be able to fund the exhibition of all the projects. The purpose of the meeting today was to decide which two exhibits would be hung in the museum, and that as curators they should keep in mind this was a professional presentation of their work to their peers.

The presentations were quite good, the answers they gave to the questions I asked of them were thoughtful and sensitive, and the class responded in role as curators with insightful questions. The answers to my questions: "If you could chose any room in the museum to display your exhibit, what room would it be?, what shape would you rebuild the room into? what colour would you have the walls painted?; what special kind of lighting would you want?" produced some extraordinarily creative answers. All of this confirmed that this indeed was a "good" class.

In fact the discussion was so lively and intense that we covered only two out of the four groups. We would continue this role playing presentation tomorrow, Thursday. What the students did ot now was that Ms _____, the regular teacher and my associate, was going to be away at a Curriculum Planning Meeting. Tomorrow there would be a "Supply Teacher" even though I would be doing the teaching. As soon as the first students began to arrive in the classroom on Thursday morning and realized that there was a "supply" the changes in behaviour appeared. The established practice in this drama class had been in effect since the beginning of the semester, some eight weeks ago. It was standard and followed rigidly. Come into class, take off your shoes, put them in the shoe cupboard, and come and sit in a circle and wait for the class to begin.

The first students to arrive glanced quickly at the "supply" and me and very quickly decided that hanging out in the hall was much better. When they eventually drifted into class, no one wanted to take their shoes off, and certainly no one wanted to sit in the circle. After a lot of cajoling, they were shoeless and sitting in a circle. "Who is in charge of leading the game today?," I asked. No response. "Ok, let's see, from the list I have, it appears that Henry is scheduled to do the game today."

"I'm not ready, sir. Let's not play a game today."

"Well, I have a game that is good at getting things going. It's called ZOOM and ZORCH." I attempt to explain this extremely simple game and am amazed that this same group of "good" students has with the disappearance of the regular teacher turned into an uncooperative group of insolent, eyeballs rolling towards the ceiling, adolescents. These were not major changes in behaviour; they were subtle, but they were definite changes. We finished the game because when I suggested that perhaps they had a better game to offer that suggestion was greeted with silence.

When we moved onto the presentation of the last two Holocaust exhibit projects, the same "smart ass get the supply teacher" attitude and behaviour continued.

That night as I thought through the days events, I was struck by two things. First, there had been no change in behaviour with the ESL Drama class. Second, I was really bothered by this change, by the way I had been treated. I could either put all those feelings into a garbage bag and toss them out, or deal with them in some way.

I thought that whatever way I would deal with the situation, it needed to be connected to the lesson of the Holocaust Exhibits and how the Nazis treated their prisoners.

The next day, _____ and I discussed the situation and both agreed that we had to talk to the students about what had happened, and we devised the following scenario.

_____ and I began the class with a fairly straight forward review using brainstorming of "How the Nazis treated their prisoners." The students offered the following reasons:

> They didn't show them any respect; they starved them both with no food and no attention; they dehumanized the prisoners; once they looked at them as non-humans they could do anything they wanted to with them; they made them wear the triangles to humiliate them; they made fun of them; they ignored their needs; they killed them; they tormented them; they tortured them; they didn't care about them

_____ then made the point that a lot of people in Germany at the time did not have direct, hurtful impact upon the prisoners, but they knew what was going on and for a variety of reasons decided not to do anything about it; they just let it happen, and so went along with it.

At this point, _____ motioned to me and said "You, come here, up in front of the class." When I got to the front of the class, she slapped a white triangle onto my chest. She went back into role:

> Well! what oh what do we have here with this nice big fat white triangle on his chest; why I think we have ourselves a real live STUDENT TEACHER here, don't we?; oh, good, he thinks he is coming here to help us and maybe learn something and try to teach us; well, we will show him all right; the real teacher is not here today, so we don't have to do anything we

don't want to to; after all, he's not a person, not a human being; he has no feelings; he's just a student teacher; we don't have to follow any of the rules we all know; he's not even a real teacher, he's a student teacher so we can give him a hard time; what can he do back to us?; we don't have to take our shoes off; we don't have to sit in the circle; we don't even have to attempt to play his stupid game; he's a nobody; we'll just see how far we can push him, and push him and push him until he breaks; he's so stupid he'll never do anything to us; besides if he squeals on us who is going to believe him; he's not a real teacher anyways, he's nothing but a pretend teacher ...

I stood in front of them in my very best humiliation pose and very quickly, like the best acting, the total belief in the imaginary situation which we had created overwhelmed me. The triangle on my chest began to burn itself into my flesh; I felt wounded; I felt branded; I tried to make eye contact with the students seated on the floor in front of me but they all avoided any eye contact. I was riveted to their faces which were ashen. I also realized that I had never felt so humiliated in my entire life. The drama had gotten to me.

_____ then gave them a journal writing assignment where they were asked to explain their actions yesterday and what understanding had they come to regarding them as a result of what they had just experienced; after the writing, we would come into the circle and talk through yesterday's events in light of their new (drama based) experience. The writing assignment took about fifteen minutes. When we were all in a circle, _____ asked who would like to begin. Silence for what seemed like hours.

Their collective embarrassment was palpable, and I wanted to get them off the hook, so I began to share with them why _____ and I had decided to bring the mirror of their behaviour into the lesson and place it before all of us so that collectively we could understand something. I assured them that we considered them a good class, that the work they had done in the drama as museum curators up to this point was filled with insights and feeling, but that the behaviour which they exhibited in the last class was indeed discriminatory, and it was a discrimination which was the result of *subtle* changes, but that it was the subtle kinds of discrimination which were often the most difficult to identify and get rid of. I then told them how I felt standing up there with the white triangle on my chest. I also told them that I did not like the feeling it produced, and that I needed to talk about the incidents in order to learn from them about what I might have done to precipitate such actions. "I am here to learn with and through you and in the course of this learning to teach you and myself something." More silence.

Finally, Martin, one of the best students, spoke, "Well, sir, we did not show you the respect we should to a teacher, but I lost respect for you when you made the sarcastic remark to Henry." The puzzled look on my face invited him to explain further. "It was when some of us were in the circle and you were waiting for the late comers to take their shoes off and join the circle and Henry said 'You can take attendance now, ya know' and you said 'I know how to run a class, Henry' well, I lost respect for you then because he was only telling ya to take attendance and you thought something else."

I was stunned because that aspect of the dynamics of the situation cited had completely escaped me. I looked at Henry and for a while he didn't want to look back even though he was looking at me. I kept thinking to myself: patience, patience, patience. Finally, Henry said, "Naw, Martin, you got it wrong. I was being sarcastic, but I was just trying to see how far I could push him." Martin: Yah, OK, but I didn't get it that way so I still lost respect for him because he came in here and busted into our group and made us uncomfortable when we've been together for a long time and now a stranger is telling us what to do. Maybe its not cool and maybe you were wrong to be sarcastic to him but I still lost respect for him because of the way I saw him treat one of my group.

Henry: Yeh, he's so stern and he don't have no sense of humour and he talks funny. At this point, _____, my associate, jumps in: Wait a minute. He. He. Him. He. Who are we talking about here? This is a person, a human being with a name. Why don't you refer to him by his name?

While I am engaged in this conversation, at the same time the resonance of another conversation with students is fighting with the available space in my mind. It happened during my previous practicum.

* * *

One day there was an assembly and I was given an "ON-CALL" assignment. I had to take a grade ll class to their assembly, sit with them, and at the end of the hour take them back to the class room and control them for another hour while the second assembly happened.

The kids treated me as just another "Supply" and tried to sit through the playing of the Anthem. I made them stand up. The Assembly was to celebrate multicultural week at _____. Since the school is forty per cent Asian, I found it odd that nothing Asian was included on the assembly program. A few black kids (definitely the minority in this school) performed the majority of the musical numbers and two Indian students performed a traditional Indian dance. The VP made some general remarks about multiculturalism and how important it was to the overall education of the students at _____, but she did not mention the large Asian student population and what they contribute to the school's "rich and varied life". When I talked with the kids in the class that I was babysitting, I raised the same issue with them. Why was there no representative of the Asian population at the assembly? Blank stares all around. Including a non response from the Asian students in the classroom. One student said, "Oh they [the Asians] are too busy getting all the good grades to screw around with stuff like singing and stuff."

I decide then and there that I am not going to give them this period to study, but that I was going to take the opportunity to talk to these kids.

"You know, I'm a student just like you now. I'm doing this so that I can get a piece of paper which will allow me to apply for a job when one comes up in order to teach in high school because I really want to work with young people. So if you could give me some advice, what would you say to someone who wants to be a teacher, to someone who wants to be a good teacher?"

Ricardo was the first one to answer. "Do more, a lot more, of what you're doing right now, sir, talk to us. All the teachers in this school got their heads stuck so far in their books they don't look us in the eyes." All around agreement. "Show us some respect" is voiced from several corners of the room. But not just voiced, the message is underlined to the point that I can't ignore it.

"I don't really know what you mean by that. Showing respect is, for me, pretty vague. Teach me how to show you respect."

This time Melissa shoots up her hand and speaks all the while keeping her hand up in the air. "Sir, learn the names of your students. I got three teachers here and I've been in their classes since September and they still don't know my name. She don't know the names of anybody in the class."

Adé, a very fair skinned kid from Somalia, asks, "What's your name, sir, you never told us your name?"

Instinctively and because I feel very comfortable with this sudden openness on their part, I say "Joe." The class breaks out in applause. The conversation takes off now and moves rapidly from the Mike Tyson case to Rodney King to date rape to their feelings about the school (very negative) and no matter how many things are discussed somehow we always seem to get back to the idea that "teachers don't respect their students". Once again Ricardo, "Look, sir, uh, Joe, don't assume that just because I didn't do my homework I'm a total jerkoff. Try to find out why I didn't get it done. How do you know, man, that my Mama didn't die last night or something like that. You won't know if you don't axe." "Ask." "Yeah, you're right, I mean ask."

Since these kids keep bringing up the topic of respect, I feel that I need to point out something to them which they have overlooked. "Do you think respect is a two way street?" No response but they have the look in their eyes of thinking through something new and intriguing. "Look, I'm not trying to excuse a teacher who doesn't know your name. That's terrible and I think you have the right to say to that teacher in a polite and non aggressive manner, Miss, I would like it if you could make an effort to remember my name and to use it when you speak to me. I'm talking about the nature of the respect that you as students show to teachers who do know your name."

"Sir, if a teacher knows my name and still makes the lessons boring, do they deserve my respect anyways? If I don't show respect to the teacher, they can make me pay for it, but if they don't show respect to us by making the lessons interesting, the only thing we can do is tune out or make trouble."

"What's the difference between an interesting lesson and a boring lesson?"

"When you can see your face in the lesson, sir, it's interesting."

* * *

"Why don't you refer to Mr. Totaro by his name?," _____ repeats to a silent group.

"It's too difficult, Miss. I can't pronounce it. It's too hard to say."

With the conversation of the other students still resonating in my head and with Martin's slightly twisted conception of the nature of student-teacher respect still hanging out there unresolved, I decided to raise the stakes a little in this exercise:

"I've been told by other students that knowing their names is important to them and that a lot of their teachers don't know their names after being together for six months. I've been here for three full days now, and I have made a very great effort to learn the names of all the students in my classes and I am teaching three classes. I know all of your names. [I went around the circle and named each of them.] I learned your names because it is important to me to be able to look you in the eye and say your name. It is a sign of respect. Now what does it tell you about the way you view your responsibilities in any relationship regarding respect? (pause) Is respect a two way street? (pause pause pause) But I can understand how some of you might find my name difficult. So why not call me Joe. When I taught at university I always told my students they could call me whatever they wanted — just as long as they could say it to my face. ... Laughter at last broke through. The tension eased. Some of the students did call me Joe for a few days, but by the end of the three week practicum, all of them had gone back to using my surname and attaching the ever present "sir".

The next to the last day of my practicum, I asked this class permission to have _____ give me the journal entries they had written after our triangle role playing exercise. They all agreed.

"I now understand that what I did to the teacher was wrong and it doesn't make me feel good at all. I feel like I intentionally hurt someone just because they were different. I really don't like that feeling, and it scares me because if we hadn't done this drama in class I might not never have had this feeling which I now understand is an important feeling to have. The more I think about it, the more important it becomes."

"I knew we was going to catch hell for what we did, but I didn't think I was going to feel this bad about it. It really sucks when you hurt someone when you could have not hurt them at all in the first place. I never thought much about it until now, but I hope I never forget it."

* * *

I don't know why I do it, but there are times when I ignore the myriad instincts racing around my mind-body-soul trinity. When I ignore my instincts which have always pushed me along paths not traditionally taken; when I cave into the pressure (is it perceived? is it real?) of a situation and behave as others expect or require me to behave, I have always come to regret not listening to my needs, my instincts. When I only hear what others want of me and when I cease to listen to me, my involvement becomes distanced. I don't like it, but for someone who views himself as a "doer" I can't seem to reverse the tide of events. I give up sometimes and "go along". It appears to be easier, but in the end it causes a tremendous sense of turmoil and personal betrayal. It is a denial of risk, and for me that is perhaps the greatest risk of all.

Having written this, I pause and my mind wanders back toward a practicum experience where I gave up, where I denied risk taking, where I gave in to an associate who made me feel less than adequate to the task of teaching French. Now that I have some distance from the events, I realize that the experience revived fears from my own schooling days ... fears I thought had been successfully calmed.

* * *

I have just completed another journey. While not exactly into another country, it was in some aspects a journey into another time period. For two weeks I was time warped. I taught in this collegiate in the suburbs. The visual aspects of the outside and interior of this school, both of the buildings and the look of the students, reminded me of what a "school" was like when I went to school. Frightening. The first image of my new school was the immense illuminated sign on the front lawn of the school, "Congratulations, Student of the Month, "_____". But my attention is quickly drawn to streams of cars driven by parents dropping off their children at the front door of the school. At 3:15 the same parents driving the same assortment of BMWs, Jaguars, Mercedes, Lexus, and Toyotas, and Hondas and Volvos and an honest to god Rolls Royce thrown in were back at the front door of the school waiting to retrieve their children.

As I enter the school lobby my eye is assaulted by visual images praising the student in every imaginable academic and extracurricular activity. After I had been there for a few days, I noticed that all of this "Here is our student body and this is what he have done and do!" was concentrated in the main entrance lobby. Elsewhere in this vast school (there are five gymnasia), I notice that the walls are bare. There is a lot of animation and excitement in the halls, but there is not the kind of NOISE that I have experienced in other schools. The difference is there is no "rock music of choice" being blasted over the school's PA system. These students gather in groups and enjoy each other's company; they talk to each other; no one wears a Walkman. As I walk through the halls, students actually leave their coats in their lockers. In fact, NO ONE wears an overcoat to class with the implied message of "I am outta here". Here the students wear clothes, real, old fashioned going to school clothes, not the bizarre costumes I have been used to seeing. These kids who are dropped off and collected by their parents are also outfitted in slacks (some jeans), turtlenecks, sweaters, blouses, skirts, and an assortment of designer footwear. Not only did I *not* see a single girl wearing unlaced black combat boots, but neither did I see a single HAT of any kind, shape, or vintage on any student's head—unless they were coming in or going out. In this school HAIR is what you sport on you head. Perfectly groomed, perfectly dressed, perfectly behaved, and, as I was to experience it, perfectly bland. It was without a doubt the most perfectly organized and efficiently run school I had been in since the beginning of the year.

By the time I finished my two weeks of 'imprisonment' and 'control' at this 'ideal' school, I began to understand why the teachers all made such a concerted effort to tell us during the first day there that "This is such a great school" It is a great school for the teachers; somewhere along the way, the students fit into the picture.

My associate had been teaching French for a long time and his spoken French was excellent. Every class, every period, every day began precisely on time with the door locked. Instructions given to the class to copy their homework assignment in their notebooks. Done. Notebooks closed and placed *under* the desks. Desk tops cleared. Attention to the board at the right. Irregular verb of the day. "What are the seven principal parts of the verb "VALOIR"? Written on the board directly under printed signs attached to the top of the board indicating "INFINITIF" "PARTICIPE PRESENT" "PARTICIPE PASSE" "PASSE SIMPLE" "PRESENT DE L'INDICATIF" "FUTUR" "PRESENT DU SUBJONCTIF" Repeat after me. Again. What is irregular? Underline it. Copy and complete your verb charts. Test on Friday.

I was immediately struck by two things: his extraordinary enthusiasm, bounce, vigor, and energy in teaching (he really seemed to love it) and the pathetic, robot like quality of his students. They were soon to become my students, I thought. I sat and observed for two days. His performances were remarkable. Over the years, he had managed to convert every grammar rule in the French language to a simple pictograph/diagram which he would write on the board and immediately draw a rectangle around it. "What is the rule?" And the kids would robot back the rule. Here is an example of the rule. Copy this in your notebooks. Open your books to Exercise A. Sentence one, Felecia. No, not correct. What is the rule? Exercises done. Reading. Reading done. Dictation. Dictation done. Class done. Package tied up in a great big neat bow. Teacher dancing on air. Students dead as doornails.

After the class, I feel cornered as he interrogates me about the ins and outs and ups and downs of his lesson. Did I notice how organized it was? Did I notice how quiet the students were? Did I notice the pattern: rule, example, rule, example? I was numb. Yes, I noticed all of the above. I also noticed that in this seventy-six minute language class, the teacher spoke for sixty-six minutes. I also noticed that in this Advanced French Immersion Class, of the students who did speak, the majority made major grammar errors. I *noticed* these things, but I did not give voice to them. Why? Partly because I am basically a polite person; partly because I have an age perspective which allows me to know that there isn't anything I can't put up with for a known period of time, and partly (maybe mostly) because of the demons of the past which still seek to attack when I feel vulnerable, and the beginning of any practicum, or new job, or new anything, renders me vulnerable. Suddenly, as I write this I am thrown back to an earlier journal entry.

* * *

The Collegiate is the site of a student teaching assignment; I am working with the Head of the French Department who is also in charge of the Gifted Students Programme. Possibly because the collegiate offers free breakfast for anyone who wants to get to the student cafeteria before eight thirty in the morning, no one comes to class hungry in this programme. All the students arrive early for class, go to their desks, get their books ready, and engage in the pre-class banter in French when the teacher is around and in English at all other times. The danger for me is that I have a tendency to regard the gifted students as adult learners and forget they are kids and need to be reached as individuals; they still require the focussed attention of an adult, and, most importantly, they have an extraordinary need to have their achievements recognized and praised. Correcting a mistake in grammar or pronunciation becomes an exercise in positive reinforcement. Somehow I am more aware of this need with the gifted kids than I was with the kids at other schools. It may be that with the gifted classes I am only teaching eight to fourteen students in each class while the average class size at other schools was thirty.

I don't know why the vulnerability of a gifted child is more readily apparent to me than the vulnerability of an average student, but it is. These gifted kids are completely centered on task accomplishment and "getting it right". When you correct a mistake on their worksheets their look of remorse and terror is immediate. I find it difficult to ignore the shattered look in the eyes. It seems that for the average student, a mistake is a mistake is a mistake—OK I'll get it right next time, if I remember. I learned quickly enough, however, that the shattered vulnerable look was preferable to the other standard response of the gifted kids, "Oh, this exercise is too dumb and too easy and too boring; I've done this stuff before." That response is as difficult to deal with as is the belligerent response of the budding "hood" in the classroom. They are linked, however, by the emotion of insecurity.

My own insecurity has been the axis of my thoughts for the past few days. I have spent untold hours at night gazing at French text books knowing I had to make a decision so I could BEGIN the lesson planning. I can't begin. Something keeps me riveted on the books and away from the decisions, the actions which will lead to a completed lesson plan and finally to bed. I had forgotten about the sources of my deep insecurity concerning my intellectual ability, but as I walked around the school's middle class Italian and Greek neighborhood during this afternoon's lunch break, it all came flooding back to me. Of course, when I was younger I was forced to deal with this, and I did deal with it, but dealing with a ghost and putting the ghost firmly into perspective does not make the ghost go away. Once an addict always an addict; once an   alcoholic always an alcoholic. In my case, no matter what I have accomplished, once I was labelled that label has always remained there in the deepest, farthest corner of my brain, especially when I am vulnerable.

When I was in Grade Six, the teacher asked me to take a large folded white paper down to the principal's office. Two days earlier, the class had been given an intelligence test. I knew the test scores were written on the paper I had in my hand. I can't remember when I decided to do it, but I whipped into the Boy's Room, went into a stall, closed the door, opened the paper, found my name on the left hand side of the paper and quickly followed with my eyes across the paper to the right side where the scores were recorded.

J.Totaro --- 90

I had an IQ of 90. I was almost certain the principal could not tell I was guilty of peeking as I handed the paper to him.

The full impact of my sneaking a peak at the paper Mrs. Laughlin had asked me to take to the office smashed into my consciousness several months later. Up to that point, I thought that the highest IQ score you could get was 100 so 90 was pretty good. It was in one of those Condensed Reader's Digest Magazines one often finds in Dentist's Offices that I read several months later (while waiting to get a cavity filled) that I was at the very *very* bottom of the average group. According to the Reader's Digest article, one point less and I was well on the road to being an idiot. But I knew I was not that because my score was 90. 90 meant that I was less than average.

My mother wondered why I had lost my appetite and appeared "a little sick" for the next few weeks. I was never able to tell my parents why I was "a little sick" because even at that point it had been made abundantly clear to me that I was going to get a university degree. Maybe even more than one. Maybe even one for each of the degrees my parents never had.

When I started Grade Seven a few weeks later, I was still feeling "a little sick". But this seemed to disappear as time went by. In my high school, at the end of Grade Seven, you and the "school" made a choice about which "track" you were going to follow until graduation. If you wanted to follow the "academic track" in order to get into university, you had to study a foreign language because, at the time, you had to have studied a foreign language in order to meet entrance requirements for universities of distinction. Also, at the time, most universities required at least two years of university level foreign language study as part of the BA degree.

We were given a diagnostic language test, and a week after the test, I was called into the Principal's Office. The results of the test showed that I was incapable of learning a foreign language, would not be able to pass the foreign language requirement for the high school diploma in the academic track, and therefore would not be able to get into a university. I should take this form home to my parents and decide which trade I wanted to learn, have them sign it, and I would be enrolled in the "general track". Even though I felt as if I was going to vomit as I left his office, it somehow seemed to make some kind of strange sense to me because I knew I only had a below average IQ. Nonetheless, I was not able to discuss this with my parents; I could not find the words. When my father was contacted by the school because the "form" had not been returned, we were scheduled for a parents visit with the principal. My father insisted I was to be present at the meeting; I was the one who was going to have to do the work, after all was said and done. It was my first lesson on how to structure a meeting to achieve what you want no matter the agenda. I was well on the road to becoming an academic administrator before I was in high school.

Parental demand steamrolled the principal into submission, and I embarked on my first course of study in French knowing that I could not do it and that it was pretty amazing I could even read a book. I did four years of French in high school, four at university, lived in a French speaking African country for two years, became completely fluent in French, and all the while, the ghost hovered, the ghost which said that no matter what I was actually doing, I should not be able to be doing it because I really was not capable of achieving what I had actually achieved!

The label still haunts me. Last night I had to peel it off one more time before I could begin thinking in French.

MEMORIES OF PRACTICE TEACHING[2]

"We will take twenty minutes, no twenty-five minutes for lunch, and then I will show you how I have planned the next two weeks." An associate and I are standing in the hall now. A student approaches to ask a question. "No, no, no, you can ask your questions in the morning. I am here every morning at seven-thirty. I answer questions in the morning." The student turns and leaves silently. My associate gives me a look as if to say, "Now that's the way to deal with that!" and saunters down the hall towards his lunch. I can't get outside fast enough to have a cigarette.

* * *

I am waiting outside the French Office door. Several staff who pass by offer to let me into the office, but I want to be standing there waiting, on time, when my associate arrives. "I am going to allow you to teach the Grade Ten class [direct quote...allow quickly runs around my head] because they are now very well behaved and you won't have any discipline problems with them at all. They were terrible at the beginning of the year, but now they know the rules and if one of them steps out of line, they have to come in at seven-thirty in the morning and wash the tops of all the desks; then I make them write out *three* times a verb chart. They won't give you any trouble. You will teach them what I started today and in seven days you will finish the unit and give them a test." She walked over to an imposing bank of lethal looking file cabinets, opened a drawer, and retrieved the file folder containing the test for the Unit. It was mimeographed. I looked in utter amazement. There were two thoughts duelling within my head for the first cut and thrust. 'She wants me to teach to the test, her test' vs 'No one has used a mimeograph machine in fifteen years, this test is fifteen, what, twenty years old!' He must have read part of my mind, because he said, "This is just an old copy; the ladies in the office have put it on one of those machines they use today and it looks perfectly lovely. So, now you have the test, the assignments, here is how I organize my grade book. Look at it while I try to organize the PD day for next week; the administration wants it on this destreaming nonsense; won't work, you know; this new minister seems like a more sensible one than the last one and I have heard through the grapevine that he is going to throw the whole destreaming mess right out the window. By the way, before you leave, I shall show you how to make the signs for the principal parts of the verbs. Invaluable things. Once they are tacked up above the board, you always know exactly where to put the different forms."

* * *

For two days, I attempted to follow my associate's way of doing things. I was also introduced to the "teach by the stop watch method". She told me every day in minutes and seconds how long I took to do the irregular verb parts, how long to review the homework assignment, how long to do exercise D. She then told me how long it SHOULD HAVE TAKEN.

"What if there are questions?" I offered knowing, in part, that my final report was now going to be based on how well I maintained her time schedule as well. "Have them write them down in the notebooks and come and see you in the morning before homeform. It's good for them. Gives them extra time with the teacher and allows you to build a better relationship with them."

* * *

For the third day, I was to begin teaching "conditional sentences" and the verb sequence required if the subordinate clause begins with 'if' (si). My associate had drawn for me one of his pictographs explaining the order of tenses, but I put it aside and decided that I had to risk teaching the class on my own in my own way. I wrote a series of dialogues for the students to prepare; dialogues which posed various problems and solutions if one course of action was taken over another. I also invented a game to play which would reinforce the required verb tense sequences. The students were going to do most of the talking in this class and I didn't care what the consequences were. I thought that it might be best if I started the class with those wretched irregular verbs and those verb charts. I then told the class that we were going to split into roups of three and they were going to rehearse a little dialogue which I had prepared for them. We would present them to the rest of the class. They quickly formed their own groups and in ten minutes the presentations began. "What's similar about these situations?" Hands up all over the place. "The kid asks his parents to do something and they say OK if you do such and so." "Right. What else?" "One scene happens today, the other yesterday, and the other tomorrow." "Right again! What do we use when we talk about these conditional things in the present?" The discussion is launched. I then drop the bombshell. "OK, we are going to play a game." I explain the game and like most games the first few times everyone screws up and laughs. I laugh too. I remark to myself that this is the first time I remember hearing these kids laugh. After the game, we tackle the exercises, and I break up the parts of the sentences between two students and have them read them as if it were one sentence. In the middle of the exercise, the period bell rings, and I realize that I only covered half of her (mine?) lesson plan.

My associate peels the skin off of me like a banana at the critique. She never referred directly to the original dialogues or to the game; she was very concerned about the level of noise in the classroom, said that I had lost complete control of the class, and that if I continued to do things "like that" the students would eat me alive; besides I did not cover enough material and no one wrote down anything in their notebooks and none of the verbs covered in class were included on the test. She kept returning to the extraordinary amount of noise that that been unleashed in class.

I finally felt that I needed to reply, but it was a reply that I was making while I was tossing in the towel at the same time. I explained to my associate that I could understand how she would consider that I had lost control of the class because of what she perceived as excessive noise. I agreed with her that there indeed was more animation in the class and that did produce more noise, but that to my ears and to my sensibility, I was willing to accept that noise in a language classroom because as far as I could hear most of the noise was being made in French.

I had made my point mostly for myself, but I knew that I would be killed in my evaluation if I tried anymore of that nonregulation stuff. I backed down from my convictions; I wasn't going to risk getting a bad report; I took the safe way. I felt numbed, but I had already accepted the idea of doing it his way in order to get a good report; now I only had to do it.

I did it as best I knew how to. I had spent the past twenty years in some form of acting—either doing it or teaching it. I did not have to be a murderer in order to act a murderer. I only had to convince the audience to believe that I was a murderer. Did I convince this audience of Grade Tens?

The day before I left, my associate asked me if I would be interested in getting some feed back from the students about my teaching. She proposed asking them two simple questions: What I liked about Mr. Totaro? and What I did not like about Mr. Totaro? The implication, presumably, was what I liked about Mr. Totaro as a teacher. I agreed to the exercise. She assured me that he would not look at their comments at all, that she would seal them in an envelope which I would address for her, and send the comment off to me.

They arrived one week later. I shall keep them for a long time, and I shall read them whenever I am tempted to take the easy path.

> I liked the way you tried to teach us things without treating us like idiots.
> I hated the way you started trying to get in good with _____.
> You were very patient with us, you didn't scream at us when we made mistakes. You taught at a speed that was normal and so that we could understand you.
> You should teach the way you want to teach and not copy other people.
> This teacher needs to find his own style.
> When you stopped using the games and things, I got the impression you gave up on us and just did what _____ does all the time.
> You made the lessons fun, but then you seemed to give up on your ideas.

The rest of the comments were similar to the ones above. As I read them, I felt the flush of shame rising in my face.

* * *

"Remember, Joe, the single most important thing about learning any language is to learn the rules of the grammar. If you emphasize grammar, you always have something to come back to; it's the safest port in the storm of the classroom. Good luck!"

* * *

The experiences of such practicums have hung about my head like the Furies in Sophocles. One of the winged beasts carries a sign saying "Language is Grammar". More than anything else, this legacy bothers me, and that image festers in my memory. I am truly in love with language and especially with the evocative power of language. As an actor, I chose to concentrate the development of my career in a theatre which was rooted in great, powerful, poetic language. As a teacher of actors, I had scant interest in the modern theatre as a source of texts for exploration. Through all of this, I know that language is a vessel for individual expression, and that the most extraordinary usage of language is intimately tied to the individual's need to communicate. As a teacher of language (or of acting), I want my students to experience a need to say something, to experience the direct connection between visceral and vocal language.

* * *

Part of the joy of another practicum is teaching two ESL Drama classes. It is beginning to take on the aspects of a religious experience: I have climbed the mountain and have seen the light. Each and every class is a bone tingling thrill. You do, you explore, and you see the results every day. You also get back from these students ten fold what you bring to them. I am convinced that this display of appreciation for the teacher is connected to these students' understanding of the privileges connected with free public education. It also has something to do with their attachment to the context of language learning: they NEED to learn and this need enables them to take some extraordinary risks in the classroom.

Like other Drama classes, the ESL Drama classes begin with the playing of a game. My associate and I have decided, however, that we want to call them "activities" rather than "games" because we want to link the doing of these things to an understanding that they are another way of exploring the skills one learns in a drama class. On one of the boards, we have printed:

SKILLS

In drama we learn:

- Participation (joining in)

- Communication (getting along with others
- Listening skills
- Writing skills
- Cooperation
- Respect for other religions, cultures, differences
- Respect for ourselves
- Confidence
- Problem solving
- Decision making
- Understanding
- Observation (watching)

Each day a different student teaches the other students a game from his/her culture and, where possible, a song. After each activity, the question "What skills did we use to do this activity?" is asked and answered by the group.

For the last two weeks of my stay with them, we are going to explore stories from their cultures. We begin the unit by doing some exercises related to memory. Their assignment for the next class is to think about something in their past, something which happened to them, how old were they, where did it happen, what time of year was it, what sights, sounds, smells do they remember, what are the details of what happened, and how did they feel about what happened. When my associate and I were going over the items to be included on the assignment, she took my list and added "something which you are comfortable talking about and sharing with the class". When I explained the assignment to the class, I left that out. Was it an oversight? or was it my attempt to raise the stakes of personal involvement in the exercise? I may never know for sure, but I suspect that I wanted to deepen the need to tell a story. At any rate, the stories blew me and my associate and the class out of the water.

I did not know what to expect when it came to the actual sharing of the stories, for the class was truly destreamed in terms of fluency in English. In fact, I believed the exercise might be beyond their linguistic capabilities. I was particularly worried about the students from Vietnam. They were timid, spoke so softly as to be nearly inaudible, and of all the students in the class they had the most "heavy" accents. In a circle: "Who wants to begin?" Reuban, from Sri Lanka, the best student in the class, raises his hand and begins to tell the story of how he was riding on his bicycle one day when gun shots and bombs began exploding all around him; he was ten and an older man tried to steal his bicycle in order to get away from some soldiers who were chasing him. He convinced the man to ride on the back of his bike and together they got away. When Reuben stopped to let the man off, the man fell to the ground. He had been shot in the back and was dead. When he finishes there is an atmosphere of electric silence around the circle. Without any prompting, the questions from the other students begin; they are excellent, well phrased, insightful questions. Fourteen different accents and fourteen different levels of English fluency achievement no longer seem to make any difference at all. There is within the group a collective need to know more and to share, and to do this is English.

"Teacher, I want go next." says Tang[3] one of the students from Vietnam. My heart sinks a lot because I am particularly worried about Tang. He is twenty-eight and looks twelve; he is frail, has a squeaky high pitched voice and of all the students in the class is the one student I find the most difficult to understand. It was such a good beginning, I did not want the class to get set back at all. Every time I look at Tang I keep thinking to myself, "How is he going to make it here; he'll get blown away."

Tang's story was about his escape from Vietnam. He was one of eight children, and his family had decided that he was the one family member who would attempt the escape. A place in one of the boats costs three thousand American dollars which his family raised on the black market by selling "pieces of gold". He was told by the captain of the boat the date, time, and place of the boat's departure. It was from an isolated fishing village at midnight next week. No baggage allowed. There were 185 people on the boat which was ten meters long and three meters wide. There was no food and no drinking water except for the private supply of the captain and his crew all of whom also had machine guns. They were on the South China Sea for nine days, and Tang showed us how he sat for the entire period. After the fourth day, some of the weak people on the boat began to die. Each morning when the sun came up, three or four people had died during the night. The captain made the passengers throw the dead bodies into the sea. The bodies did not float very long on the surface, however, because soon huge sharks came swimming by and ate them up. Sometimes the sharks would bump and shake the boat.

More questions and more answers flow.

Jimmy, from Guatemala, begins to tell a story. I can't believe it. This is the first time he has spoken in class. Jimmy was a soldier and fought against the Communists. At the beginning of the war, he had six brothers and four sisters. Most of them were dead now because Jimmy's father was a colonel in the government's army. Jimmy and his brother were hiding in the jungle trying to get some sleep after having fought all night long. They were sleeping in a trench when he woke up from the sound of a "flying bomb". It landed next to his brother, exploded and killed him. Some of the shrapnel blasted into Jimmy's stomach. He waited for the shelling to stop and then dragged his brother into the jungle and tried to bury him. He passed out from the effort, and when he came to he was back in his camp surrounded by his friends who had found him and brought him back. It took him three months to heal. Because the wounds made it difficult for him to walk, his captain put him in charge of guarding the Communist prisoners they had taken. One day, he heard his captain torturing a group of prisoners. He recognized this man and his wife because they were from a village near his own. He also realized that it was pointless to torture them. They didn't know anything. Jimmy asked the captain to stop beating the woman because it "make my heart break into pieces". The captain flew into a rage and ordered Jimmy to take his machine gun and execute the man and the woman immediately. "The man he look me in eyes and no speak but talk and say me with eyes its okay you kill me, you only do what he makes you not want to do; if you not obey him he kill us everybody; I see you good man, you try to be good with us; it's okay. My captain he make me burn these peoples after; so that my memory my country."

There are no questions this time. My eyes are brimming with tears. I look around the circle; grim faced wide eyed students are transfixed, some crying, some slowly shaking their heads; all in some way thinking through their own story of how and why they have arrived at this story circle; the feeling of understanding and acceptance is palpable. The language I heard has given me a new and profound understanding of the real relationship between language and grammar and context.

The language I heard has taught me something about the nature of eloquence.

POSTSCRIPT AND THE PROMISE OF THINGS TO COME

Every young actor at the beginning of his career shares a common bond. The telephone. You wait for that call from your agent or from the producer to come in and audition, to read for the part, or to tell you that you got the job. As a young actor, I hated that dependence, and I am old enough to remember how filled with a sense of freedom I felt when home answering telephone machines were finally affordable.

Twenty-five years later, I am an older teacher searching for my entry into a different branch of a profession which has nurtured me for fifteen years. When I went to the Faculty two years ago in order to get another degree and the Ontario Teaching Certificate so that I could work in the secondary panel of the public school system in Ontario, I knew it would be a new beginning for me, but I did not know I would find myself back at the same level of dependence on the telephone I experienced as a young actor.

Supply teachers for the Toronto Board are required to be near their telephones from 6:30 until 8:00 each morning and from five to seven each night. I sit and sip strong black coffee, read the "Globe and Mail" and wait for "DIC" to call. "DIC" is the acronym for Dispatch Information Computer. My early morning and early evening life revolves around DIC. "Sorry, I can't make it to the seven o'clock movie; I'm waiting for DIC to call."

"Something there is that does not like a wall" and something deep in me does not like the depersonalization of a computer invitation to go forth an participate in one of the most personal forms of communication—teaching.

It is ironic that if you get a contract job (and theoretically even if you don't) you get a telephone call from a real person, the principal. I would have used "human being" instead of real person, but some of my experiences with principals have (sadly) left me wondering if that description is apt and true.

Having spent last year as an LTO teaching French, I began this new school year having been placed on the A List of Occasional Teachers for the Toronto Board. "Oh, you'll work EVERY day" I'm told by everyone who seems to know anything about public education which seems to be everybody. That's nice, but it also means waiting for the telephone to ring.

The first time DIC called me, I was so excited I forgot my Personal Identification Number (yet another PIN to remember!). Four permutations of the last three digits later and finally the bright, male computer voice says, "There is an occasional teaching position available at (pause) .... on (pause) Tuesday, October 1. The subject is (pause) Dramatic Arts. Special instructions are none. If you wish to accept this assignment and receive the Job Number, Press 1. I press 1, and my life changes.

I know where the school is because I passed it every day last year on my way to teach French. The school had a bad reputation, but my first impression of the building puts me at ease. The school is spic and span clean. The office manager is warm and friendly and remembers to give me a key to the washroom. When I find the Drama classroom in the bowels of the building, I begin to relax until I see on the desk the file folder marked in vibrant red "SUPPLY". As soon as I open it, my stomach begins to tighten. I have not been left class attendance lists. I am dead meat before I begin. I know it, and as soon as I say to the class that they will need to please print their names and home forms on the attendance sheet which is being passed around they already know that I have no idea of who is supposed to be in this class. Moreover, I don't know their names.

I have come to realize that the readiness of students to identify themselves by their names is an instant and, in my experience, unerring indication of the kind of a school I am going to be teaching in for the day. In the "marginal", "difficult", and "tough" schools the first encounter between student and supply teacher is characterized by wariness, suspicion, and aloofness. Scene: Empty classroom. You, standing by the desk. First student enters.: "You a supply?" Although this is meant to be a question, it is always uttered as an indictment. This first verbal encounter is followed by stone faced visual assessment with the eyes revealing a script of "What buttons can I push?; how much can I get away with?" Or before I can even answer the indictment, they turn on their heels, and you never see them again although you can hear them gleefully telling everyone in the hall, "Let's get the hell out of here! There's a supply today." In this scene, even before the class starts you have been dehumanized and depersonalized. In the so called "good" and "academic" schools, the characters are the same but the dynamics are very different. "Good morning, sir. Are you going to be our teacher today? What's your name, sir? I'm Jeremy. What happened to Miss? Is she sick?" All during this scene, the eyes are bright and the stagiest revealed is clearly one of "This could be interesting. Here is someone who will teach us something in a different way."

But the scene at . ... this morning is closer to the scenario of the first example above. Facing those students who either did not get the message that there was a supply today or who decided they were going to give it a try, I begin the task of attempting to take attendance without a class roster. "What's your name?" "I'm a human being." Not a good beginning. "I know your a human being, but I need to know your name so that I can take attendance. You see, according to the Education Act, I am responsible for you during the time you are enrolled in a class which I am in charge of, and in order for me to fulfill my responsibilities I need to know your name." Most of the time, this works, but often I spend an inordinate amount of time simply attempting to identify the kids in my charge for the next seventy-five minutes. Why are these kids so suspicious of a new teacher? Or are they simply suspicious of a new male white authority figure? Why do they desperately hang on to the identity of their names? They seem to be as afraid of giving up their names as they are of giving up their walkmans and hats and huge coats. I know you can't teach a subject until you reach a kid, but how do you reach a kid when she won't share with you—in the first instance—her name?

Most of the rest of the class is spent in vain trying to get them into a circle so that we can do a warmup and explore the lesson on building a sound machine which the "real teacher" has left for me to do. Don't leave me a lesson plan, don't leave me directions or a key to the washroom, but please, please, please, leave me a list of the names of the kids in the class.

I'm exhausted at the end of the class which the students have decided ends five minutes before the timetable in front of me says the class ends. Suddenly there is a flurry of big coats and walkmans marching irresolutely towards the door and the hall to freedom. One student stays behind to talk and console me: "Don't worry sir, they're just as bad with Miss .... But why don't you just yell at them the way Miss .... always does. She always yells at them all the time."

"Oh, I don't like to yell; it's a waste of my energy."

"But Miss .... does it all the time."

"Does it do any good?"

"No, sir, they just do what they want to, but they should be yelled at!"

When she leaves, I look at the timetable and realize that the last two periods of the day are Grade 9 Drama Classes. Christ. Grade 9 after lunch with a bubbling mix of too much sugar, too many hormones, and too much of anything else they might have put into their tireless bodies. Luckily, I have a spare now and I sneak out of the back of the school, get into my car, and speed home to retrieve my secret weapon . If it's not there, I *am* going to be toast.

I spent the lunch hour in the teacher's cafeteria networking and giving my name and telephone number to anyone who would take it. I found out a lot about the school and its recent troubled past, but I remark about the positive atmosphere in the school.

I am a teeny bit late getting down to the Drama classroom. The door to the room is locked and the hall is a zoo. Sinkers of "SUPPLY" are hissed at each other as I pass through the center of the masses climbing the walls of the lockers. I open the door and they rush in, but I can't get the damn key out of the lock and when I finally arrive in the drama room they are on the walls, the floor, the ceiling, the scene lights have been hooked up to the disco mode on the board and are flashing like crazy; paper missiles and assorted hacky sacks, hats, and empty chips boxes and Pepsi cans are zooming past my ears. I am hit on the back of the head by a paper clip flung from a rubber band clutched in the hands of someone in this maelstrom of adolescent giddiness.

"I need everyone to sit down and please be quiet so that I can begin the class and take attendance." Zero effect. I try several variations of this with rising volume. Zero effect. I plough ahead with attempting to get names and am greeted with an extraordinary number of "human beings" and names like Roberto Alomar and Muhammed Ali. This is not going to work. The class is clearly out of control—both mine and theirs. The Pepsi can hitting my head is when I remember my secret weapon. I go behind my desk, reach into my briefcase and pull it out. I begin to take Polaroid pictures of this hysterical group. With the first flash, the noise in the Drama room turns into a frenzy; with the second flash, the kids clam up; with the third flash, the only noise in the room is the sound of the camera motor spitting out the incriminating evidence. They are stunned, wide eyed, and they are quiet. I have their attention. "I'm always willing to try something new, and since you all have refused to help me with the attendance by giving me your names, I'll just attach these pictures to the end of day report that I am going to leave for your teacher. I'm sure she'll be able to recognize each of you. I'm Mr. Totaro and I am your teacher today. We are going to start by playing a name game."

* * *

What a difference a phone call makes! Today I am introduced to a new collegiate. It is not one of the ones mentioned in breathless hushed reverence when the "top" collegiates are discussed, but it is in an "immigrant" neighborhood. As I approach the front steps of the collegiate, fifteen to twenty students are chatting and hanging out, but one of them opens the door for me and says "Mornin', sir". This is a good sign. The halls are filled with groups of kids sitting and reviewing work; mainly European, Asian, and kids from Somalia. The first class on the timetable is Italian, and I don't speak Italian despite my last name. When I get to the room, there are six or seven kids sitting at their desks and chatting. They are open, friendly, immediately ask me my name and introduce themselves, inquire after their teacher, and giggle when I tell them that I don't speak Italian. "But you speak French, sir, so we'll all learn something today, won't we?" Yes ... we did. Why do these kids reach out to a stranger and allow a relationship to evolve through a class period while other kids immediately throw paper clips and Pepsi cans? In this school, I observe kids in class with no hats, no walkmans, no overcoats, no overt messages of "I'mm outta here". They all have notebooks, paper, pens, pencils, and their books are with them not in their lockers. They speak easily with a strange adult and show civility and good social manners. Most of them carry themselves with a sense of high self-esteem. Although I have no way of proving it, I feel that if I needed to contact the adult or adults in their lives, I would be able to talk with them even if through an interpreter.

DRAMA ON IMMIGRATION IN INNERCITY SCHOOL[4]

There is a hole in my halftime timetable teaching French in the grade nine gifted programme, and it is decided that I will go out into the feeder public schools and conduct Drama workshops with the grade eight gifted programme classes. It really is PR work, but I am thrilled to be able to use some of the Drama in Education stuff I have acquired because I have been struggling with how to incorporate Drama techniques into the teaching of French. Participation in Drama work requires a level of linguistic achievement on the student's part in order to participate in and help create and explore the imaginative circumstances which are the heart and soul of the drama work.

We decide to approach the teacher at Public School because we have heard she is not only teaching in the gifted programme but that she herself is a gifted teacher. European born and a former professor at one of the province's prestigious universities, she turned to public school teaching when her university department was abolished. At first sight of her, I like her immediately. There is an Old 'World' atmosphere in the classroom; this has got to be one of the oldest public school buildings in the city; huge room with enormous windows and twenty foot ceilings; there is a feeling of ordered clutter about the space; this room is used. The kids are writing something when I arrive which gives Jane and me the opportunity to chat quietly and get to know each other. An open, friendly manner and an immediate desire to explore the uses of Drama in her classroom because she feels these kids are extremely confident in their abilities to reason and think (she explains as she points to her shoulders and head area) but they are less secure in learning and exploring from their hearts and emotions. Because she has no formal training in the uses of Drama in Education she has never introduced this work; therefore the'kids will probably be slightly resistent at first because it is new to them. Then she asks the question which lets me know this has the potential of being a productive association: "Would it be OK if I participate in the drama work along with the students rather than sitting on the side and observing?"

Because of scheduling problems(I don't believe the average layperson realizes just how many additional "Programmes" and "units of study" have been mandated and imposed upon the regular subject curriculum at the public school level.),I can't get back to begin work with this class until next week. However, I can return before that just to sit in on a few regular class periods in order for the students to get to know me and so that I can acquire a feel for the class. When I return I arrive as Mohammed is beginning to present his independent study unit to the class. He begins by turning what appears to be a massive` paper he has written on the subject. ` He is going to compare Newton's Theory with Einstein's Theory and show how Newton influenced Einstein. I am already lost, but I spend the time watching the class. Although this is obviously a class which knows and understands polite behaviour, what I observe is not polite silence. These kids are really listening; they follow the entire two hour presentation, and when he finishes he is deluged with all kinds of questions for additional information, additional clarification on some point. At one point, one of his classmates challenges him on one of his mathmatical6 examples and computations. Some of the kids whip out their calculators and some flock to a computer. There is a real sense of animated inquiry. I am amazed and in awe. I can't wait to begin working with this class.

I decide to start the Drama workshops with very simple name games so that I can learn the twenty-eight names of the class as soon as possible. Stand in a circle; the teacher makes a sound and a motion and the class repeats the sound-motion sequence; then, in turn, 'each student does a sound/motion sequence which the class repeats; finally, each student picks an adjective which is a self-descriptor and is alliterative (wacky Wayne or Merry Miranda) speaks the phrase and couples it with a motion. It was s if I was attempting to pull their teeth out without anesthetic. Jane was accurate in her description of this group. They were extremely comfortable and alive and aggressive in their head work, but the affective learning was difficult (alien?) to them. Slowly, the class realized that this could be just plain silly fun if they allowed it to happen, but what this group of kids could comprehend about Newtonian physics in two hours had no relationship to the amount of time it was going to take to get them to learn from within themselves. It might have been that their teacher was participating in the work as well and it might have been that eventually they accepted me (they did respond it my wit—they even recognized it as '"wit") and after two additional "drama activities" sessions, they brought to the drama circle the same kind of energy they brought to Mohammed's presentation on Newtonian Physics.

The class had been doing a unit on Immigration, and Jane wanted me to give the kids an emotional experience with the theme of immigration. The overwhelming majority of the kids in the class were either immigrants themselves or first generation of immigrants. I decided to add one additional workshop of pre-drama preparation before we launched full blown into the actual drama. I explained that they needed to acquire some basic drama skills or tools before we could begin to build this house of drama. We spent the next class period learning about tableaux (frozen pictures which tell a story), teacher in role and class in role, and we spent some time on an explanation of the rules of drama making: you must participate in the drama; you must go along with the imaginary circumstances, and you must not say or do anything which would destroy the circumstances of the drama or which would bring it to a crashing halt. This class went surprising well. Perhaps because the practical aspects of the workshop were coupled with some abstract explanations of concepts. What was important was that the class was beginning to like acting out roles within the drama.

I began the next class with a very simple, friendly activity which produced a lot of laughter and silliness—the activity SHARK (cf L. Teoli's story of the same activity). Very abruptly I left and room for an instant and suddenly came storming back into the room "in role" as a very nasty "police officer". I shouted directions to everyone about cleaning up the room, moving the chairs, forming a LINE — I said STRAIGHT!! straight-line with five centimeters distance between each student, eyes forward, NO TALKING and wipe that smile off your face. I then went down the line and gruffly picked out all the kids with black hair. You, you, you, you over there. I made all the kids with black hair form a double line facing the back wall.

The kids had very quickly figured out that I had gone into role and that the drama had begun. After getting the kids segregated, I stepped out of role and congratulated them on how well they had accepted the imaginative circumstances of the situation and to remind them that this was an imaginary situation in which they were going to play roles. That sometimes they would have to figure out which role they were going to play and sometimes I would assign them roles. OK?? Everyone, including all the kids with black hair said yes and I went back into role as the nasty Police Officer. I told them that I had just come from an emergency meeting the the Government and that the Ruling Council had decided that all the current economic and social problems of the country had been caused by people with black hair. Therefore it had been decreed that all people with black hair had to leave the country immediately. I deputized all the non-blackhaired kids and told them they were to search through the country and arrest all people with black hair and bring them to the police station for immediate deportation. The kids with black hair could not leave the room but they had to attempt to disguise themselves or to hide or to avoid getting captured. This was a risky move because it could have resulted to chaos. The kids, however, enjoyed this game and found the safety of the roles they were playing protected. A few decided to practice passive resistance; some quickly disguised themselves with with their clothes; some found clever hiding place; others tried to negotiate or bribe their captors. These kids loved to solve problems. Eventually I got everyone to form a huddled group at one end of the room. I stepped out of role and praised their ingenuity and cleverness. Then back into role quickly as the nasty Police Office. This time I began with: I had no idea there were so many people in this country with black hair. Just to make this official you are ALL under arrest and will be deported shortly. Suddenly all the kids without real black hair took on the role of someone with black hair. "Because you do not fit in this country any more, it has been decided that you must leave this place. We will give you three minutes to go to your homes and gather together your belongings. You must report back to the police station in five minutes. Go. One group of kids attempts to escape through the closet door. I stop them and send them packing. I look around the room and see many group improvising the scene. They are doing an improvisation and they have never been introduced to this, but they have bought into the circumstances of the drama. While they are` preparing for their voyage, the teacher and I set up tables for the next stage of the drama; we place large black markers on the table and quickly get together sheets of paper on which to write.

When the class reassemble, I inform them that they are to follow me onto the boat; we go through an imaginary boat boarding, a storm, and an disembarking procedure. (All of this is building belief in the drama) When they are disembarked, I herd them into the New Immigrants Hall and inform them they are to submit to an interview process. Jane and I conduct the interviews during which we attempt to find any pretext to deny them entrance into the new country. The conclusion to each interview is assigning each immigrant a new name. Before giving them a new name, we rationalize the choice by telling them we can't pronounce their real name, it sounds funny, or they won't need a name no one can pronounce in this new country. They meekly accept their new names and name cards and go back and stand passively in line until _____ approaches the desk. She was one of the first students in the class to really dig into the imaginative side of the drama; she had already emerged as a natural leader, but I was not to learn until after the drama had finished that up to that point, her participation in all other class activities had been marginal. We went through the usual interview routine, made fun of her real name, assigned her a new name, and handed her the name card. She looked at the paper, looked back at me, and crumbled the paper into a ball and threw it back at me shouting:

"I am not taking that name!"

"You must or you won't get into the country!"

"I won't use that name." {She begins to drill me with her eyes.}

"Why?"

"Because my name is me and NOBODY is taking that away from me! When you take my name from me, you rob me of who I am!"

At that point, I stepped out of role and congratulated her for having the courage to stand up for her beliefs no matter what the consequences. We have a quick and animated discussion about the nature of personal responsibility. Some of her classmates do not agree with her actions because they fell she might have endangered other members of her family who did not agree with her; some think your name is no big thing, others disagree, and the conversation continues for at least fifteen minutes.

Suddenly I am back in role as the immigration officer. I tell them that the rulers of their new country have decided that they can only take one possession with them into the new country. They are given a few minutes to decide what it is from among the things they have taken with them they wish to bring into the new country. Once they have chosen what it is, they are to write about it and explain why they have chosen it, and what it means to them.

* * *

I am teaching Drama in a collegiate on the other side of the city and the world. I am told this will be a multi-day assignment. They wanted me yesterday but I was booked, and the supply they had "didn't work out". Some one in the second period class picked up a desk and threw it at the supply. But don't worry "she has been suspended". When I enter the classroom, one of the three students drawing pictures on the board, looks at me, throws the chalk on the floor, stomps it into dust while yelling, "I don't want no fucking supply; I want my teacher; why did she have to go away?" I think he realizes that he might have revealed too much about himself not to me but to his classmates and so he stalks out of the room. The message is clear and the three actors played their parts: suspicion, anger, betrayal. I notice from the class attendance lists that this class has nearly perfect attendance this term (it is now early December). So these kids outwardly "bad kids" are coming here everyday because it is a safe, warm, friendly place, a place where they are getting the focused attention of an adult, and when they see the supply the message is that another adult has abandoned them. Do I have time to answer the ....? racing through MY head? Do I care about getting through the day? or Do I care about you? I remind myself that they are angry not because I am there but because their teacher, their adult, their focus of concern is not there. On the theory that unproved anger will sometimes dissipate in the presence of passive resistance, I sit at the desk and begin to read whatever is available. I create my own isolation from them. I give them a passive target to react to as they filter into the room. The difference is they still keep coming. No one takes off when they see me. They mill about and eventually they take their seats. "Are we going to do something today, sir?" It is a question, but it is an invitation to begin.

ENDNOTES

[1] I received permission from this drama teacher and the principal of the school to include the episodes that follow in my narrative.

[2] Some of these memories have been fictionalized to preserve the privacy of the parties involved.

[3] Permission for this episode has been sought.

[4] Permission for this material is received.

In: Teacher's Stories, Teacher's Lives
Editor: Carola Conle, pp. 67-83

ISBN 1-59454-472-7
© 2006 Nova Science Publishers, Inc.

Chapter 3

SHAFTS OF LIGHT: RECOLLECTIONS OF MY SCHOOLING

Loreen Teoli

These are days you'll remember. Never before
and never since, I promise, will the whole
world be warm as this. And as you feel it,
you'll know it's true that you are touched
by something that will grow and bloom in you...
These days you might feel a shaft of light
make its way across your face. And when you
do you'll know how it was meant to be. See
the signs and know their meaning...you'll know
how it was meant to be. Hear the signs and
know they're speaking to you, to you.

Lyrics from "These are Days"
by Natalie Marchant and Rob Buck, 1992

I purchased the compact disc on which this song is found shortly after I becan classes at FEUT (Faculty of Education at the University of Toronto). "These are Days" immediately found its way into my consciousness. I often wake up mornings with it rolling through my mind. It has been the musical accompaniment, the soundtrack, to my year of learning how to teach.

I have spent much of this year remembering and looking back at myself in both the distant and recent past. Reminiscence, or reflection, has certainly been encouraged at the faculty in many of my courses, but I believe that my mind's backward-looking activity has been aroused by the process of becoming a teacher in mucht the same way that Proust's was by the taste of a madeleine. Each time that I entered a classroom this year, as a teacher or as a student, I remembered a teacher from my past or an event from my past as a student. I believe that these memories are signs, or signposts, which are speaking to me and attempting to be understood with regard to the teacher that I am becoming.

My first clear memory of school coincides with my parents' discovery that my father had cancer. I was an only child at the time and we lived in the basement apartment of my paternal grandparent's home. My parents had purchased a home in a new subdivision of Toronto just before receiving news of my father's illness. They decided to go ahead with their plans to move, in spite of, or perhaps because of, my father's diagnosis.

I was six years old. I did not understand what "changing schools" meant. I had only been in grade one for two weeks and now I had to say goodbye. The school I was leaving was old - the ceilings were high and an early Indian summer made the classroom uncomfortably warm. My teacher, whose name and face are gone from me, announced to the class that I was leaving to go to a new school. The children fidgeted and crumpled lunch bags, but no one said goodbye. It was to be the first of many academic leave-takings for me.

My new school had only recently been built. Sod had not been laid yet and there was mud and the smell of fresh plaster everywhere. My mother registered me and left for home. I was escorted to my classroom by one of the school secretaries. When we arrived, my teacher, Miss Bea, stood with me at the front of the class and said, "We have a new girl today. Her name is Loreen Teoli". My future classmates had been engrossed in some desk work, but most were curious enough to look up and examine the "new kid". I was extremely self-conscious and uncomfortable. I remember feeling my bowels loosen. Many of the children watched me as Miss Bea led me to my desk. She gave me a pencil and paper and then proceeded to the blackboard to explain the work which I was now to begin. My anxiety increased as she completed her explanation. I know that something was expected of me, but I had no idea what it was. I pretended to understand the instructions, printed some letters on my paper, and slid the work inside my desk, praying that Miss Bea would never see it. Miss Bea, however, noticed that I was finished before anyone else and asked to see my work. I know that it was wrong. My face burned, my stomach churned. I was terrified. I slowly pulled my paper out of my desk and handed it over. She became angry. I could feel her disappointment and I cowered. I fought very hard to keep from crying. Miss Bea left me alone for awhile after that episode. Eventually I was able to understand her instructions and become one of her best students. But I learned two things that first day: I hated being the "new kid" and in order to win teacher approval, I had to do exactly as I was told.

My family continued to move annually and I was the "new kid" in class every year for ten years. I continue to be aware of the difficulty and necessity of adapting to a new educational environment. I spent the better part of the summer before I was to begin classes at FEUT worrying about my initial encounters with students and teachers. My first day was like so many other "first days" at schools in my past: The school building was oppressively hot; the facial expressions of my peers seemed hostile; everytime I opened my mouth to speak, my heart pounded. The mere idea of raising my hand to respond to a professor's question increased my pulse rate dramatically. I was sure that everyone could see and hear my heart beating. My voice shook when I spoke in class and I had difficulty breathing. I wondered how I would ever have the courage to stand before a class and teach.

I found that courage and strength in my Drama class. I entered this third class at FEUT with the same old fears: would I be liked and accepted by the students and the teacher?; would I appear foolish and stupid? The professor asked us to stand in a circle and choose an adjective that began with the same letter as our given name. We were to choose an action to accompany this adjective. Each person would then step into the circle and say their adjective-name aloud while performing the brief accompanying action. The professor was the initiator: "Cheerful Chuck" (he grinned broadly). The students continued: "Melodramatic Michele" (she put her hand to her forehead); "Jovial Jim" (he extended one arm in a handshaking gesture); "Joyful Joe" (he raised his arms above his head); "Risky Randolph" (he slid sideways into the circle); "Aloof Alex" (she turned her head away and raised her eyebrows); "Lovable Loreen" (I hugged myself). After everyone in the class had stepped into the circle, we repeated this activity with a slight variation: each time a person entered the circle, said their name and performed their action, the rest of the class would then simultaneously echo that person's words and movement. When it was my turn, I stepped into the circle, hugged myself and said, "Lovable Loreen". Everyone immediately stepped forward, hugged themselves and said, "Lovable Loreen". It was difficult to express how wonderful this felt. To have everyone in a classroom say your name and reflect back to you the way in which you have chosen to be seen is wonderfully affirming. I was safe here; I loved this class.

The professor continued with this type of activity for several weeks. He engaged us in dozens of co-operative, non-competitive activities. The first time he used a lecture format, I was completely relaxed and comfortable. I could hear him instead of my heartbeat; I could learn, because I was not afraid.

I had powerful new knowledge to accompany me on my first day of practice teaching: All students have private fears in a classroom, expressed in very different ways which are sometimes disruptive and almost always counter-productive to the learning process. If I could assuage some of these fears, both my own and the students', then teaching would become much easier and more effective.

During the course of this pre-service year, I have employed many of the drama activities taught to me at FEUT in order to create a safe environment conducive to learning. The most remarkable successes I have had with these techniques have been with ESL students. During my third practicum, I worked with two ESL drama classes. Here were students who were not only new to the school, but new to the country and the language. Their fear in the classroom was palpable; they were terrified of speaking. I worried that drama work would be difficult, if not impossible, with students who had little to no English. It was the beginning of a semester and my associate assured me that I should begin with them in much the same way that my drama professor at FEUT had begun with us: with "comfort-building" games.

I purchased a ball of twine and brought it to class. I sat in a circle with the students and held the twine aloft. I told them that I would begin the activity by saying my name, followed by the name of someone else in the class. After I had called someone's name, I would roll the twine to that person who, holding their strand of twine, would roll it to someone else in the circle, after calling that person's name. I started with Gibrilla, who smiled broadly and received the string. He passed it to Billy, who passed it to Ahmed, who passed it to Chien, who passed it to Rosa, and so on. Initially, everyone was hesitant. We were unsure of each others' names and the game progressed slowly. As we became more confident of each others' names, the pace quickened and the string rolled rapidly, forming the web-like structure I had hoped we would create. I stopped the game after about fifteen minutes and asked the students to look at what we had made. I asked them to tell me what they thought it resembled. They responded: "electrical wiring"; "a road map"; "the branches of a tree"; "a spider's web"; "the inside of the human body"; "ice-skating tracks". I suggested to them that the things which they described, and the "network" which we had created, were symbols for our class and our relationship to one another. They smiled and nodded; they said they understood. Chien, who had been so shy earlier, suggested that we now retrace the path of the twine, so that the "net" which we had made would not become a tangled mess. My associate later remarked that she was pleased I had honoured his contribution.

I believe that this activity was successful because the "names" for it came from the students. I later learned that the names of some activities can also have disturbing meanings for some students. In another ESL drama class at the same school, I introduced a game called "Life Raft". I had played it with my peers at the Faculty, and it had achieved both a freeing of inhibitions and group bonding. I placed five large pieces of paper on different parts of the floor in the drama room and told the students that these papers were life rafts. The water in which these rafts floated was shark-infested. The students were to move about the room quickly, pretending to swim, and when I yelled out "shark", they were all to find a space on one of the rafts as quickly as possible. I emphasized that everyone was to help everyone else stay on the rafts -- the object of the game was co-operation, not competition. When the activity began, I noticed that Thanh, Viet, Judy and Donna were not engaged. They walked slowly around the outer edges of the classroom and only grudgingly found a raft on which to stand when I yelled "shark". As the game progressed, I removed some of the life rafts so that more and more students had to crowd together and really co-operate in order to all find space to stand or balance on the few pieces of paper. While some students were giddy with laughter, as I had been when I took part in this game, others appeared very uncomfortable, even frightened. When I spoke to my associate abouth this lesson later on, she apologized to me. She had known that this activity was part of my lesson plan, but had forgotten that a few of the students had escaped from their countries on small boats and that some of them had seen people eaten by sharks. I was devastated. How could I have been so insensitive? My goals had been to increase self-confidence and establish an atmosphere of trust and safety. For some of the students, the results were the complete opposite of what I had had in mind.

I tasted the madeleine again. This teaching experience evoked a memory from grade two. I have only one school memory from that year. This is remarkable because I have such clear memories of earlier and later school years. My father died when I had almost completed grade two. Miss Clark was my teacher. My father had been ill for some time before his death, but I do not recall equating his illness with the knowledge that he would die.

I had not been allowed to attend my father's funeral, but I was kept home from school until my mother felt comfortable letting me return. Miss Clark was a "stickler" for notes explaining absences, and the adults at home had failed to provide me with one. When I tried to explain to Miss Clark the reason for my absence, she interrupted me quite abruptly and said again that she required a note. I waited until the class had begun quiet work and I approached Miss Clark at her desk. I bluntly said, "I was away from school because my father died". I remember that Miss Clark looked strange and that she said I would not need to bring in a note and then she left the room. I was quite pleased with my news and the effect that it had produced and I proceeded to tell all my classmates. (Twenty years later, when I read Agee's "Death in the Family", I was amazed to see some of myself in one of his characthers).

Recently, my mother told me that the school phoned home that day. Miss Clark went home and was replaced by a substitute for two days. School staff and administration apparently watched me closely for signs of depression. They told my mother that I appeared well-adjusted and unaffected. But, I remember nothing else from that year. Except that Miss Clark looked like the Wicked Witch of the West from "The Wizard of Oz".

In hindsight, Miss Clark may have reminded me of the "wicked witch" from "The Wizard of Oz" because she persisted in seeing me only as a student inside of her classroom. The "wicked witch" only saw the ruby slippers on Dorothy's feet; Miss Clark only saw a student who had been absent from class for three days. Students and teachers have lives, whole histories, outside of and prior to their entrance into a classroom. Students are not "blank slates" onto which educators record facts. When we enter a classroom, we do not leave parts of ourselves outside.

I always liked the Scarecrow in "The Wizard of Oz". He suggested to Dorothy that she had several directions in which she could go. He asked her where she wanted to go, and then he gave her some choices of how to travel. He was her guide as well as her travelling companion.

At the end of the practicum, in which I taught two ESL drama classes for two weeks, my associate suggested to me that I had a special gift for teaching these students. She cited my warmth, enthusiasm, and ability to give very clear instructions. She told me that she believed me to be very "relational". My associate hugged my the day that I left and said she felt as though she were losing a friend. I was reminded of all the teachers with whom I had shared a relationship, a special friendship. In grade six, my teacher adored me and I loved him. In one memorable parent-teacher interview, he told my mother that I was intellectually gifted. (Years later she told me that she was very uncomfortable because he gushed over me for twenty minutes). His gift to me at the end of the year was Shakespeare's "The Merchant of Venice".

One other teacher with whom I shared a special bond was my grade thirteen English teacher, who signed my yearbook: "At the risk of being maudlin - it has never been so difficult to say good-bye to a student". The first reflection that I wrote this year at FEUT was about this teacher.

We moved frequently when I was a child, and it was not until I entered high school that I was allowed to continue in an educational institution for more than one year. Westview C.S.S. was the school which, for the above reason, most impressed me and it is of this school that I write.

We lived in an Ontario Housing high rise behind the Jane/Finch mall. Walking to school was a noisy, stressful endeavour. There were several factories and government housing projects in the area and my friends and I often joked about the proximity of the hospital to our school. The school itself was large and over-populated (over 2700 students at that time). In spite of all of this, I loved going to school. It was there that I felt that I was heard. I was very involved in student activities and it was great to be a part of something.

One of the most memorable experiences I had was in Mrs. Mayerson's English class. She had a reputation as a very tough teacher and when I found her name on my timetable, I was worried. We had to read "The Turn of the Screw" for our first class discussion. I was surprised when she asked us to describe the ghosts in the story to her, so surprised, in fact, that I blurted out: "But they're not real! They're only in the governess's head". Her astonished reaction further surprised me: "We're not supposed to be able to discuss that for several classes!". I now see that I messed up her lesson plan, but she was so pleased with my outburst, and I was so affected by her pleasure, that our interactions continued in this vein for the remainder of the year.

This relationship caused many of my classmates to resent me, to label me "teacher's pet" and "browner", but I was excited by the friendship that was developing between myself and Mrs. Mayerson and was usually unmoved by their taunts. Her recognition and celebration of what I now regard as my intuitive talents, elevated my level of self-esteem such that I was "protected" and unaffected by any negative comments which were directed at me.

If I sense that a teacher cares about me, if I understand that we have a relationship, then my learning accelerates. In another reflection, I wrote about what happens when the teaching is not "caring" or "relational".

I am lying on the table at Jeff's. Jeff does what he calls "Mind-Body" work. He refuses the title of Therapist because he does not see himself as a "fixer"; he sees himself as one who "meets". I love going to see him because I get to talk about myself for a whole hour while he massages me. It is a self-indulgence in the best sense of the word.

Today I am complaining about a professor at FEUT with whom I am having difficulty.

Me: This man has lost everyone in the class! He doesn't even see us. The people in the class offer wonderful ideas and he doesn't even acknowledge them.

Jeff: I wonder what would happen if you tried to talk to him about this. How could you approach him? It might be quite beneficial for both of you.

I immediately think of a dozen reasons why I should not approach this professor: He would not welcome the comments and would be angry with me; he would feel threatened by my comments and this would colour his evaluation of my subsequent work; he would throw my comments out to the class as a whole, and because he is so intimidating, no one would "fess up", I would be seen as an "isolated case" and his teaching would remain unaltered.

I say some of this aloud to Jeff and he is surprised that I already know how this professor will react to something that I have not yet said. Jeff suggests that this is unfair to both myself and the teacher. I say that part of the problem for me is that I don't really know what to say to this man.

Jeff: Stay with what you know. Don't tell him how the rest of the class feels. Tell him how you are feeling.

Me: I feel invisible. I feel uncertain. I feel stupid. I don't know if his knowing any of this will change how he is in class. I am angry that I am having these difficulties. I do not want to teach in this fashion.

Jeff: I hear from you that you know what kind of teacher you do not want to be.

I am becoming the kind of teacher that I want to be, but I find myself wondering if it is possible to sustain this style of teaching without considerable personal risks.

At the end of my first practicum, the students gave me a surprise going away party. They purchased a huge cake on which was inscribed, "Good Luck Ms. Teoli" and they all signed a giant card which read, "You'll be missed!". Inside the card, one student wrote, "You are a teacher who will be loved by all of her students". I remembered hugging myself in drama class while saying "Lovable Loreen". Here I was, 34 years old, and still wanting to be loved everytime I entered a new classroom. The need makes me very empathic: I understand that the students, too, want to be loved, or cared for, by a classroom teacher, but it also makes me very vulnerable: what if I am not liked? Furthermore, do I want to send students outside of my classroom and have them capable of learning only when someone cares about them? Do we eventually reach a phase of development where we can learn without being liked?

During my final practicum, I taught a group of non-credit ESL students. My associate had them for 2 1/2 hours every morning and was preparing them to take a written test which would indicate whether or not they were prepared for credit ESL courses. This was an adult high school and most of the students had children. The classroom in which I taught used to be an auto shop and all of the windows were 15 feet above eye level. Our area of the school was referred to as "C BLOCK". The ESL students sat at quite a distance from each other and rarely spoke. My associate had them writing and reading for most of the morning while she rotated amongst them, providing individual tutoring. My "relational" character regarded the climate of the classroom as arid and, after some amicable negotiating with my associate, I engaged the students in drama activities.

Once again, I asked the students to form a circle and learn each others' names. (They had been together for two months and did not know the names of their classmates). I stood in the circle with them and, indicating the space on my right, I said: "The space on my right is free, I would like Abdihakim to come and stand by me". When he did, the space on Aster's right was free and she was to repeat this phrase, inviting someone else to stand beside her. I felt that the game was going well. Everyone was smiling and laughing, and they were learning each others' names in a very invitational manner. My associate suddenly interrupted saying, "You are helping them too much". She then stood in the middle of the circle and told the students that they were each to invite her to stand beside them. Sameya was to be first. She struggled through the phrase and when she was finished, my associate curtly responded, "no". She proceeded to say "no" to each student after they invited her to stand beside them. Her comments to me later were, "You can not be their friend; you are their teacher". I spent the next 2 1/2 weeks waiting for her to leave me alone with her class so that I could "be myself" with them. Whenever she left me alone with them, I included myself or my family into the lesson. On St. Patrick's Day, my daughter was in a parade and so to explain the meaning of "parade", I showed them a picture of her in the OISE newspaper. There was a sudden flurry of activity as everyone in the class pulled out wallets and purses. Everyone had a picture of a child or children and I was to see each one. The class assumed a party atmosphere, with everyone sharing stories of their families. Frantically, I wrote vocabulary on the board: "brother", "sister", "sibling", "education", "university", "tricycle", "roller blades", and "nurture" were only a few. When my associate returned, she was pleased to see the words on the board. She gave the class a spelling test based on their new vocabulary. They did remarkably well.

On the day that I was to leave, Maria, a woman my age who is from El Salvador and has two children, presented me with a card and a hug. When I began to cry, she said to me, "Do not worry. We will be okay". I was amazed that she understood my tears. I felt that I was abandoning these students; I wondered how they would ever survive without me.

I recently dreamt that I returned to this school. I had forgotten that I was only a student teacher, and that I was now to return to FEUT. It did not make sense to me that I was not to stay. I was crushed. Why were they making me leave? I could not convince them. I had to leave again.

My frequent experiences as a new, frightened student have provided me with some important strengths as a teacher: the ability to empathize with and to care for the students in my classroom. But is there a danger in placing too much importance on these relationships? Do I need to distance myself from the students? Can I not be their friend? Would Maria be okay? My good teachers had been facilitators; they had created an atmosphere of safety and caring and had said goodbye when that time came. They helped me to leave, to move on, and because of this, they will never leave me.

Now I'm looking through a tunnel
Back into the room
With the genius of a druid when the
sunlight floods the tomb.
And I'm never going back there, and I
couldn't anyway
'Cause though I made the great escape
I never got away.

Lyrics from "Katie"
by Jimmy McCarthy 1987.

My year at FEUT seems very far away now. I have moved again and I have a second daughter--Leni--now 5 months old. When I think of teaching, I worry that I have forgotten everything that I learned and that I will be an ineffective teacher. There is, however, a part of me that understands that this is not so. That I will always be an effective teacher because of my experiences and the person that these have helped to create.

I just got off the phone with a friend of mine who also has two kids and who teaches part-time. She has been supportive throughout my short-lived teaching career and continues to call me whenever she hears of a suitable job. I am surprised to discover that I do not want a job outside of the home right now. I am enjoying raising my young family and I am loathe to miss Leni's baby years.

While Leni sleeps, I write. My older daughter, Kate, is outside playing in the snow with a friend from her kindergarten class. I can see them from where I sit at the computer. They are collecting chunks of snow and depositing them in a red toboggan. Their pink and purple snowsuits glow in the grey landscape of this particularly dreary January.

My children bring such joy and clarity to my life at present. When I try to explain this to well-meaning friends who imagine that I must need outside stimulation, I am reminded of the narrative which I wrote during my pre-service year at FEUT. I ended this narrative with an expression of need for the students. Some of my colleagues suggested that this "need" was in danger of sounding neurotic, even dangerous. It is important to me now to clarify what it is that I mean by "need" because it is similar to the need I feel to be at home with my children.

Again, Leni sleeps and I write. I can hear her over the baby monitor while I sit at the computer in the basement-she is snoring. The wasing machine and the dryer are both running and so I feel completely able to justify sitting and writing. The pervasive aroma in my office is Ivory Snow. The floor is littered with the remnants of my morning play session with Kate--Play-doh, tea set, blocks, old high heels--we played tea party, her favourite game. I ignore the ringing of the telephone because it is important to me to record my thoughts about a class at which I was one of three guest speakers at FEUT and, if I do not do this now, I will lose my window of writing opportunity to diapering and breastfeeding.

I left Leni at her grandparents' home when I went to FEUT so that I would not have to leave mid-class in order to nurse her.

I travelled from my in-laws apartment building in North York to Bloor and Spadina by subway. I do not have much time away from my daughters and I wanted to relish my independence. I purchased a Kit Kat bar at a subway concession and boarded the train at

Finch--I was breathless with excitement and anticipation. I had had no time to really consider what I was about to do. I had not been in any kind of academic setting for over a year and here I was, with very little prepared in the way of notes or plans, blithely travelling to Toronto to speak to a group of pre-service teachers about some of my teaching experiences, both as a teacher and as an adolescent, and why it is so valuable to write about these experiences.

I decided to concentrate on the other people riding the subway in order to alleviate the nervousness which I could feel creeping into my armpits. I tried to imagine what their days experiences had been. The woman with the bright yellow boots and Honest Ed's shopping bag looked alert and expectant--she was possibly travelling to some new adventure, as was I. The young man sitting next to me was slowly drifting off to sleep, his tattered knapsack slipping slowly from his shoulder--maybe he had just completed an essay and was on his way to deliver it before a deadline. I had forgotten how much I used to enjoy this "game": watching for visual clues to a person's inner life. It occurred to me that this was something which I also did in the classroom. I watch the students closely for signs of their experience, both immediate and previous. This self-discovery was valuable in that it both calmed my sudden case of nerves and suggested a focus for my imminent encounter with a group of students. I would watch them for clues and respond, react, all-right, maybe even teach accordingly.

I was not prepared for my own reaction to a building that I had not entered for some time and which was now full of bustling students. I could barely contain my excitement. My ears began to feel hot and I knew that if I looked in a mirror, the lobes would be bright red. I hurried up the three flights of stairs and arrived breathless in a corridor where students were quickly disappearing into classrooms--I was late!

Leni woke up just as I was remembering how it felt to be late to class. An entire day has passed since I wrote about my arrival at FEUT and I find myself again with time to myself because Kate is playing at a friend's house and Leni is once again slumbering. Today she coughs over the monitor and the pervasive aroma is of Vicks Vaporub and coffee--I have been up with her much of the night and cannot go on without my coffee--a mother's elixir.

As I scurried down the hall at FEUT, I could smell coffee everywhere. This was to be the last class of the day for many students and the only way to survive it, I remember, was with a healthy dose of caffeine. I met Gill in the hallway, who was both

late and lost and, after a hearty embrace (we had not seen one another since I practice taught under her guidance), we entered the classroom together. The room was bright and busy. Joe, who had been seated behind a desk at the front of the room, jumped up to greet us. I could feel myself relaxing as I smiled at Carola--this was all very familiar and not at all forgotten. It was not until I sat down behind the desk with Je and Gill that I looked at the people to whom we would be speaking. Loosely grouped around circular tables, they also were in the process of greeting one another and settling into their seats. Some students were alone and quiet--they sat at the back of the class and watched us and their peers from under lowered eyes. One young woman at the front of the classroom slouched backward in her chair, put up her feet and met my gaze with a welcoming smile. I liked her unusual eyeglasses and her casual attire--she appeared self-confident. A young man seated front row and centre seemed to be the most sociable member of the class. He spoke to everyone and was comfortable making direct eye contact with the guests at the front of the class. I felt confident he would have questions for us throughout our discussion.

While Carola introduced us and explained what flow our discussion would take, I had a small but meaningful revelation--I was studying this group of people so that I would have an idea as to how I should speak to them. Their physical attitudes, attire, expressions, even beverages were clues which would help me to unravel the mystery of how to speak. This was the need of which I wrote and which I have been trying to clarify ever since I recorded it. I need the students to show me how to teach them. This seems like an obvious enough statement at first glance, but when one considers the recent report on learning drawn up by the provincial government and its emphasis on a "common curriculum", it is perhaps not obvious to a great many educators. How can there be effective teaching if it is not student-centred?

The physical attitude of a student seated at the back of Carola's class reminded me of myself as a student in high school. His posture and attire suggested to me that he preferred not to be seen: shoulders hunched, torso turned away to the back of the class, baseball cap pulled low over his forehead, and eyes that looked everywhere but at the speakers in front of him. Carola had specifically asked me to speak about my adolescent experiences of schooling, of being a student "at risk". While I did not feel that this young man was presently "at risk", I surmised that he had been at one time during his schooling and that his present classroom demeanour was a hangover from some past educational experience.

When I began to tell the story of my adolescent experiences in the educational system, I could feel my focus shifting from the present to the past. I remember my first day of high school with remarkable clarity. I awoke early and stepped onto the balcony of our fourteenth floor apartment. The weather was hot and muggy and there were ominous clouds in the distance. The back parking lot of the Jane/Finch Mall, which was directly underneath our balcony, was empty except for a few delivery trucks and a lot of sticky garbage.

The rest of my family slept on. I hoped to be able to leave for school before they awoke because I did not want to be a part of another mind-bending conflict. I wanted no harsh words, no hurled abuse or objects, before I ventured into this new experience.

I wanted so badly to go to school and to have a fresh start. We had recently moved, again, and I longed for some recognition of my difficulties, of my life. For various reasons, this recognition could not happen at home, and I had yet to develop a voice to ask for it.

My two younger sisters and I shared a room. I gingerly stepped through their silence and the debris of our attire, to choose an appropriate outfit in which to be seen: denim overalls, old grey t-shirt, no socks, a pair of black, negative-heel oxfords that were all the rage in the '70's. I must not appear to be trying to look good; I must look as if I could care less about clothing, when, in fact, thoughts of clothing which I could not hope to afford were a daily source of unhappiness. I resolved to be silent and make people work to know me. I looked at myself in the mirror hanging inside our closet. My long, shag-cut, black hair was greasy and half-covered my face, which sported the requisite acne before a first-time event. I would not groom myself, I decided, but I would apply deodorant.

My sisters slept through these "preparations" and, before I turned to leave, I studied them. I felt like crying, as I often did whenever I left them to go anywhere. How could I abandon them to their day, when I knew how troubled it would be? I rubbed my face with my hands. No one must see me cry, but perhaps this time someone might see that I must.

The route to my school, along Finch Avenue, is a noisy one. I see dozens of other students walking together and singley. I watch them from lowered eyes for clues: is anyone as unhappy and nervous as I am? Are ther any friends here for me? Who has money for clothing, accessories, make-up, movies? If anyone looks in my direction, I look away quickly; no one must see my need.

(This is all so difficult to think and write about. I often pride myself on having left this part of my life behind, neatly compartmentalized and labelled "difficult youth" or "troubled childhood".)

I enter the high school and spend an anxious few minutes locating my homeroom. In my continuing efforts to hide myself, I sit at the very back of the room and quickly slouch so that my hair hides my face. My homeroom is a shop class. There are mysterious tools and benches everywhere and the clean smell of sawdust. My teacher has a British accent and a bemused expression. He says very little to us before going up and down the rows to hand out papers that tell us our schedules, locker numbers, room locations, school rules. He pauses at my desk, looks down and tries to peer through my hairy camoflauge. He says, "I'm sure that you're in there, somewhere". I respond with a grunt and a gutteral expletive, but inwardly I am shaken. Somehow this teacher guessed that I am hiding, to him I am transparent.

My subsequent encounters with teaching staff over the course of the week are similar. I am not left alone to wallow in my chosen cloak of invisibility and resentment. I continue to sit at the back of each classroom in brooding silence. When I am addressed or asked a question, I grunt or glare. I am not to be easily won over. I am not yet conscious of the rationale behind my behaviour, but hindsight suggests I was testing these teachers: how much effort were they willing to put forth, how much of their time and energy would they invest in such a hopeless case? I looked for hope in their eyes - a dim reflection of myself.

My history teacher seemed always to be watching me. Whenever I glanced up from my post at the farthest recesses of the room, he was looking at me. He never failed to greet me when I entered his classroom and was never offended when I ignored him. I had an ally in this class, a young woman who was illiterate, and would now be labelled "behavioural", sat next to me. We exchanged dirty jokes and asides throughout the class. The teacher chose not to separate us, but to continue to give us joint assignments. One day he asked me to stay after class. I thought, with grim satisfaction, "Well, here it comes, the punishment which I so richly deserve". To my surprise, he thanked me for helping my "ally" and asked if I would be able to assist another student of his who was also experiencing language difficulties. My response was taciturn: "Okay - if you really want me to". He smiled and said, "Yes - I really want you to". I quickly left.

My hasty exit was a disguise for the happiness I felt. This teacher had persisted in his efforts to find out more about me and had resolved to value what he found. Many other teachers would be tested and challenged by my behaviour over the next few years and, while there efforts were not in vain, I was not an overnight success. My physical education teacher suggested that I attend a leadership camp. I responded with an incredulous stare and walked away in silence. My math teachers urged me to enroll in the enriched math program. Again I declined, informing them that they must be "nuts". My American history teacher told me that I was a good writer and I dropped out of his class. I laughed derisively when he suggested I audition for the "Reach for the Top" team. It took my teachers four years of persistant efforts to reach me.

By grade twelve, my academic performance began to improve. I became involved in extra-curricular activities and I began to take an interest in post-secondary education. All of these changes were remarkable considering my home life. School became my salvation: it was a predictable environment in which I was valued for my distinct talents. I blossomed.

As my schooling improved, my home life became more difficult and at the age of seventeen, I was forced to move out. I was terrified. What would become of me? Communication (what little there had been) with my family ceased, as did any financial support. I moved in with my boyfriend and began to receive student welfare. The visit from the social worker, a well-coiffed woman in a three-piece suit, frightened me. I remembered a similar social worker visiting my mother years before when she had applied for mother's allowance.

My behaviour at school regressed: I became sullen and withdrawn. This time my French teacher reacted. She called on me to participate in spite of my continued silence and eventually spoke to me after class one day.

French teacher:	Do you need to talk with someone about any problems you might be having, Loreen?
Me:	Who cares?
French teacher:	I do.
Me:	What can you do?
French teacher:	I don't know unless you tell me.

I promptly burst into tears. I cried so hard I was sick to my stomach. This teacher led me to the staff washroom and stayed with me. She took me to the guidance office and, after a hurried and intense conference with a counsellor, drove me home. We spoke little. I continued to cry noisely. I was appalled I had been found out, but felt safer knowing that someone in a position of authority had taken measures to help me.

Some kind of emergency teachers' meeting regarding my situation must have ensued, because many of my teachers approached me with offers of help: my English teacher offered her home; my history teacher offered financial support; my guidance counsellor met with me daily and gave me her home phone number.

These individuals' actions changed the course of my life. They persisted and refused to allow me to remain invisible. Their dogged efforts to see and hear me did not go unnoticed by me. I eventually responded by allowing them to know me better; I let them help me. Complicated applications for universities, grants, bursaries, and scholarships were simplified for me by several of my teachers-- even the Principal of the school helped me to obtain a scholarship. I obtained entrance, with scholarships, to the university of my choice.

I ended my high school career as class valedictorian. My drama teacher, sensing my nervousness, gave me a little push from backstage toward the podium and whispered, "They want to hear what you have to say".

I return to the present and look closely at this group of pre-service teachers. They are silent, some look incredulous. I think, they need to hear what I have to say. They must hear that their caring, their attention and concern, can make such an enormous difference to a student. The young man at the back of the class, who I thought might be hiding earlier, asks a question: "What are we supposed to look for? How do we know if a student is at risk?". He sounds skeptical, not entirely convinced that a teacher could make such a difference in someone's young life. I respond by saying that there is no hard and fast rule, that we must be keen observers of our students, that they will reveal themselves to us in some fashion, that we must be receptive. We must be ready for the revelation, for the shaft of light.

In: Teacher's Stories, Teacher's Lives
Editor: Carola Conle, pp. 85-102
ISBN 1-59454-472-7
© 2006 Nova Science Publishers, Inc.

Chapter 4

TEACHERS ARE...

Robin E. Hoffman

sympathetic listeners well-dressed liars understanding writers protective parents relentless researchers hockey players actors backpackers computer freaks bookworms moviebuffs skiers skaters good cooks bad cooks smokers drinkers polite abstainers painters dancers dog lovers cat fans riders card players cyclists vegetarians vegans carnivores gardeners drivers pilots passengers villagers city goers campers musicians hunters collectors authors singers farmers lifeguards divers photographers feminists liberals conservatives fence sitters honest learners mothers fathers sisters brothers uncles aunts unfriendly giving patient wise inspiring long distance runners armchair jocks brides bridegrooms partners friends caregivers therapists mediators pacifists decorators chess players carpenters midwives social convenors renovators builders patients healers land owners renters finders keepers sellers shoppers knitters sewers buyers designers illustrators scrabble players advocates assistants servers creators butchers bakers candlestick makers

If I am a woman friend writer feminist gardener cook waitress I mean server speaker reader healer partner daughter sister mother to be why are my tales so hard to write? My teaching stories are like smells in a kitchen sometimes mixing together quite well into something familiar, other times mixing together into something new and strange needing to simmer for a while until the true flavour comes through.

What do teachers eat? What do teachers wear? What do teachers do? What happens after school? Where so they go on vacation? What do teachers teach? *Who are my teachers?*

What are the ingredients for making parents, Sunday school teachers, brownie leaders, coaches, tutors, instructors, bosses, professors, mentors, guides, trainers, assistants and advisors?

School was a popular topic around the dinner table at our house. We talked about what we did at school, who we played with at recess, who we sat near, what we heard about other classes, who brought what for show and tell, friends and enemies, happenings in the lunchroom. We talked about teachers: teachers who inspired us to complete unusual feats, teachers who treated us fairly, unfairly, teachers who taught us well, teachers who took advantage, teachers my parents had had. We talked about teachers and school more than other things--we lived in a small town and boarded the bus at 8:15 and returned home at 4:15.

SMELLS OF HAIR SPRAY

Mrs. Linzer[1] wore more spraynet than anyone I knew
she taught my dad when he was little
and now I had her for grade one
I was always in trouble for talking
once she took me by the hand to the principal's office
I was red faced and sniffling within minutes
tearfully, I negotiated a new seating plan
so we turned and went back to class
I moved to a different desk and it turned out for the best
because right after that the girl I used to sit with
threw up all over the desks
I was surprised when Mrs. Linzer didn't try to clean it up
she called the custodian who came with a mop and towels.

The next year Mrs. Fellner proudly escorted me
down the hall to Mrs. Linzer's class
she knocked on the door and waited
Mrs. Linzer opened the door and Mrs. Fellner beamed, "We just
wanted to show you how much the printing has improved."
the two of them smiled down at me
and I felt proud and small and mad all at the same time
this had to mean that
teachers talked to one another about their students

SMELLS OF SMOKE AND COFFEE

Miss Beighton taught grade three
she didn't look like other teachers
she wore short dresses high heels and burgundy nail polish
she drank cold coffee and smoked at her wooden desk
one time her boyfriend Bill sent her flowers at school
and at parents' night my mother told her
that she was a *household word* around our place
she was quiet for a moment then she smiled
showing her very white teeth and said thank you

SMELLS OF SOAP AND CRISP LINEN

My piano teacher Sister Mary Anna
smelled like those old yellow bars of Sunlight Soap
I wondered if that was the soap nuns were allowed to use
did they pick out their own shoes?
did they wear a white dress when they got married to God?

I got a red star in my book if I played with no mistakes
a blue one if it wasn't quite right
once she hit my hands with a ruler when I said I hadn't practiced
I couldn't lie to a nun
my mom said I didn't have to go back after that
but I finished the year somehow feeling sorry for her

SMELLS OF HOT CHOCOLATE AND CUPS OF CHICKEN SOUP

Mr. McDougall was my skating coach
he had black figure skates unlike the hockey skates I'd seen
he wore a yellow coat and a taupe coloured cap
his voice was soft but sure the group would listen and we did
we heard he had a pacemaker and that he was 68 or 78
this amazed us--everything he said and did seemed like a miracle
he was very patient and he always gave us a break

so we could go off the ice for a hot drink from the vending machine

SMELLS OF SUNDAY PERFUME

My Sunday school teacher Miss Harriger was young and pretty
we tried not to worry that she didn't have a husband
I loved these classes--extra social time when there was no school
I kept going even when my little brother quit--he hated wearing a tie
We would listen while she read to us, then we'd tell her who we helped that week
I remember when she asked me if my mother had the baby yet
and I said yes it was a little girl...
she said that was wonderful news and then I almost didn't want to add
...but she died.
We said a little prayer for her after that
and she squeezed my hand when she helped me with my coat

SMELLS OF CEDAR CHIPS AND SWEAT

We had a guinea pig in grade four--*Googie* was his name
each weekend one of us could sign him out to take home
Since I often finished early I took on some extra duties
changing the cedar chips in Googie's cage
washing the sink after painting
refilling the glue bottles--the back of the class felt like mine
my parents were not pleased with this set up but it was not until
the report card came home saying I was anti-social
because I would not hold hands with a boy
during square dancing in phys-ed
my mother went to school without me to see *Mrs.* Layette
(she wouldn't call her *Madame*) and afterwards
I didn't get to clean Googie's cage anymore
but we could choose whoever we wanted for gym partners

SMELLS OF OLD SPICE

All of the male teachers smelled like Old Spice Deodorant
I guess there were only a few kinds back then
Mr. Selby had a brush cut and a beard
he was my first man teacher
he wore high-top running shoes with his dress pants
I remember that he had a high regard for books
and since my parents let me read pretty much anything I wanted
I read almost non-stop. I generally had a book in my lap at my desk
and it amazes me now that I thought he never noticed

We had to do oral book reports--Mr. Selby would ask us questions about what we'd read and then he'd initial our book cards. I did seven or eight and then forged his initials for twenty-five more. I really did read those books--I just hated having to go up to his desk after every single one and tell him about it. He's a principal now and I did like his class because he really believed we could do anything. We went to court and made a class movie. We had a sale to pay for our trip to the science center. We grew plants in the class and had a weather center so we got to do the weather over the announcements. I guess we did all kinds of neat things. I've thought about tracking him down to explain the book thing...I guess at the time I thought he didn't notice, but now I wonder why he didn't say anything?

Mr. Michaud taught phys-ed. I had him the year Grandpa died. My mom said my dad sat with him till the end just talking to him because hearing is the last to go. The day we found out I still wanted to go to school, so my mom let me. Then during phys-ed we had to jump on the trampoline--one at a time while everyone clse stood around watching to catch the jumper in case of an accident. Mr. Michaud was very strict about spotters. I crept to the library and read my book because I didn't want to be watched. Mr. Michaud was furious--my mother had to come to the school. The good thing was she always listened to my side of things first. Mr. Honeywell was very nice when he found out about my grandfather. Mr. Michaud was too, and I remember the next day he brought in slides from when he lived in the Northwest Territories.

In grade 7 we had Mr. Booth for music. One day the school was called by Tracy Shuslip's mom. Then Mr. Booth had to make an announcement that when we were studying the lyrics to *Fool on the Hill*, it was just a *possibility* that the writer was referring to God as the person on the hill. Mr. Booth emphasized that he had not meant to imply that God was a fool.

SMELLS OF NURSES' SHOES

High school was a pretty good experience for me
I remember my English teacher in grade ten, Miss Burton
she always wore *Oomphies* brand hospital shoes
and big loose floral patterned smocks
she had a round face with bushy eyebrows
her low rumbling chuckle was a little disconcerting
she joked with the boys but never the girls
my first week there she chuckled to the class,
"and I hope you're all proud of yourselves--the new kid
did the best on the test. That's right--the new kid with glasses
in the back corner."
oh great I am mortified conscious of my glasses nervous
knowing I am blushing feeling proud happy and mad all at once

I heard she died a few years later and I thought about her
for a long time. How did she die? Was she lonely?

EXPECTANT SCENTS

In grade 12 Mr. Hodges made me rewrite the chemistry test because he knew I could do better. I did. How did he know? That same year Mr. Knuth (my math teacher) summoned me from class to tell me he didn't approve of one of my male friends. He felt he had to say something because he was 'bad news.' I didn't know what to say. I thanked him for taking an interest, and I wondered about stories in the staff room.

It's funny because when I went back to that school to assist with an English class, Mrs. Rogers assigned me to a difficult student in one of her classes. She thought I could make some progress because if I'd managed to see the potential in Neil Thomas (the same one Mr. Knuth talked about) then I'd probably be a great help in her behavioural class. I was.

For several years during university, I went to a high school as a teacher's assistant. One day the woman I worked with was called to a meeting, so I was left with the grade nine class. I was told that the on call teacher would be dropping in shortly. This class was geared toward kids that who had problems with the standard English class in that school. The school was interesting because most of the parents who lived in the area were *certain* that *their* children would definitely be attending university--and therefore should be taking only advanced level classes; however, a few had relented and allowed their kids to go into this small class for some extra help.

When I arrived, the students were in the hall making lots of noise--understandable--the door was not open yet. I found a caretaker to open the door and we went in. The class would generally begin with about 20 minutes of reading. The teacher often put soft music on to start with but I couldn't find the tape. Most of the students were reading already except John. John had to move around the class often. We all knew about this and had no problem with it.

One of the on call teachers popped his head in the door to see if everything was OK. He was visibly annoyed. "Everything under control?" I nodded. He continued, "Because you know, I *can* come and sit in here." Then he muttered, "They're like a bunch of animals." He closed the door behind him.

I didn't know what to do. I pondered the idea of running out after him and explaining that John is hyperactive and that yes, the noise level in this class is a little higher than others but it *works* this way. I decided against going after him when they began to remove almost everything from the bulletin boards while I was taking attendance--just to see what I'd do. I gave them a minute and then said, "If you'd like to rearrange things, I'll give you five more minutes and then we can get to writing on the computers." They put most things back and eventually settled in to work--though it might not have seemed that way to a passerby in the hall. The kids *seemed* unaffected by the comment that teacher had made, but it stayed with me for a long time. I think I felt an awareness of teaching from a different place. A louder place?

SMELLS OF DONUTS

My first full time teaching job evolved from my experience at a literacy centre where I volunteered when we moved to Toronto. The smell of donuts makes me think of this school. The training centre was a project sponsored by the Ministry of Education and the Ministry of Labour for laid-off workers who needed to upgrade their English or math before going into a college course or an adult day school. I was hired to teach English. They wanted someone without preconceived notions about how long it would take for people to complete their upgrading. Did they have the right person!

The first day I had three students. Talk about intense. I was really nervous and so were they. They were such good hearted people and so glad of the chance to go to school. We believed in each other so it really worked. We read and wrote--I told them they had to be ready for their tests in less than a year--and that of course they would be. Since none of us knew any differently, that's exactly what happened. We talked a lot. They really wanted me to know that they had lots of experience even if it wasn't in school. They did. I learned so much about culture, language and struggle. I loved reading their writing, and I told them how much I'd learned from their stories.

We had a good relationship because all of us understood that I was simply helping to improve their reading, writing, and speaking abilities. These were skills I had that they didn't because they had been working and raising families, coping with small children and aging parents...doing things I would also need to develop skills for. This statement seemed to underline our mutual respect. It really eased my nervousness too--and I guess as much as anything they had to know I believed in their learning abilities. It was so simple--sometimes just saying, "You can do it," seemed to make it possible.

Our centre has grown a lot from those days but my initial exposure to the ones who slipped through the cracks has stayed with me--some people had high school diplomas and their reading level was only grade six. Others hadn't really had any formal education in English. Some had degrees from other countries and couldn't access jobs because of language and racial barriers. Not all, but some of the learners had given up prestigious jobs in other countries to come to Canada to make new lives for their families. But you know they did well because they wanted to be there.

It's funny because when I left to go to FEUT they gave me a beautiful candle and a bracelet. *You've been a wonderful teacher. We'll never forget you--all those times you made us coffee and picked up donuts.* I smile when I think of those heartfelt words--and I remind my feminist voice that making coffee is a nurturing sort of thing and that's what all that meant--caring--not *just* making coffee.

And you know standing around the coffee machine at break time was and still is when special conversations take place.

Getting ready to attend FEUT I sign up for the course *Teacher's Lives as Narratives*. In between picking courses, I stumble across a poem by Bronwen Wallace:

> ...I didn't mean to go into all that
> didn't intend to get all confessional
> and tell you how every time I read a good poem
> by a woman writer I'm always peeking
> behind it trying to see

if she's still married
or has a lover at least
wanted to know what she did
with her kids while she wrote it
or whether she had any
and if she didn't if she'd chosen
not to or if she did did she
choose and why I didn't mean
to bother with that...

Bronwen Wallace
from "A Simple Poem for Virginia Woolf"

I wonder what teachers keep in their kitchen cupboards? Do they look like mine? Were the spices once in neat little rows? Are the wooden spoons stained with sauce? Do bags overflow from the middle drawer? Is the garlic fresh? Do plants take over the sunny window? Are there drawings on the fridge? Is the dish soap phosphate free? Does the aroma of coffee make the morning any easier?

SMELLS OF COFFEE WHITENER

I wasn't sure how I would fit into the role of student teacher. I could only remember one student teacher while I was in high school. He was tall with a soft voice and he always wore a suit and tie. He looked too big for the desk he occupied at the back of our English classroom. He taught us a writing unit. I still remember his comments on my story he had read so carefully.

To ease my growing nervousness over my first teaching placement, I had driven past Grantley the weekend before. I knew the bus route, so timing would not be a problem. When I arrived the other teachers were very welcoming. They gave me a coffee, and asked all about the faculty. It took all of us a good half hour to realize I was not who they thought I was, and they were not who I thought they were. Although I had driven past the school in advance, I hadn't noticed the change of address sign (the very small sign) on the practice teaching board at the faculty. What a nightmare! The staff at Grantley *Secondary* School (as opposed to *High* School) assured me that this happened to supply teachers *all the time* since the new school had only been built two months before.

In a taxi on the way to the correct school, I cleaned my glasses three times, tried not to bite my nails...We had been warned that you might as well forget about a good evaluation if you were late *even once*. I had phoned the principal to explain what happened. She said not to worry--just go straight to the main office on arrival. The office staff didn't react to my lateness. They contacted the associate teacher by intercom. The guidance teacher pointed me toward his class. "He'll be at the top of the stairs wearing a pale green suit."

We went straight to the English office where Mr. Daedalus poured us stale coffees with heaping spoonfuls of *Coffee Mate*. Once in the classroom I felt more at ease. The teacher had a great rapport with the students. From day one he told me, "We teach *kids* here not subjects."

After a short time I formed a connection a grade ten student named Tina. Tina was a quiet, tough-talking kid who apparently had her own apartment and lived on student welfare. Her only obvious friend in the class appeared to be another girl, Lori who could be described as hard. The associate teacher had warned me about both of them. He described Tina's friend as someone who would stab you if she had the chance, and Tina as a smart, tough little thing.

I learned that stories about the students are readily shared among the staff--of which I clearly was a part since I was privy to such information. I must admit I was wary of Lori after hearing about a violent episode the previous year. They seemed so young. I asked Mr. Daedalus, "Don't you wonder what they've been through?" He told me the school is literally full of what he calls the walking wounded, and that you have to just do what you can with the ones who will let you.

Lori's attendance was periodic. Tina's was a little more consistent--although when she was in class she was often disruptive. I kept reminding myself that at least she was there. After the third class I realized that she became frustrated when she couldn't understand instructions because she absolutely refused to ask for help.

The class had been working on writing assignments, and Tina could not figure out how to move the cursor fluently on her computer. At this vocational school there was almost no money for computers, but Mr. Daedalus had gone around with his truck and collected the old Commodore PET's--basically these are outdated word processors--but the effect they had on the class was fantastic-- just being able to say they were printing off their writing pieces gave the students an enormous amount of confidence. Anyway, I went over to Tina's computer and sat down with her to explain how confusing I found the mouse on my own computer. She grudgingly accepted my help and completed the assignment. The next day when they were doing journals on computer I helped her set up again. This time I put some topics on the board for the ones who couldn't quite get going. The topics were ones that allowed the learner to be the expert by writing from experiences with their best friends, worst enemies, favourite vacation--anything they could write a description of.

Tina stayed on the computer for the entire class. She handed me two pages and confessed that she was not finished yet. That evening Tina's writing was near the bottom of the pile.

I just went to his house to hang out--you know? And then the guy wants sex--he was bigger and stronger than me too. I finally got away and locked myself in the bathroom. In the end I climbed out the window and I even left my jean jacket. I was friends with him too. How can I have been so stupid? I'm never going there again. I told my best friend about it and she got mad that I let it happen. We fought about it but she understands now. It's strange how you have to trust your friends to fight with them.

I wrote a long response, including several numbers of community service organizations for girls and women who have been sexually assaulted. She came up to me after reading my response and said:

Miss--I think you didn't understand my story--if he had gotten away with it -- it would have been different. But I got away before he did. I have to finish it still.

Had I said too much in my response? I didn't want to scare here off--but as a teacher and as a woman how could I not have responded? I approached her at the end of class and thanked her for sharing her story. I told her that even if a threatened crime is quite carried out, the experience can still be terrifying for the survivor. She nodded and said, "Yeah, it was pretty bad, but I can handle it. I have to."

I can handle it. I have to. She's right. And she's strong. Maybe as strong as she is tough. Her words echo in my thoughts. They survive so much. The walking wounded. If only wounded was the adjective not the noun.

Tina did finish the story--she even put it in her folder (her first completed piece) and she did continue to attend most of the classes I taught. I wonder if she had any other woman teachers? I wonder if she'll finish school, if she'll find a job where she's treated well, if she'll keep writing?

THE SMELL OF ROSES

During one of the grade eleven classes Mr. Daedalus was probed about his son's death.

They know somehow these kids. Some say they heard it on the news but really it happened seven years ago--most of them would have been nine or ten. They pepper him with questions. Who did it? Where did they get the guns? How long did it take you and your wife to get over it? In Round Lake? You buried him in Round Lake?? Did you want to get the kid who did it? Just pummel him? I would have wanted to just wrap him up.

Finally, the teacher goes and runs off a story from his computer. It's a wrenching account of his grief--a letter of sorts to his son, who would have been nineteen by now. The class is silent--preoccupied with who might be crying--Mr. Daedalus included. When he is finished reading they ask more questions-- amazing questions. What do you do on his birthday? Have you been back to the grave? Who do you blame? Do you talk to the other boy? What happened to him? Maybe you should talk to him.

-No, we couldn't stay there. He was like my shadow. Everyone was always looking for him. I built an arena there and he was the first person to skate on it.

Turns out he brings a rosebush home every year on the boy's birthday for he and his wife to plant somewhere near the house.

I was amazed by his honesty. No wonder the kids love him. At the end of the first week this same man stares me straight in the eye, "I know what it's like to *really* care about this job and I have a sense you will too if you don't already; however, to keep yourself sane you *have* to have an outside interest. If you don't-- you'll never last. Mine's skiing.

SMELLS OF RED ZINGER TEA

I find out the last practice teaching session is a twenty-five minute bike ride from my house. I'm not sure I can cope with riding in heavy traffic, but I tell myself it's a great way to exercise and it's getting to be the end of the year so I know transportation costs could go to other things. I don't mention my cycling plan to my mother--I know she'll have a fit. It snows the first day so I take the streetcar anyway.

All I know about this school is that it's an alternative school. I have no idea what an alternative school is--I think there was *one* in my hometown but I'd never been in it. I look at myself nervously in the streetcar window. Pants, casual cotton sweater, god--I can't believe I'm worried about what I'm *wearing*. I silently curse everything I've ever read about first impressions. Once I arrive at the school a tiny woman with glasses notices me. She is surprised to hear that I am a student teacher, "Just come with me. I'll take you to the staff room. She tells me her name is Margaret. She teaches science and society, and computers.

The staff room is a small sunny place with plants and pictures everywhere. I am introduced to Rena who looks about 25, wearing denim overalls, a t-shirt, and red cowboy boots. She smiles and explains that Mark hadn't told her when I was coming. She has classes only in the morning so I am free to observe any other classes in the afternoon. I find out quickly that the kids at this school are quite politically active. They are involved in fund raising for various women's shelters and many have been on peace marches. There is a full recycling and composting program in operation. Much of the curriculum happens outside of the classroom. The students are quite free to leave classes if they need to. Though there is a fairly strict attendance policy, teachers are flexible about make up assignments and the students seem to have a fair amount of input into the course content.

This is a big change from another school I taught at where the students were not allowed to leave class--even to go to the washroom. Mark, one of the English teachers here, has the OAC Writer's Craft Class *at his house* every Wednesday night. I go to the first class and participate as a student. He watches my actions and listens to my feedback carefully. He tells me that I can lead the class the next week at my house if I want to.

The next Wednesday I rush around making coffee, red zinger tea and putting out muffins. I try to remember the ingredients in case of allergies. The doorbell rings. Students arrive in clumps of three or four. We end up sitting on the floor in the living room and the computer room. The cats are good ice-breakers. They are unusually friendly, purring and jumping into any available laps. I realize that the students were nervous too. But the nervousness ebbs away as we talk about pets, writing, and music. They are a very creative bunch and in some ways almost intimidating--they seem old beyond their years. They are, I guess. A few live away from home, two are trying to get into art college, another to a film program, another to a dance program. Already they have chosen creative paths, owning their voices.

They tell me my place is great and ask me if I ever jam with my husband's band. I laugh at this, but softly. They are so sincere. They study paintings on the walls, books on the shelves, food that's in the fridge--they didn't see that the milk was out. It comes to me that they trust me. Maybe because of my cats, torn carpet, or unorganized fridge, at any rate they expect this to be a *good* creative writing class. It is.

The group is very open. We complete several writing exercises. They love sharing their work. We do (I say *we* because the teacher shares in this setting too) a timed exercise about bread. We share our writing and then take a look at Margaret Atwood's prose poem, "Bread." I am relieved. They are impressed with the class, their writing, my writing. So am I.

The next day one of the teachers approaches me in the hall, "I heard you had the writing class at your house last night. The kids were just thrilled. They said you had the most beautiful cats they had ever seen."

"Well poor Sue couldn't take it; she has really bad allergies. But on the whole it went really well. They're a great bunch."

The next day Alice is working on her application for the film program at Ryerson. She has an interesting proposal for a documentary about women in manufacturing. Mark and I help her edit her letter of application. He pushes her, "What do you mean? What are you trying to get at here?" Her voice will be strong. Alice and I talk a little as we continue editing when he leaves for his meeting.

"So, what do you want to *do* ?" she asks me. "Did you ask for a placement at an alternative school? Do you want to teach?"

I am taken aback. "Well," I answer tentatively, "I didn't ask for a placement at an alternative school, no. But I am very impressed with the way it works here. I like it that the teachers are responsible to the students--*not* the administration. I guess that's partly because there is no administration."

"Yeah. Did you know that three students sit in on teacher interviews?"

"Wow. That's great."

"So, you didn't finish. What do you want to do?"

"Oh yeah. Well, yes I want to teach. I really have had success with literacy students, but I've loved working with Writer's Craft Classes too. I've been reminded, I guess, of how much I love literature. I want to continue writing too. I struggle balancing that with my teaching. Maybe I always will." I am conscious of a blurriness of roles here. But it's OK. I don't have the answer she wants--or maybe I do. At least I have been honest. "What about you?"

"Well, I really want to do this film thing. But I love literature too. I guess I see myself eventually teaching." She looks sideways at me

"That's great. I don't know much about film but I think your idea is fantastic. It seems like whatever you choose, you'll take your creative flair with you. Teaching is a great field--it looks like you've already done some dance teaching. Keep track of this for your experience profile." We both laugh about this. I had told her another time about trying to choose the right words on my application to the Faculty of Education.

I think about our conversation days later. Alice is typical of many of the students at this school. Very open. Very creative. Very focused. I like the relationship dynamics between students and teachers in this place. I think teachers going by their first names works here. Maybe because the school is small? Conversations are definitely warmer.

The last day approaches quickly. This is harder to leave than the other places. I guess because it's been three weeks and since it's so small, I feel like I've really connected with some of the kids--many of the kids. The atmosphere is so honest. It's refreshing too, to see that the students have a voice--individually and collectively--that counts.

I wrote a letter to one of the teachers:

> Dear Rena:
>
> We talked a little about perspectives and points of view while I was with you at Center School. At this point in our work together, I'd like to offer you a glimpse of your work as seen through my window. The grade eleven class is unlike others I've seen. Coffee brewing at 9:00 creates a kitchen like setting from the first moment of class. The circular formation of the desks, the familiarity of students calling you by your first name, and the relaxed dress code are all factors that contribute to a seemingly high level of respect for the students on your part. This respect appears to be mutual.
>
> I wrote down parts of our conversation during the first week.
>
> Rena -*As you can see I'm really learning as I go. I hope I'll be of help to you. Because I have so many questions myself--I sometimes wonder what student teachers think.*
>
> Robin-*Well it makes me less nervous about asking questions--It's interesting that there's no administration here. It seems like, for a teacher, the important people to answer to are the kids.*
>
> Rena-*That's for sure. When I came for my interview, three of the kids were part of the committee that interviewed me. It probably worked in my favour because they (the kids) thought I was going to be a student at first. I guess that's what I like the best (answering to the kids, I mean), but it's also what I find the hardest --they question everything they are presented with. It keeps me on my toes. I've had them ask me, "Is this just busy work? Why is it important for us to learn this?" Then I have to ask myself why they need to learn it. It's hard though because there's this fine line--if I question myself all the time I could look like I don't know what I'm doing.*
>
> I have appreciated your openness. It's thought provoking to hear about some of the struggles involved in the first few years of teaching. It seems to me that part of the openness at Centre School comes from a fairly equal relationship between students and teachers. I noticed how involved the students are in terms of developing the rules and school policies. This must be challenging for teachers because roles are not clear cut--maybe they never are? I don't mean that a blurry role is a bad thing--just different from what I've been taught to expect--though not necessarily different from what I've experienced. What is your opinion? Do you feel that a "blurry" role gives you more freedom? Does it make your job harder?
>
> During the second week you made a comment:

"I'm having a little trouble with professionalism--the whole idea of it. I'm not sure of the boundaries. I'm trying to learn from Tom because he seems very professional and very sure of himself."

This particular comment popped into my mind during the grade eleven class when we were having a discussion over coffee and donuts. This was after Bina and Omar spoke to you privately about the rest of the class holding them back. You told me earlier that they had voiced their annoyance during lunch the day before. You told me you were concerned because they said they were tired of you stopping the class for people who were half an hour late to re-explain things that you had just said. To improve the situation you decided to have a class meeting the very next day. Again, I jotted down a few notes as I listened to the points raised by you and by the students.

Rena-*I've had several people come to me privately to say that they are unhappy with the number of people coming in late. It seems that this disruption is interfering with their learning.*

Theresa-*Who are the people?*

Rena-*If they want to come forward they will. I wanted to raise the issue with you people to see if we could come up with some ideas. Frankly I feel like I've tried everything I can think of to deal with the lates and absences.*

Sam-*Well, I think after 20 minutes you should lock the door.*

Joe -*I think after 10...*

Rena -*Actually I have a real problem with that. This is a classroom and I don't believe that anyone should be locked out.*

Jan-*But if people can't make the effort to get here on time maybe they should be locked out.*

Rena- *Well if the lates bother any of you, you should say something about them.*

Jan-*But you're the teacher.*

Rena-*But this is your classroom.*

Allison--*But, I don't understand--you're the teacher and isn't it your job?*

Rena-*OK, that's fair --I don't mind telling them that we've come to some policies in the class but I won't enforce them on my own. If people come late and they're talking, it's up to you to tell them that they're interfering with your learning.*

Bina-*So what we should tell people is that we've decided that after half an hour they'll be marked absent--but they can still come in; however, they can't interrupt the rest of the class to find out what's been going on.*

Toni-*When should we start this?*

Rena-*Next period.*

Allison-*Wait that's not fair for the people who aren't here.*

Jan-*But that's their problem.*

Joe-*OK let's vote.*

(a vote is taken)

Rena-*It's solved then? Two days' grace for those who are not here to find out about the new policy. Then people are marked absent after half an hour. If people are being too loud whoever it's bugging will say something it. Deal?*

Students-*Deal.*

I didn't see the grade eleven class again after the new policy went into effect. I wanted to ask you a few questions about the discussion and I was hoping we could set up some sort of dialogue to 'enhance the learning process.' I'm using quotation marks because we've joked about 'eduspeak' jargon. Seriously though, I would appreciate your response. Observations can be so difficult because I am looking out from my own window of experience--so I could be missing or misunderstanding something vital in the process I'm observing. Does that make sense?

At any rate I really was wondering how the others in the grade eleven class reacted to the new policy? Did their classmates tell them, or did you make another announcement? Looking over my notes from the discussion, I am reminded that certain students voiced expectations about your 'job' as teacher. Did you notice this? My observation about the sometimes "blurry" role of a teacher comes to mind. As a beginning teacher, I might feel inclined to discuss the role or job of a teacher and the role or job of a student. Especially in a school like Centre School--the roles are not clearly defined. In your opinion would a discussion like that be valuable? I also wondered, Rena, if you thought that your own questions about professionalism contributed in any way to the discussion in class? These questions sound a bit leading, but I'm trying to base them on my observations so I keep steering them back to the discussion with the grade eleven class. Please respond when you have some free time; I hope we can develop some sort of ongoing dialogue about teaching. Hope to hear from you soon.

Bye for now,
Robin Hoffman

Rena read this but did not say much in response. I guess the decisions are mine.

So now the paper work begins. Again choosing the words to say what I'm all about and what teaching means to me. Application forms don't have enough lines to explain my vision of a classroom.

There will be lots of windows--natural light. A blue box will be in place. Student work will be displayed on the walls. So will pictures and inspirational words. Plants will be overgrown in the window sills. The book shelves will be full of books, magazines, and newspapers--old and new. The stories in the books will be stories my students can connect with. Stories of women, stories of men, stories of immigrants, stories of First Nations People, stories of students, stories of artists, stories of writers, stories of homes, stories of prisons, stories of the streets, stories of homes, stories of animals, stories of life. I want them to love reading and writing. The class will be colourful and safe.

It will be our classroom. I will try to avoid labels, to teach about critical thinking, to bring learners' experiences and interests into the classroom, to create an atmosphere of tolerance and respect, to inspire students to want to learn, to encourage people to speak out and to have confidence in their voices. We will learn together.

There will be many challenges I will continue to face as a teacher--many that I haven't even imagined; however, I have a growing wealth of stories--stories of my colleagues, my teachers, my grandparents, my parents, my siblings, my friends--all connections with my own stories. These stories are stored in my mind as my personal practical knowledge like a kitchen cupboard full of ingredients to add to whatever happens to be cooking.

One last stroll through the almost empty halls at FEUT. One last meeting. I close the window just a little--the pigeons are awfully close. I drain the last of my coffee from my faculty mug. For some reason I feel sad and happy and strong all at the same time.

ENDNOTES

[1]All names mentioned in narratives are pseudonyms. Permission for the use of the accounts has been obtained from anyone who is featured (not simply mentioned in passing) in reflections or narrative accounts.

In: Teacher's Stories, Teacher's Lives
Editor: Carola Conle, pp. 103-148
ISBN 1-59454-472-7

Chapter 5

THE CHALLENGE TO CARE: A PERSONAL NARRATIVE OF TEACHING AND LEARNING

Michele Pinet

I've come to a frightening conclusion that I am the decisive element in the classroom. It's my approach that creates the climate. It's my daily mood that makes the weather. As a teacher, I possess a tremendous power to make a child's life miserable or joyous. I can humiliate or humour, hurt or heal. In all situations, it is my response that decides whether a crisis will be escalated or deescalated and a child humanized or de-humanized.

Haim Ginott
Author, Child Psychologist and Teacher.

1995 - JULY

I started to cry the other day. I haven't cried like that for a long time. Later, I tried to tell a friend about it. I choked. I could barely speak.

Feelings overwhelmed me, as I thought about all that I have written and my experiences of having been a student and now a teacher and the path that has led me here.

Not so much as a child, but as a teenager, I experienced the kind of 'abuse' a person in authority can exercise over a young person. I had to struggle through it and its consequences on my own. In those days, support systems were not so readily available.

I was crying because of the 'contrast' of my experiences then and now.

Days away from being 46 years old, I am a teacher who still feels the student within me. That student is overwhelmed by the positive feedback and support that I now experience as a teacher.

If I didn't have them in the past, I have wonderful role models now in the professors that I had at the Faculty of Education; other teachers that I have met; the head of my department; and particularly the principal of the high school where I am presently employed.

It is a wonder, at times, that I survived and made it here, to where I am and that I am what I am. More than a survivor, more than someone who has broken free, but someone who has used those experiences as a launching pad, I have taken flight.

1991 - STUDENT TEACHER BLUES

I have been sick for a week now. I have been dragging myself from class to class from meeting to meeting with fellow presenters. My head is in a fog and I can't really think. Because I work through the weekend, I have not been able to take any time to recuperate. I am feeling sorry for myself because of the stress of presentations and papers that are already closing in on me.

I hate deadlines. Without them I would probably accomplish very little, but with them I feel as if there is never enough time to do the job properly. I know I agonize over every little thing but that's because nothing seems to flow easily out of me.

At 43, a person doesn't often experience many revelations about oneself. This 'epiphany' (one of my favourite words) is a critical one for me this year. I have discovered that I cannot write at night. This is serious information since I have a great deal of writing to do. I am a night owl (and would prefer to sleep in the morning). My natural inclination is to do my work in the afternoon and/or evening.

Hours of staring at the computer, producing nothing but garbage, is torture. I rework a few sentences to death. Finally, throwing up my hands in surrender, I retreat to my bed. Five a.m. comes. My alarm shakes me out of bed. Sitting bleary eyed at the computer - low and behold a miracle! Words flow easily from my brain in a logical sequence onto the paper. An amazing feat! Truly amazing! I discover that I can write in the morning and that I should not waste hours of my time trying to be creative, sequential or articulate at night. Perhaps it is the moon that bedazzles me. Befuddles me?

> "She's a bright little girl, but she's always in the moon! "
> *A statement, made by more than one grade*
> *school teacher, told to me by my mother.*

*   *   *

Carola: *Themes...the reason I brought the theme question up is because I want to make sure that you are comfortable with the themes that someone else would see in your writing. I was thinking of the hurtfulness that is woven through your writing, being hurt, or other people being hurt, and sex.*

I hadn't really thought of that. I wrote without the thought of my writing being for others. It was something that was simply a personal uninhibited expression for our eyes to see and our mouths to chew on...for me, for you, for our group and sometimes for the class. Should I be afraid that others will judge me? I stopped being a victim a long time ago.

1993 - 1995 MONOLOGUES AND DIALOGUES

Carola: *Do you see any kind of link to your teaching? Are we working still on the same issues, but in a different form?*

Michele: *I think these are some of the same issues that are still swimming around in my brain. I have such a mixture of emotions about what I'm doing. I seem to delight in the teaching process from moment to moment, but somewhere out there I am still fighting the role of even being a teacher. It's ironic because I feel I go into the classroom and one of the things that I think hits people about me is that despite the fact that I'm in my mid 40's and am overweight, I go in with an incredible amount of energy and passion. I get excited; I get creative; I do crazy things to get the kids' attention; I challenge them; I engage them constantly; I'm pulling them in all the time trying to get them excited about the learning process..."Did you know.....? Isn't this exciting?...This has never happened before! This is amazing!" I'm telling them this is amazing instead of just feeding*

> *them facts. I'm getting excited and they're getting excited and we're all getting excited together. This amazes me about myself. I am enjoying this so much. Yet, there's a little part of me out there that's saying "I don't know about this. I don't think I want to be a teacher. Am I a teacher? Can I do this? Is this me?" It's weird. Very weird.*

Joe: *Fight that. Fight that part out there.*

Carola: *What part of you is that little voice? Why is that there?*

Michele: *I don't know why it's there. Perhaps it comes from having a dream of being in theatre and being an actor. As they say, "Those who can't do, teach". I think that's sort of where it comes from, and yet people have said to me all the way along, you'd make a really good teacher. There is something inside of me that feels I'm compromising my dream. Yet, I go to school and I'm challenged and I'm creative. More so than when I was trying to run my own little theatre company.*

Some of the kids I have taught have been involved in criminal activities. Others are into drugs and alcohol. I am devastated for these kids because I think they are terrific. They're bright. They're creative, but they're throwing their lives away and their education away minute by minute. It makes me so sad. I go home and feel weighted down by the burden of this realization. I guess the troubled kids are the ones who challenge me. I love them. A lot of teachers don't. But I want them. I feel, "Send them, send these kids to me."

* * *

On Parent/Teachers' Night (1), as a beginning teacher, I felt very uncomfortable. I was nervous because one of the students I was teaching was going around telling everyone he hated me. I could see him across the room as he entered with his father. He was angry because I wouldn't let him 'go to the washroom'. Instead of going to the washroom, he'd go outside and smoke like crazy. He'd take off for fifteen or twenty minutes and then come back. There was a thin layer of smoke that covered him like a veil and floated behind him. The smell assaulted my non-smoker's nose as he passed by. He was stunned when I confronted him about the smoking.

He: *How did you know?!*
   (His response was like that of a child, when a mother knows the child is lying. Reinforcement of the myth of the all-knowing teacher/mother.)

Me:*I can't trust you. Make sure you go to the washroom before class, because you won't be allowed to go during the class. You lie and then you take off for twenty minutes; that's almost a third of the class. I'm sorry, but I can't allow you to do that any more.*

When he was in class, he wouldn't shut up. He was undermining my job, not allowing me to teach the other students. I was getting very frustrated, so I decided to be strict with him. He was getting into a lot of trouble outside the classroom as well.

On Parent/Teachers' Night, he and his dad made their way around the room. I noticed, as they sat with other teachers, it was the student who appeared to be conducting the interviews. They finally arrived at my desk. How in the world was I going to handle this? After all, going to the bathroom is a basic human right. The student said, "And this," as he looked at his father "is Ms. Pinet." Subtext: This is the teacher I was telling you about.

He had an attitude, a chip on his shoulder and a real 'expression' on his face.

He: *Okay, now my work is fine. I just talk too much and you don't want me to go to the washroom.*

Suddenly everything fell into place.

Me:*Hold on. Let me get your file.*

I pulled out his file. I was so proud of myself for being that organized. Two months had passed. It was the beginning of November. Out came two pieces of paper.

> This is what you have done since the beginning of the year. Yes, your work is good, hen you do it, but you don't do it. Here, let me see your attendance record: Late, late, absent, absent, absent, absent, absent...you're not here to do the work. When you do come, you talk. You undermine the class. Listen, I know you hate me right now. I know you are angry with me, but you know what? I don't care, because I'm fighting for you life. I'm fighting for your future. I'm fighting for your education and I'm not going to give up. I'm not going to let you get away with it!

(1) Part of this episode has been fictionalized to protect the privacy of those involved. However, permission for the inclusion of this section has been attained from the principal of the school.

The 'attitude' just sort of washed away from his face. His father was very supportive, very positive. It was strange. The words just came. Everything fell into place, everything was right, the words, the emotion, the passion. The teacher sitting next to me said, "Wow! I wanted to cry. That was so good!"

....I keep amazing myself. I keep coming through for myself and for the students. But, for some reason, I'm afraid that it's pure luck. I don't always believe in myself. That's an old problem.

> Carola: *So what you are saying now that is quite interesting, is that your present experiences are not like your personal narrative generally, are they? I am thinking back over your earlier stories, which were kind of on the negative side. It's interesting that things are very different.*
>
> Michele: *Not negative really. Occasionally 'dark'. I'd say. Amusingly dark sometimes.*

I remember doing a collage of myself for an art course in university. The collage was two sided. I explained to the art professor that the black and white pictures were 'me' on the inside. They were sad photos mostly. 'Me' on the outside were photos that were bright and colourful and whimsical. I guess my perception was that, though I projected an outgoing personality, I felt I was hiding a rather dark and depressed psyche. The professor looked at the collage and said, "No dear, you have it in reverse. The colours and the whimsy are on the inside. The black and white are your outside." I was taken aback. I realized that when looking at the collage from another perspective there was truth in what she said. An epiphany!

Most of my experiences as a young student were rather mundane really. But, I am a very theatrical person. Dramatic moments leap out at me from my memories of what I consider to be an ordinary life dealing with ordinary problems. All of my family is 'dramatic'. Big voices that carry. Histrionics. Extreme emotions. I remember writing in a Valentine's Day card to my parents once, "For French Canadians, we are rather Greek." (as in Greek Tragedy).

So, when I describe my childhood and my experiences as a student, the dramatic moments are those that I remember, whether positive or negative. Mostly negative, I guess. Things that are slightly off centre fascinate me. The bizarre within the banality of life. Faulkner's *AS I LAY DYING* or James Reany's *THE KILDEER* are examples of the kind of literature that engage me. So, when I look at my life 'the strange',' the sad' and even 'the sexual' leaps out. Fueled perhaps by Roman Catholicism. It's all those lives and deaths of the martyrs, I was fed and relished as a child.

My reflections 'accent' my life, but they are not my life or a complete picture of who I am. These experiences, and the sense I make of them, have helped to shape me and I believe have contributed to the kind of teacher I want to be, strive to be.

On the other hand, I don't want to trivialize what happened to me either. As an older teenager, still a high school student, I was exploited and abused emotionally by teachers (in various forms) who had authority over me. Sometimes sex was a factor. That is the reality. The impact of 'that' to my life and what I did as a consequence is also the reality. To hide, by omission, what I did would go against the grain. I did cut my wrists. I did have a breakdown at 19. That experience coloured who I am now. It was a long time ago.

During the group's dialogues, I discussed the fact that I resisted the impulse to become a teacher for a long time. I said that I didn't know 'why'. I came up with rationalizations relating to being a professional artist. Sometimes if a person stands too close to a painting the shapes and colours are lost swallowed up in the blackness. Stepping back helps you to see what is there before you. Perhaps my experience of 'teachers' had something to do with my not wanting to become one.

Like a child who is abused, you can either become your role model or you can do something different.

The other day, I was in a line at the bank.
In front of me, three generations stood before a teller.
The little girl must have been about 5.
She was acting up.
Her mother pinched her once,
then again for good measure.
The child's face screwed up with pain.
Within seconds she began to pinch her grandmother's breast.
"What are you doing?!" yelped the old woman.
The little girl giggled and wouldn't stop.
It was suddenly a game to her.
In telling the story to my friend,
she pointed out that the pinching was probably coming full circle.
I hadn't thought of that.

It takes a great deal of effort to do something different because there is tendency to become what one has experienced.

Michele: *Mine wasn't the most positive of educational experiences.*

Carola: *You pulled yourself out of those experiences and maybe this is what gives you the confidence that those kids can do it too.*

Joe: *The really interesting part of your story is how you made that change. How you decided to take the garbage and put it into a bag and put the tie on it and say whew, I know it's still there but it is not part of my baggage any more then go on. That's the learning part. That's the essential part.*

Carola: *One of the students I have this year said that as a teen he was a punk. He said in his experience, when he is out in the schools, the people that he likes best as teachers seem to be all those who themselves had problems in school and have risen above them. He, himself, did not have a very good experience. He now wants to teach the kids who have problems, the tough ones.[........] Michele, you said something in the piece that you wrote for admission to the faculty that you were a person that doesn't get upset by things that freak other people out.*

Michele: *Yeah, I can handle issues that embarrass other people.*

Robin: *You were basically saying, "What's my role model?" You grew up as a child and your role models were a disappointment. They weren't role models at all.*

Loreen: *There must have been something.*

Carola: *I think the impression I got was that you became your own role model. You knew you weren't really that terrible little kid. Somehow you are more than what has happened to you. The part of you that survives and is successful through all that; it's your role model.*

Michele: *I don't know if I actually am that role model, but I think it's what I want to think...*

Joe: *Yeah, well, that's to what you aspired. Role models are by definition unattainable, really.*

Carola: *I wonder if you have ever explored the connection of acting and drama in your life. You hint at it every now and then in your stories. I mean, has acting and drama helped you to live your life better? I speak as a non-drama person, someone who has never acted. It seems to me though, when you act you are pushed to put forth something; to perform no matter what the present conditions of your life. Maybe you have just had a fight with someone but whatever happened, you are performing tonight, and you do something with yourself that puts that other part away. It seems to me that you have to do that when you are teaching as well. You put all that energy out in the classroom and act appropriately no matter in what direction your life's going.*

Michele: *Well, you either put it aside or you take it and use it.*

Joe: *Or you bring it into the classroom and torment the kids with it, and that's what some people do.*

Carola: *But maybe as an actor you already know that there are some things that you don't bring into your work; there is a higher purpose. In a way, you draw on resources somewhere within yourself that help you walk that bridge, make that jump.*

Joe: *Your analysis of what should happen is accurate. I mean, **that** is what **should** happen. Some actors are able to do **that** a lot better than others. Now, it is eight o'clock and you must perform **Romeo and Juliet**. You perform **Romeo and Juliet** no matter what's happened at six o'clock with your husband. Or what happened at 7:59, which is more often the case.*

Carola: *Some of us don't get put into that kind of position! We have jobs where we can say to ourselves and others, "Well, I am having a bad day today. Don't ask me to do this or that, because I'm in a frazzle. My husband did such and such..." But, on stage, you can't do that. You can't say, "Excuse me, audience..."*

Michele: *I certainly think that I have a strong sense of what it means to be a professional. The show must go on!...no matter what. Even as a little child that was given to me, in a sense, by my mother. I remember once being very, very sick with a high temperature and my mother saying "You don't let people down." I had to recite a poem for a school concert. She bundled me up and packed me off to school. "You don't let people down."*

It really is an actor's credo. I have fallen off stage. I have fainted on stage. Someone fell on my head once on stage and almost killed me. I remember screaming in pain. Luckily, I was in the tail end of the dragon and there were loud sound effects. I would go off stage and wail while they packed my head in ice. Then I would go out and do my thing blocking out the pain. Luckily, the scenes were short. Then I would go backstage and wail again.

You put 'whatever' aside and you get on with it. You do what you have to do, come hell or high water. But, on the other hand, I do think that you take what has happened to you too and you redirect it. You take that energy and you re-focus it in a way that is going to be of most benefit to you and others.

***

During my practicums and my two years of teaching, I have seen how the labeling of students can destroy their self-esteem.

Student: I can't do it. I'm stupid.
Me: *You are not! You can do it!* (A look of disbelief from the student.)
          *You **can** do it!*
She: *I'm stupid!* (I walk over and face her.)
Me: *Say, "I'm smart".*
She: *What?* (A confused look comes over her face.)
Me: *I said, say "I'm smart".*
          Come on.
          Say it.
She: *I'm smart.*
Me: *Say it again.*
She: *I'm smart.*
Me: *Again.*
She: *I'm smart.*
Me: *Good. Remember that.* (And she did.)

The students look at me and in their heads they say, "She must know. She's the teacher." Powerful stuff 'that'.

THE TEACHER AS A STUDENT

Three and a half years old. The first glimmerings of awareness. I was dancing. It was a ballet class in Churchill, Manitoba. We were practicing for a recital. Children were in a circle hands raised high, like little steeples. The teacher wanted me to go in and out of the circle underneath the arms. She repeated her instructions a number of times. Sometimes I did it. Sometimes I didn't. I really couldn't understand what she wanted me to do. The times I managed to do what she wanted were accidents. To my great disappointment, she gave another child the part. No matter. I stole the show by falling asleep on stage.

When I look back and think about that time, I feel as if I was in a kind of half sleep. My mind hadn't quite woken up yet. Nothing penetrated. I couldn't follow instructions. It was like people's mouths were moving but I couldn't hear them. And yet obviously, I was starting to put some things together.

Kindergarten (Manitoba)

I don't remember her face, only the outline of her body.
She is sitting, holding a book.
Its pages are open, pictures facing us.
We are on the floor, in various positions, looking up.
She is young...and smart.

"Let's each of us make our own book", she says.

I love to draw
It is my primary preoccupation.
I take two pieces of paper and fold them down the middle.
Inspired, I put crayon to paper
two images emerge,
one large, one small.
The smaller is done quickly.
It is the larger figure with which I take great pains

Hands up.

The time has come to share.
Anticipation aches within me.
First, this one...then that one.
Finally!
My book.
She turns the pages.

Not a ripple of shock or emotion passes over her face.
I wait...and am disappointed.
She is smart.

I take my book home.
Mummy is having coffee with some of the other navy wives.
"What did you do in school today, Michele?"
I hand her my book.

(Pause)

Ha!

Finally!

My mother's face goes pale...then red.

I don't really hear what she is saying to me.
I feel only my delight.
A reaction worthy of my artistic efforts.
It is my first consciously wicked act -
a graphic drawing of myself and mummy in the shower,
breasts, nipples, vulva and pubic hair.
I am an excellent drawer for 5.

That teacher was smart.

I started Pre Primary late, because by that time we had moved to Dartmouth, N.S. My dad was an officer in the Navy and we had to pack up our 'kit and kaboddle' every 2 to 3 years. I remember, at the end of the year, all the children were yelling with excitement when they got their report cards. I smiled and jumped up and down with the rest of them, but I really didn't have a clue. I couldn't read very well yet.

They kept me back in Pre Primary for another year, because I hadn't finished my blue and yellow readers. All I can remember is that I was constantly looking over shoulders trying to copy other children's work. *I still hadn't woken up.* Or, maybe that was from the previous year. I'm not sure.

'Sleeping Beauty' must have had her kiss at some point, because by the time we moved to Montreal the following year -

Grade One

I skipped it.

I do know that when I did learn to read, I loved doing so out loud, particularly when there were visitors. I would show off my booming voice. It always brought rather stunned looks to their faces. I loved that! In Grade Two, I was even chosen to make a presentation before the whole school to the newly appointed bishop.

Grade Two (Montreal)

St. Claire de la Innocence[1]
Grade Two.
English speaking teachers were scarce.
She was 17 years old,
a recruit straight out of high school.
A pretty, giggling girl
with dimples á la Shirley Temple.
She took me behind the classroom door
because my hair was long
and told me the story of
Lady Godiva.

She delighted in playing games,
at our expense.
2 spelling mistakes
Down to the principal.
7 spelling mistakes
Down to the principal.
1 spelling mistake
Down to the principal.
It changed everyday.
I was a lousy speller,
having skipped grade one.
Me….and a line of little boys.
The principal warned me,
"Next time, I will have to give you the strap."
I never went down again.

4 girls and 16 boys
She made us pick who we liked best in the class.
She paired us up,
making little romantic liaisons
on St. Valentine's Day.

She made a fuss
the day of the class picture
and sent for the principal.

Too shy, she said, to
have her picture taken alone.
'He'
must be there, as well,
to have his picture taken too
and
to give his support.
'He'
looked like a movie star.

***

Two boys were fighting in a park across from a row of apartment buildings. A crowd of young people had gathered to watch the fight. Everyone was yelling and screaming, egging the two boys on. A little girl, who was only about 7 or 8 years old, saw the excitement so she ran to where the fight was taking place and joined in. There was one boy she disliked so she began cheering the other one. Somehow, the boy she disliked must have picked out her voice from the crowd or else it had all been planned, because suddenly that boy stopped fighting. He turned towards the little girl. Slowly he walked over to her and slapped her across the face. He then turned, went back to the other boy, and they walked off arm in arm. The crowd dispersed leaving the little girl stunned and standing alone.

I've always hated getting my face slapped.

One Saturday, as I was playing with my doll carriage outside of my apartment building, two brothers, who were in my class, grabbed me. My arms were held behind my back, while a line of little boys took turns kissing me. This went on until my mom stuck her nose out of the window and screamed, "What's going on?!"

Bless Mom, who must have been on a 15 second timer whenever her children were out of sight.

Grade Three

Her name?
I forget.
Her nails?
I remember.
Long

Red
Sharp
Buried in my neck
Out of anger
Because inside
my desk
was a mess.
Brushes and chalk
would fly past our ears.

Still,
we liked her
because she was pretty.

One day, a sweetheart sent her
a beautiful bouquet of roses.

Years later,
while camping down East,
I met some people who lived
in Ville LaSalle.
They knew her.
She had been suspended
for slapping a student.

Grades Four and Five

Lost in the Bermuda Triangle of my mind.

Grade Six (Victoria, B.C.)

Mrs. Hines -
She reminded me
of
Même.
(my maternal grandmother)
Plump and pleasant.

I wasn't the popular choice among the other girls for the role, but Mrs. Hines chose me anyway – to play the part of Queen Marie Antoinette in the school pageant.

I have a photograph. I look older than eleven. My hair was in a chignon decorated with an ostrich plume. I was arrayed in an off the shoulder dress that one of the sisters had pulled out of an old trunk. My face was covered with heavy make-up, some teenage girl's artistry. It was evening. I was tired and look slightly cross-eyed.

One of the great sadnesses of my life is the 'lost photograph' of Dianne Barry (her real name) and me. [*]

```
                 «                                        «

        «
           «                                         «

        «       «                              «
             ««                                    «
    «                                    « «
         ««         T                          «
                                           « « « «
                    w
                      o                    t      ««
                   school                                i
                   girls.                  e
                   Tunics,                s
                       white        blouses,
                       black        stockings
                        and    Oxfords.
                       Me,
                        sitting
                        in a tree
                       Arms out
                       flung. Legs
                       dangling.
                       My face
                       full of
                       suppressed
                       laughter
                       and bubbling
                       joy. D i a n n e,
                       my bosom buddy,
                        standing at its base
                   hands       clasped together
               as if about        to sing a hymn.
                   Her smile          full of sweetness.
```

[*] With great emotion, in 1999, the photograph was found. It had been at the bottom of one of my mother's dresser drawers and was discovered when she decided to move from her condo. It had been lost for 26 years!

Dianne and I collected holy cards. Every week, she and I would race to the school store to go through the cards. We'd argue over the prettiest pictures, each costing a few pennies. The store was located on the way to the borders' dormitory. One day, in a fit of curiousity, we continued to climb the old wooden stairs that seemed too narrow. They deteriorated the higher we went. We chickened out and fairly flew down the steps in fear. They say that the ghost of Emily Carr walks the halls of the old convent. We didn't know that at the time.

I loved to read about the lives and deaths of the Saints (particularly the deaths). I had aspirations of becoming a virgin martyr, whatever that was. It sounded like such a wonderful thing to be. What a romantic! The concept of martyr, by that time, I had grasped. It was the 'virgin' part that eluded me.

Our uniforms, topped off with tams showing the school crest, declared that I was a Roman Catholic. Every day, I would take a shortcut home through a field and a small wood. Victoria was primarily Protestant. One afternoon, as I walked from the bus stop home from school, a group of kids started yelling religious slurs at me. I ignored them and walked slowly with my head held high even when they started to throw stones. "Forgive them for they know not what they do," I said out loud to myself. They must have thought I was nuts.

My sense of religious fervor unfortunately didn't extend to my sister who suffered a great deal at my hand. She will never let me forget.

From Grade 6 to Grade 8, I loved to stay after school to chat with my teachers. In many ways, I preferred their company to that of other children. I must have been a real pest. I was a talker and wanted to tell them...God knows what. My mother said that if I came home the first day of school saying I didn't like the teacher, it was probably because the person had not wanted to listen to me and had told me, in no uncertain terms, to 'cease and desist'.

So, I stayed after school to talk with my teachers, as my sister waited for me in the schoolyard. Each day, it got a little later. Eventually, we were arriving home at least an hour after we should have. It happened so slowly, that I was terrified my mother would eventually start to realize that something was wrong. I was anxious to move from Victoria, so I could start fresh. It was a burden to me because, even if I wanted to go home early, I couldn't because Mom and then Dad would know the truth. It became a nightmare. I really have no idea why Jacqueline (my sister) didn't tell them. One day, Jack-O-Lantern, who was in Grade One, got fed up of waiting for me and took off. We had to take two buses to get home. She was a bright little girl and made it without a problem. Unfortunately for her, hell broke loose because she was not supposed to be on her own. I made her out the villain. She got a spanking. I never confessed (except to the priest).

Grades Seven

BLANK, BLANK

...and Eight

Mrs. Smith
had a diabetic husband
who was the school caretaker.
He had seizures.

From B.C., we moved to Quebec. I was in Grade Eight again. I hadn't failed. It was just a 'Quebec' thing. I was going into my first year of high school and in Quebec that meant Grade Eight.

Grade Eight (Quebec)

Sister Mary Jowls
looked like a Bulldog.
She showed us no mercy,
terrified us into submission.
1963 was the only year of my life
that I did my homework religiously
out of fear.

Sister Mary Jowls was the only teacher who took me aside and told me I was special, 'a leader'. She insisted I get better grades, so I did. She was tough. I don't think I ever saw her smile. I must admit to remembering her with mixed feelings. She traumatized me once. She did 'a number on me' about being perfect in a performance.

I played the role of a herald in the St. Patrick's Day Pageant. The sisters decided that at the end of the evening, I was the obvious choice to thank the various people who had helped. During the rehearsal, I kept stumbling over the music teacher's name. It was a German name and difficult to pronounce. The sister admonished me saying that there was no bigger insult to a person than to make a mistake with regard to their name. After the performance, as I proclaimed our 'thanks', I 'tongue stumbled' over that same person's name.

I was devastated. Once off the stage, I became hysterical. I sobbed. The sister, in a fluster, opened the windows to give me some air. She left me alone without a word of comfort.

Grade Nine

A 'lazy' student
I worked so hard on a piece of writing,
that it made me feel sick.
The result -
I won a citywide essay contest:
First Prize
in the Senior Division.
My photograph was in the newspaper.
I still have the clipping somewhere.
The prize was only 10 dollars,
but in those days, that was a lot.
My award was given to me at a special luncheon at the Château Frontenac.
I remember my teacher wanting me to sing 'Oh Danny Boy',
but I wouldn't do it, unless she agreed to some rehearsals.
Over 200 people attended.
The priest,
who presented me with the prize,
said none of his Grade 11 boys had entered the contest,
because the subject matter was too difficult.
Wouldn't it have been more appropriate
to congratulate
a 14 year old girl
who had taken on the challenge of writing about the
"Symbolic Meaning of Celtic Design"?

Grade Ten

Sister Mary Biology
A favourite teacher
She made school exciting.
After they banished the Latin Mass

She left the convent
On a motorcycle.

Grade Eleven

My last year at Catholic High.
The only things I can remember are:
I was voted Class President.
I won second prize for my Careers Poster.
and
I was finally old enough
to go to the parties
on the ships
coming into port from around the world.
But, I never even got to go to one.
Dad retired from the Navy.

Grade Twelve (Ontario)

1967 EXPO
Hi Ho Hill High School
Co-ed.
Culture shock.

My mom tried to get dad to stay another year in Quebec City, so I could finish high school. It wasn't an issue for him. It was the way of the world in those days, I guess.

Anyway, it was a very difficult year – the beginning of a period in my life that had a nightmare quality to it. The principal of Hi Ho Hill High School told my parents that it would be a miracle if I passed, even though my average was in the 80's. Students didn't do well when transferring from Quebec to Ontario. Big surprise! I was a uniform clad Catholic school girl from Quebec City who was being uprooted and tossed into a coeducational public school setting requiring street clothes (I didn't really have any!)

Though I had been to school dances in Quebec, I was shy and awkward with boys in the classroom. I spoke to only two or three boys during the whole school year. My shyness was interpreted as snobbishness. I always appeared to be self-assured. (I still do.) I was completely the opposite. (I still am.)

My education in Quebec had been traditional - English, French, Religion, Latin, Algebra, Geometry, Health, Geography, Biology, Chemistry and History. No options. The Ontario school system was like an alien environment. It was too late (I didn't have the prerequisites) to take options I would have loved, like art. To get the credits for my high school diploma, I had to take subjects like Grade 11 Physics, Business Studies, New Math and English. Grade 12 New Math, particularly, was not a treat. I couldn't make 'head or tail' of it not having had any of the previous years' courses.

My average for my first set of exams was 56, even though I had worked very hard. My confidence was shaken to its very core. I knew what the nuns wanted from me, but these lay teachers? I didn't have a clue. I stopped trying and my average was the same at the end of the year. They gave me my credit in math, only if I agreed not to take it in university. They said I would have to take it again, if I wanted to do that. What a laugh! They needn't have worried!

My mother encouraged me to take a Special Grade 12 One Year Commercial Course at a downtown high school. My best friend had decided to attend, so I decided to tag along. I had been accepted to art college but my mother couldn't cope with the idea of my leaving Ottawa for an apprenticeship in Toronto...so I stayed in Ottawa and studied typing and shorthand, skills which I didn't excel in. I couldn't stop myself from reading or thinking about the material I was typing. Not the way for anyone to improve his or her typing speed.

Again, I found myself in a rather alien environment for one who had always been in the Academic stream. Higher education didn't seem to be an issue for my parents where their daughters were concerned. Office work would have been fine. On the other hand, it was important that Pierre, my brother, be well educated – a not uncommon attitude, perhaps for the times, particularly in French Canadian families.

(Pierre became a mechanical engineer; Jacquie, a nurse; and moi, an actress. I was the black sheep of the family. The odd ball.)

At least at this new school, I got used to the boys. I joined the choir and finally felt at home. It was here that I got into trouble for the first and only time of my educational career.

Grade Twelve Commercial

A still life
in the art room -
a small loaf of bread
a glass of (red ink) wine
and a dagger.
Inspired
I plunged the blade into the loaf,
trailed the (red ink) wine down its
doughy opening onto the little plate
and called it
'Consecration'
(In honour of my catholic upbringing.)
Two weeks later -
a summons to the office
by the VP and the art teacher.
Confronted with the taboo of touching a still life!
(and called a destructive pervert)
"But, I thought I was creating!"
They were sure if they looked at
my school record, a flawed, warped character
would be revealed.
In truth,
my record was an exemplary one.
They would have found no such thing.
It was my first and only infraction.
I was an innocent.
I wept.
It shook them up.
Hurriedly they left the room,
tossing kleenexes at me as they exited in panic.
Tears had been unexpected
and yet I knew instinctively,
they were required.
The tears stopped almost before the door was shut.
My heart was cold.
I smiled at my wickedness.
(Later I was told that my tears showed I was truly sorry)

It was around that time,
I decided to go on the stage.

One day, at the school's performance of Die Fledermaus, a man came running up to me afterward.

He: *You were terrific!*
Me: *Who me? You must be mistaken. I was just in the chorus.*
He: *Yes, I know and you stuck out like a sore thumb!*

He invited me to sit in on a rehearsal of a musical being put on at a community theatre. It just happened that someone had dropped out of the chorus. Her costume fit me and I was on my way. To what? A career in the theatre, of course!

I dated one of the young men in the production.

Epiphany

We fought.
I threw a rose at his feet, in anger.
That was when he told me,
'You should be an actress."
Trumpets blared!

My mother always blamed him for putting the idea of becoming an actor into my head, but I think it had always been there. I loved being involved in school plays. That it could actually be a career had never dawned on me. He turned on the light. Big difference. If not an actor, I would have been an artist.

It was a difficult year. My parents were extremely unhappy with my 'career' choice. I felt rejected because I had decided to go to university and study theatre. It was about the same time, I guess, that I stopped going to church.

My parents insisted that I work a year before returning to high school for my Grade 13. I got a job at a large company and took night classes 4 nights a week. To prove myself, since my marks had been so poor in Grade 12, I took Grade 13 English and French. My marks had to be over 60, before they would consider supporting my decision to go to university.

It was a year of betrayal and abuse, by those who had authority over me.

***

John was in his 30's.. He was very charismatic...to a naive 18 year old anyway. I met him when I signed up to take a workshop that he was offering in the evenings at my high school. The following year, I found out that he was teaching Creative Drama to children and I begged him to let me assist him. He agreed. After class, we would go for rides in his car. He would stop at some isolated place to kiss me. At eighteen, I was still years away from any serious sexual conclusion.

I heard other storiesabout him from a friend. John came crashing down from his pedestal.

The accumulation of three years of stress regarding my education, in combination with the distress I had experienced in a number of close relationships, became too much. My disillusionment with John and, in effect, the destruction of my emotional innocence was the final straw. He had been the only adult, I thought I could turn to for moral support. I felt totally alone. I walked around, for a month, as if in a trance. I kept falling asleep. The emotional pain was too great. In the depths of depression, I finally ended up in emergency. My mom had to stop Dad from calling the police. In those days, it was against the law to attempt suicide.

On the following Saturday, John looked at my bandaged wrists and asked, "Did this have anything to do with me?" I lied and he never pursued the subject. He went on to bemoan the fact that he had some financial problems. I still hate him.

The next year, I went back to high school. For the longest time, I was never left alone. My mom hid pills and razor blades under her mattress. She had trouble sleeping. In the middle of the night, I would cry. She would always hear, even though her room was at the other end of the hall and my door was closed. She would come in the dark and rock me in her arms.

The following September, I left my job and returned to high school. Another little girl in my Theatre Arts class wasn't so lucky.

Grade 13

She dressed herself in a green uniform
(even though we went to public school).
She locked her bedroom door,
caked her lips
with white lip stick,
lay herself down
on her bed,
placed the Bible
on her chest,
by her left hand
Black Marigolds
(a book of poems)
and took
a bottle of
sleeping
pills.

I remember I had a barrette that she liked. It sits somewhere, in a box of junk in my house. I still feel a twinge of guilt that I didn't give it to her.

Laura was desperate to find her own little bit of genius. She had tried all the arts: dancing, music, visual arts, theatre. She felt so inadequate. I remember her putting a garbage bin over her head while doing an improv exercise in theatre class. In a sense, the possibilities overwhelmed her, particularly because she just didn't seem to fit in.

She could have done anything with her life.

It is strange, but we were all the same. Not 'hippy dippies'. Just ordinary kids. We agonized over our souls, the meaning of life and our place in it. Our biggest challenge was deciding on a career. We were overwhelmed by our options. We knew we could be anything, have anything. But, we couldn't cope with the richness of possibilities.

University of Ottawa

I was obsessed with theatre.
I didn't care about anything else.
The professors basically followed the same technique of teaching

that I had experienced in grade school and high school
ESP
Let's try to guess what the teacher has in his or her mind.
because that's the right answer.
Heaven forbid!
that a teacher might try to develop
a student's thinking skills.

This is a fragment of my educational history, with a few other bits thrown in for good measure.

I can't say there was ever anyone who really was a mentor to me. What strikes me though is that in many ways, as a student, I felt my trust betrayed by teachers. I think that this has had a tremendous impact on me as I enter the profession of teaching.

Following university, I moved to Toronto; worked as an actress for six years; studied sign language; started a small theatre company to work with deaf actors; and began to teach multiply disabled youth and deaf youth. (Please do not confuse the two.)

***

I got a part time weekend job at a Centre for the Deaf. I remember listening to the despair of the Sunday school teacher trying to imagine what these young multiply disabled residents might contribute to the Christmas pageant. Getting them to 'sign' a song was agonizingly tedious work for everyone concerned. I remember saying "Start with where they are at."

I took up the challenge believing that each child was capable of doing something. Mary, Joseph, the Shepherds, Wise Men and Angels. Those who were required to walk followed a masking tape path on the stage. Others, like Lori, were already on stage before hand. She was dressed like a little angel. For once she sat quietly, not screaming or pulling at her skin. Her little fingers stole between the chair and the Virgin Mary's behind. Peanuts! She munched on them for the time that it took us to present our Christmas Tableau. Another boy, with sparkling eyes filled with the pride of accomplishment, brought in the star of Bethlehem that was suspended over his electric wheelchair. Another little boy who couldn't walk, replaced for those few moments, his protective head gear with a tinsel halo. He quickly pulled his tiny body all over the stage, almost off the stage! Finally, he ended up at the Virgin Mary's feet. He pulled himself up and planted a kiss on Baby Jesus' cheek – a bit of Christmas magic that had not been planned.

Through 'A Show of Hands,' the company I set up with members from the deaf community, THE SIGNS OF SUMMER a theatre training program for deaf youth, was established. It was because of this experience that I eventually ended up at the Faculty of Education.

***

"I don't have a name for what I do. As a person it seems to me I simply stand midway between all that has happened before I arrived and what is now. What I do at this moment obviously shapes up some part of what is to come."

Dorothy Heathcote
Drama Teacher Extraordinaire

A little more than a year has passed, since I agonized over the questions on my application to the Faculty of Education at the University of Toronto. As I submitted my application, I saw others scribbling down at the last minute, what had taken me two weeks of hard labour to accomplish.

The importance of one question comes back to me now in light of my experiences this year at the Faculty of Education.

As a role model what contribution can you make to the school community?
I remember answering very thoughtfully:

As a role model, I believe I have a great deal to contribute to the school community. I have a healthy life style. I am punctual, courteous and respectful of other people's rights and property. People trust me. I am dependable and fulfill my commitments. I respond quickly and effectively in crisis situations. I believe in open communication combined with a non-judgmental attitude. I am comfortable dealing with issues others find embarrassing. I have a positive attitude and handle problems creatively. I can be a team player but I am happy to carry the ball. I enjoy life. I have an open mind and an open heart. I care about people.

In another part of the questionnaire I stated:

Life for these young people (Intermediate/Senior students) is often like a roller coaster ride, at once exciting and terrifying. I want to be able to help them develop the resources needed to arrive at a safe and steady place.

It was a description of what I thought I was and what I hoped to do. That hasn't changed really and yet after what I've been through, it sounds so 'Pollyannaish'. I have descended from my cloud in a 'freefall' wondering at times whether I had a parachute.

***

Teenage violence in Toronto has doubled in the last year. After our first TOP Day, Joe comes back in a state of shock. A gang of teenage thugs drags 5 students out of school and proceeds to beat them senseless. Three escape, two end up in intensive care. The last day of my Practicum, I am told that one young girl in the OAC class is beaten up because she complained to the office that some boys had torn down Halloween decorations. In English Class, back at the University, I listen in horror as one practice teacher tells of a student who had a gun and was threatening to kill another student after school.

Many of the children of the '60's are asking for help from their parents. Going back to the nest. They are requesting food and shelter, while their own children are on the street. Our children will never have what we threw away. Those of us who are going into teaching - we are now in the frontlines facing...what?

Practicum Experiences

Students: BANG! CRASH!

Books slammed down on desks.
Chairs kicked.
Anger?
No - just another way of saying 'I'm here'.
I am sitting, at the time, at the back of the class...

Students: *Who the hell are you?*

I smile.
I feel more relaxed this time.
I don't know why.
The reputation of these kids, this school has preceded them.

One of the students has scribbled all over his desk.

Teacher: *Jim! Clean that up.*
Students: *Woosy! Woosy!*

Jim is enraged.
He hesitates.
He's caught between a rock and a hard place.
Damned if he does.
Damned if he doesn't.

Me:*Do you mind if I borrow that?*
My desk is a disaster.

I take some paper towelling and the spray bottle of cleanser.
I start to clean, praying that they have never read *Tom Sawyer.*

I don't know why .
It just feels good to be working on a fresh, clean surface.

I say this to nobody in particular.
Jim is very quiet.
He starts to get into it.
The other fellows pause, then...
grab some paper and begin to clean their desks too.
Tim even cleans the desks next to his.
My heart leaps!

Later in the week

Students: *How long are you staying for?*
     Why do you give us so much work?
     I can hardly wait till you're gone,
         so we can get back to doing nothing.
Me:*Yeah, right.*

I laugh and tease them.

             Didn't I tell you. She's going ,
             (I point to their regular teacher)
             and I'm staying.

Students: *No way!*

They all yell.
They are having trouble getting down to business.

Me: *Sit down, please, and get to work!*
Students: *Are we getting to you, miss?*
Me: *Ha ha. It would take more than you.*
Students: *Oh, a challenge!*
Me: *No, not a challenge - a simple statement.*
              Don't you think that you could put your energy to better use?
Students: *But that's why we're here at Dumbvale, miss.*
              *Were **not supposed** to think!*
Me: *Sorry, I don't buy it.*
              I saw you thinking yesterday. Too bad.
              You gave yourself away.
              Now you're screwed , 'cause I know what you can do .
              Oh well, them's the breaks!

They glare at me.
They are not amused.
They are dumb.
Everybody knows it.
What is wrong with this person!

Students: *But miss, we're basic.*
              *You're giving us **general level** stuff!*
Me: *That's because, I think you can do it.*
              I want to challenge you.
Students: *Geeze miss!*

                              ***

We are studying *Raisin in the Sun...*

Students: *I hate this play! It's stupid! It's not real! Why do we have to study*
              it?!
Me: *Let's see if we can figure that out together.*
              What should Mama do with the insurance money?

Students:	*Buy a house! Buy a liquor store! Go on a holiday!*
Me:	*What about the children's education?*
Students:	*Naw! No way! They should do something good with the money.*
Me:	*But education is an investment in their future and their children's future. It will break the family's cycle of poverty and ignorance.*
Students:	*Not education!*
Me:	*RAISIN IN THE SUN is about dreams. Do you have dreams?*
Students:	*Yeah.*
Me:	*How are you going to get your dreams?*
Students:	*Well, I am going to college...etc, etc.*
Me:	*Do you need education for your dreams to come true?*
Students:	*Yeah.*
Me:	*If you had to choose between a nicer place to live and your education, which would you choose?*
Students:	*Education.*
Me:	*I rest my case.*
Me:	*Let's have a vote. Like in court. Lawrence, please be the spokesperson for your group.*
Lawrence:	*No way! I don't want to be a nerd.*
Me:	*Lawrence, not a nerd, a leader.*
	Take centre stage.
	Everyone respects you.
	No one would ever feel that way about you.

Lawrence slowly gets to his feet and takes his place at the front of the class.

***

She looks at me with hard eyes as she hands me the paper.

Me:	*But you've only done half the assignment.*
Her:	*I have nothing more to say. Besides, there isn't enough room on the paper.*
Me:	*Well, you can turn the page over. There's a whole other side.*

She glares at me.
I look at the sheet of vocabulary words that the students are to reflect on.

LIFE: When I think of LIFE, I remember my babies being born.

She is barely 17.

Me: *You have babies? How wonderful! Giving birth must have been an incredible experience. You gave them 'life'. Now, I am sure they are your life. You must have more to say about them. I know you do.*
Her eyes soften.
Her: *Yeah, that's true.*

The hard edges melt away. We speak quietly for a few more minutes. Our heads almost touching, like conspirators. Later, she hands me her paper. I am touched by the feelings and experiences that she has chosen to share with me. Her hardness is the armor of a survivor. The next day, I hand back her paper. Without looking at it, she grins.

Her: *Aced it eh, miss?*
Me: *Absolutely!*

I think back to my own experiences as a student. Teachers seemed acutely aware of their power. They still are, according to many young people.

These young people touch my heart. Many of them are abused and beaten down. Filled with low self esteem. Not even trying, out of fear that they'll fail. Slowly in written reflections, they share their lives, their pain, sometimes even their joy and strength.

***

Me: *It was a great class. Thank you.*
Student: *Drop the positive reinforcement crap, ok miss. Makes me want to puke.*

And they think they're not bright!
They are capable of so much more than they give themselves credit for.

***

Tall.
Black.
Sweet faced.
Bizarre hair.

He calls me *Mish*.
A combination of Michele and Miss. ***Mish.***
He says it tentatively...
Smilingly.
He likes me,
and he is testing it out.

At this school, the teachers want to maintain a distance.
As if distance is a guarantee of respect.
Don't get too close.
The teachers care....
but, they have been burnt trying to be the students' friend,
and allowing too much familiarity.

I don't know why I have made a connection with this young man.

That's not true.

I know why
and it makes me sad.

He is at peace within himself.
He is alive and full of hope.
He cares about other people.
He is a giver, not a taker.
He is polite and respectful.
He is creative, imaginative and intelligent.
He has a future and he knows it.
He reaches out.
He takes a risk.
He smiles.

He is one of the few.

He comes up to me after class on my last day.
He puts an arm around my shoulders and gives me a hug.
My associate is standing near.
"I'll miss you," he says. He doesn't say 'Mish'
"I'll miss you, too", I say.

It makes me sad.

Imagined:

Students:	Who the hell are you?
Me:	I don't know.
	I wish I could tell you.
	Someone who cares about you, I think.
Students:	Why should you care about us?
Me:	Someone should.
	Hopefully, many people care about you,
	but just in case
	...here I am.

***

On Tuesday night, I had a dream.

I was looking down into a basement or a garage. It was dark and dirty. There must have been about 50 large black rats. I went down some stairs into the garage. I felt safe at first because they seemed asleep or frozen. Still. I had to get something. I wasn't afraid. But I was cautious. For some reason, I didn't feel comfortable going back the way I came. Close by, there was a door out of the garage. The door locked from the inside. I was concerned that I wouldn't be able to lock it from the outside. I decided to exit by this way . I looked back. They were like frozen statues - no longer rats but large black gorillas. I opened the door and saw that there was a small insignificant bolt on the outside. I decided to leave anyway and to lock the door. I didn't want to go back the way I came. I went around the outside of the garage and returned to my position looking down into the garage. There was movement everywhere and a large black shadow was pulling at the door. Pulling back and forth. Pulling and pulling, as if the door would surely break.

Something extremely disturbing is happening in our class and I am at a loss to understand it. In my teaching subjects, we share a common interest, a common passion. I can only assume that it is the same for others whose commitments are to other interests. There is warmth and camaraderie in the classroom, a respect for the professor. But in other classes, I can only term the attitudes and behaviours as being somewhat bizarre. I find myself asking the question, "These are people who want to be teachers?!"

I have seen displays of rudeness, intimidation, insensitivity, ignorance, prejudice, narrow mindedness, intolerance that shock and overwhelm me. La creme de la creme?

They say (whoever *they* are) that 'To know all is to forgive all'. But, I don't know the hearts and minds of the people in the class and it is difficult, therefore, for me to maintain my objectivity. Being non judgmental is very important to me. I want to have as open a mind as I can, but what in hell is going on with some of these people?

It was the same last term and the discomfort is palatable.

***

Dear ESL English Class:

I remember when I found out that I was going to have my third practice teaching session at Downtown Collegiate and Technical School. Your reputation preceded you. Maybe not your class specifically, but all the ESL English Literature classes that had gone before you. Everyone at the University spoke of those students warmly, as if there was 'something' about these particular classes that made them special.

On my last day, I felt sad because you had just handed in your assignments and I wouldn't get to see the results of our work together. You struggled so diligently on the questions of the short story, that I wanted to hear your voices once again, through the work that you had completed .

When I first arrived, your teacher warned me. So had others. "You'll have difficulty with these students...but in one area only." Can you imagine what they were speaking about?

Your voices were like whispers. One day, in class, I told you that I felt as if I was becoming deaf. I teasingly threatened to start teaching you sign language, but instead I had you all do voice exercises. I got the feeling that you thought I was a little strange, but you were too polite to protest. First, you yawned to open up your throats; projected your voices with "Ha, He, Hi, Ho, Hu" (it's easier being loud in a group, isn't it?); and some articulation exercises " Good Blood, Bad Blood, Red Leather, Yellow Leather", including my favourite "Theopholis Thistle the thistle sifter..."

'Someone' came running up to me after class full of enthusiasm.
You wanted to learn more. You had many questions about voice training - where and how and when. I looked at the rest of you and wished that you all felt that way. Your voices were important to me.

One day 'someone' would not speak up in class.

I asked you to repeat your answer many times. You were angry at me. I am not sure why. You didn't want to have to speak up. Later, when everyone was doing desk work, I slowly made my way to you. You looked at me and I said, "You are such a big guy. To look at you, one would never know that you have such a soft, gentle voice." My comment seemed to give you real pleasure. You said "Thank you." This surprised me, because I thought maybe you would feel it was a silly compliment. But I think, you took it as it was meant, 'an opening of the door between us'. The next day you answered my questions in a beautiful full voice, that reached me from the back of the class.

'Someone' wouldn't look at me.

Your eyes didn't meet mine for the longest time. Your ultra politeness disturbed me. It made me feel as if perhaps a teacher or a person in authority had been cruel to you. I am not sure why I felt this. Perhaps it was the serious look that never turned towards me, but stayed cast downward. Perhaps it was the tone of your voice "Yes, Miss." "No, Miss." Up to that point, it was the only time I heard you speak. One day, I stopped and said a few words to you that required

more of a response. You looked up at me. I smiled down at you. I made some silly remark. I can't remember what. All I can remember is your face. An expression slowly spread across it and settled there. One that I had never seen before. A smile.

The next day 'someone' came into the class distraught.

You were late. Your courses were a confusion. You had to straighten things out after class. I asked you to tell me what the problem was and you did. You wanted to be a doctor. Your courses were all wrong. You thought, "Perhaps being a doctor is too much to hope for." "Talk to your counselor." I said, " I am sure you can work it out. Being a doctor is a wonderful dream. Go for it!" The next day a different young woman walked into the classroom. Everything was going to be ok. You had voiced you concerns and taken the next step towards a meaningful future.

Two 'someones' stood listening and speaking to me after class one day.

It was a short school day. Everyone had hurried away, except the two of you who stood by my desk. You weren't anxious to leave. I almost felt as if time was standing still and that you would linger there forever. There was a softness as we spoke together. A feeling of amazement filled me because you cared to stop a while to listen and to share a little part of your own lives. I wondered what would hold two young people on a day when they could have done anything else. A chance to be heard perhaps. Only you can answer my question.

Even though your class came at the end of the day, I had more energy, more passion in teaching you than I had for any other class. What happened between us, do you think?

'Someone' kept falling asleep in class.
I touched your shoulder. Your head came up. I looked into your eyes and saw - nothing. I was worried about you because something didn't seem right. You have a beeper on your belt. What is it for? Are you ok? Do you need help? I wish you would speak to me.

'Two someones' were always smiling and laughing.
Were you laughing at me? You told me "We wish you would be our teacher always." Why? Because I made you laugh?

After a time, when we were alone, your voices were no longer whispers. In class and in your journals you had things to say. Your voices were eloquent. It didn't take me very long to feel heart connected to you.

It was interesting when my English Professor from the University came to observe me teaching. You all closed up, like the petals of the delicate white flowers of my brother in law's Christmas cactus. It was as if the feeling of intimacy and caring we felt was not to be shared by an 'outsider'. Perhaps part of it was the bond of trust we had established that made you feel it was safe to speak.

Now that I am gone, do you still speak softly? Is it because of your accents? Or is it out of politeness, or pride or fear? I work with many students whose voices are like yours... at the beginning.

They are still important to me, your voices. Understand that you have a right to be heard. (2)

***

One day a substitute teacher, who had sat in on two days of my classes the previous week, settled down across from me. After the two days, he had written a glowing report about me to my associate. He was an older man, a former actor. He had yelled at a student that morning in class but 'he didn't feel guilty' about it. (he repeated this at least three times). He then talked to me about 'power-tripping' as a teacher. "We are alike as teachers", he said. "We have a similar style". "Hmmm...interesting", I said. I assured him that I was very sensitive to teachers 'power tripping' and that I am ever wary of this in my own behaviour with students. "Well, I thought I would talk to you about it, since I doubt anyone else will." he said.

***

(2) This is part of the Narrative Letter Exercise, we worked on in Carola's class.

Religious instruction provided me with my own code of ethics. I think back with some irony to the Sisters who, in trying to instill in me a 'moral' education, filled me with the fear of God. To burden a child with the belief that her rather innocent sins could result in eternal condemnation burning in the fires of hell seem, in light of time and maturity, to be somewhat morally inappropriate. I remember going to confession once as a fourteen year old with a sin that was weighing heavily on my conscience. I was extremely distressed that the priest's response wasn't filled with moral indignation and anger at my transgression. His kindness and understanding left me confused and worried that he must not have understood.

I believe that many of the people who had authority over me as a student, my parents and teachers and bosses made mistakes. They were rarely aware of their impact on me. As a teacher, when I make mistakes and I know I will, I hope that I am able to see them when they happen or to at least have a trusting relationship with my students so that we can feel comfortable communicating about any real or imagined wrongs.

The archetype of 'teacher', is deep within our collective psyches. All the myths about teachers hit me in the face: the teacher as another all wise, kind and judicious parent. I had been at the other end of the stick. I adored my teachers. Some were wonderful; I looked up to them; trusted them; was blind to their flaws. At times, there were some major ones.

So many experiences forgotten until this year, as I step into the role of 'teacher'. I had never given much consideration to the burden of the image that I was taking on.

As I begin to teach, I realize how uncomfortable I am with the unearned deference and respect automatically accorded me by strangers . Even the students who are rude at times, are still affected by the image that is projected onto the teacher from within the students themselves and society at large.

If one, therefore, presumes to take on the mantle of teacher, one also accepts a profound responsibility.

As indicated in my response to the question of being a role model, I obviously felt a year ago that a nonjudgmental attitude was the right stance to take. In light of my experiences, I am starting to think that, perhaps I need to write some addendums to this personal policy.

What happens in the classroom where I teach must be dictated by my goals as a teacher and the need to impart knowledge. My impulse is not to censure or to judge another person's opinion or moral stance, and yet I feel that at times this will be absolutely necessary. For teaching and learning to occur, there must be a feeling of safety and trust in the classroom. If an issue arises, I believe that the majority of students want to perceive the teacher as being someone who will 'do the right thing', who will not accept prejudice, or obscenity or violence, whether it be physical or emotional.

***

During one of my practicums, an experience occurred that made me feel I was going in the right direction.

I was teaching a Grade10 class and we were doing 'role on the wall' for *The Interview*. The board was covered with characteristics describing the two roles of Pinter's sketch. Under Miss Piffs, someone had written 'lesbian'. As we examined the words that had been written, one of the female students said, "That's a stereotype! Just because a woman is aggressive, it doesn't mean that she is a lesbian". I could have acknowledge the statement and moved on, but something in me held back. I felt something stir within the students. Something was happening that needed to be addressed. So, I said, "Let's continue to talk about this." remembering that "No lesson is so important that it can't be put aside for a lesson in life". I felt on edge as I listened to these young people. I wanted to make decisions that would move them forward in their reflections. I had to stop them repeatedly to ask them to listen to each other. Each wanted to have their say, but seemed entrenched in their own opinions about racism and whether hating homosexuals was in any way related. At a certain moment, as Heathcott would say, I....

'dropped to the universal'.

Me: *There are all different kinds of prejudices.*
   I'm fat.
   People judge me without knowing me and it hurts.
   How many people here have felt that they have also experienced prejudice?

Most of the hands in the class went up. I pointed to one student...

Student 1:   *As a little girl, I was called butch because I was a tomboy and liked sports. I didn't understand.*

One after the other, each person shared a little of the pain they had felt.

Student 2:   *I was smart, so nobody liked me.*
Student 3:   *I was a Christian.*
Student 4:   *I don't look like a macho man. I have glasses and allergies. People call me a nerd and a wimp. They don't know me. I like heavy metal music just like the rest of them.*
Student 5:   *My parents are Black and Chinese. People look at me as an oddity. A man approached me once and asked if his child could touch me!*

For the first time, there was silence, as each person told their story.

                                    ***

This is not a conclusion. This narrative has taken on a life of it's own. It may not be coherent at times, but there will be time later to work on that.

This year at the Faculty of Education, I learned more in the classroom by watching the professors, their teaching styles and their attitudes towards their students than from anything that was presented to me on paper.

The theme that ran through my life as a student and as a beginning teacher has been one of moral responsibility. This quote from our class readings has had great meaning for me throughout the second half of the year. It expresses far better than I can, my philosophy of education and my hope for the future.

Our classrooms should be places in which students can legitimately act on a rich variety of purposes, in which wonder and curiosity are alive, in which students and teachers live together and grow...I believe that a dedication to full human growth will not stunt or impede intellectual achievement, but even if it might, I would take the risk if I could produce people who would live nonviolently with each other, sensitively and in harmony with the natural environment, reflectively and serenely with themselves.

                                            Nel Noddings
                                    The Challenge to Care in Schools

Teaching: Year 1

Michele: *Right now, I think I am a very, very positive person. When I go to school in the morning, I really feel uplifted and the kids, I think, respond to that.*

The sun breaks through the morning fog on my face.
I smile...
What is it about this place?
Or is it just me.
I can't help myself.

Hello!
Hi!
Good Morning!

Why does this feel so good?
Storm clouds approaching.
Undeterred.

Good Morning!

I catch their eyes.
Courtesy requires a salutation.

Student lounging in the hall.
Great stockings! (Wicked Witch black and white stripes)
The girl looks up.

Her face becomes a mirror of mine.
She is delighted by the comment.
Thanks!
It takes so little...sometimes.

Michele: *I feel sort of weird because a lot of the students call me Michele. I gave them the option of calling me Michele or Ms. Pinet, whichever made them feel most comfortable. Other teachers do not want to be called by their first names. If I got a sense, that there was a lack of respect connected with calling me Michele then I'd probably say, "I'm Ms. Pinet to you", but I haven't gotten that feeling at all.*

***

Me: *Why do you think I am upset with you about being late for class? Why do you think I am being so strict?*

Student 1:   *Well, maybe it is because you are pissed off at someone at home. Maybe someone did something there and you are still angry.*

Me: *Really? Is that what you think? How interesting! I am glad I asked you. No, nothing happened at home. If someone at home annoyed me and then I came to school and was angry with you, that wouldn't be professional of me. I hope I never do that. No, in fact, I am not even really angry with you. 'Worried' would be a better word. If you don't have good work habits now, you'll have a very difficult time later. Do you think a boss would be happy with you being late for work all the time?*

Student 1:   *No.*

Me: *What do you think would happen?*

Student 1:   *Well, my boss would probably fire me.*

Me: *That's right. If you are late all the time now, why should you be on time later just because you are being paid.*

Student 2:   *But if you are really talented your boss will put up with it.*

Me: *Interesting. You think that? Let me tell you that I have been a boss and good work habits are more important than talent. Hmmm. Let me put it this way. You play hockey don't you?*

Student 2:   *Yep.*

Me: *Are you any good?*

Student 2:   *Yeah, I'm the best on the team.*

Me: *So, you are really talented?*

Student 2:   *Yeah, I am.*

Me: *Do you think your coach would put up with you coming late all the time even though you are talented?*

(Now this is *a moment every teacher hopes for...it sounds 'too good to be true' but it really happened!*)

Student 2:   *Actually, I've been suspended from the team.*

Me: *Why?*

Student 2:   *Because I was late sometimes and missed practices.*

Me: *Ahhhh. So, even though you are talented, the best player on the team, the coach suspended you?*

Student 2:   *Yeah.*

Me: *That's my point. Whatever you are doing, whether it's sports or school or work, it is critical to have good work habits. If I am upset with you when you come late or waste your time in class or don't do your homework, it is because I am thinking of your futures . School prepares you for life. Everything is connected. These are not rules that we make up to make you miserable. A boss will accept a less talented worker if that person has a good work ethic. The habits you establish now are the ones you will probably have for life. It is very difficult to change them later. So, please believe me when I tell you I am not in a bad mood and taking it out on you. I never want to do that and if you think I am please talk to me about it. Does all this make sense to you now?*

Student 1:   *Yeah, it makes sense.*

***

Student: *I can't do it. I'm stupid.*

Me: *You are not! You **can** do it!*

You can. You can. You can! I want to scream at them. Whether you are good with your hands, your head or your heart, you are of value; you can think; you can achieve.

The problem is not that these young people can't do the work, but the motivation to even try has been sucked right out of them. Once or twice, I saw a student break free of their label. It was like they had broken out of a cage.

One young man said, "I don't know what has happened to me. Last year, I was doing so poorly in school, but now I'm doing great!" Somehow, he got a different message that lifted him out from under the label to the truth. This boy no longer cared that the other students might make fun of him because he wasn't maintaining the general attitude of "If I don't try, I can't fail." He reveled in his new found sense of self and achievement.

I remember reading an article once about people generally believing what they are told. We can't imagine people telling us a lie, because we place so much value on honesty and truth. So, if someone is told by the system and subsequently their teachers, their peers and their parents that they are such and such, can we blame young people for buying into what they are being told?

Most of the time, if I remember my own teenage years and those of my friends, we agonized over the question WHO AM I?

We are so vulnerable at that age. We don't know who we are and are desperate to be given the answer. We want to be told wonderful things, that we are special, unique, intelligent and talented.

Instead, a large portion of our youth is being labeled 'substandard'.

Why? Because they are not 'intelligent' enough to enter the academic stream. What bull! How narrow!

So, we succumb to labeling. Labeling that boosts some children up and tears others down.

***

One day my mother told me that my father thought I was 'retarded'.
It's interesting, now that I think about it, that his statement didn't surprise me.

Mom: *Don't be ridiculous. She's in university.*
Dad: *I don't know how else to express what I feel.*
         She's not married. She doesn't have children like her cousins.
Me: *Perhaps, he meant socially retarded. (I said to her later)*

From the time I was six years old,
until I was in my thirties,
my mother said,
my father and I
were like
fire and water.
I was like some strange creature to him.
He often seemed to have a pained,
frustrated expression on his face,
whenever he looked at me.
He didn't understand me,
so, I guess, he thought
I was stupid.

1991

It was the long weekend before I was to go back to university.
I had decided to become a teacher.
I was relaxing at a resort with a friend,
squeezing out the last little bit of summer.

One night, I cried out, *dreaming* of my father.

He was *sitting* in a rocking chair.
I asked if it bothered him that I had questions to ask.
He said, it did.

Me: *Can I still ask my questions?*
He: *Yes.*

For some reason, that response made me feel so profoundly sad, that I sobbed in my sleep. The feeling was so deep within me that the physical jerking of my body woke me up.

A few weeks later, I dreamt of him again.

Suddenly, I am transported from my bedroom into a brightly lit kitchen.

My father is there, taller than the 5 feet 10 inches, I know he is.
"Do you want coffee?", I ask him.
"Yes", he says. It's so good to see you".

Strange comment...considering our past relationship and his present circumstances. It was the second time in the last four months that he had come to see me in this way.

I called to Mum who was in the other room.
"Do you want coffee?".

She also said, "Yes".

I went to prepare the coffee. I poured the liquid into mugs but as I poured, it turned to sludge - a strange, glutinous texture. It seemed to become suspended in the air. There was a television in the kitchen. The image of the earth was being telecast from a satellite dish and it was being sucked into a huge black hole. I was being sucked into a huge black hole!

The coffee exploded in a flash of light. Everything was exploding.

Suddenly, I understood....everything.

The question is, why do I keep conjuring up my father - who has been dead and buried these past 8 years.

***

I am grateful that before he died, there was a peace between us. This was made possible, I believe, because Dad mellowed as he grew older. The sting had been taken out of him. Perhaps there was no more understanding on his part, but there was an acceptance of me and who I was.

Unfortunately, I still struggle on a daily basis with his legacy, a perception of myself that makes it difficult for me to believe that my successes are legitimate. I grapple with the discomfort of sudden support and positive feedback. I guess it's the same for my students. Telling a young person that they are intelligent and creative, that they can and are doing something valuable, doesn't necessarily mean they will believe you or buy into it. It all depends on what has gone before.

My students and I will confront our inner demons together and we will succeed.

Peace and Tranquility,
Amen.

ENDNOTES

---

[1] Pseudonyms are used throughout my narratives.

In: Teacher's Stories, Teacher's Lives
Editor: Carola Conle, pp. 149-169

ISBN 1-59454-472-7
© 2006 Nova Science Publishers, Inc.

Chapter 6

My Road to Narrative Inquiry in Teacher Preparation: One Educator's Story

Carola Conle

At times one may "find oneself on a logging road." In German this turn of phrase is commonly used to mean that one is trying something that won't work or that the views that one espouses are wrong-headed. The philosopher Martin Heidegger, who often hiked in the mountains of the Black Forest in south-eastern Germany, used the metaphor as the title of one of his books (1950), focusing on the image of a road that suddenly ends, seemingly having led nowhere, and forcing the hiker to backtrack. Nevertheless, as Heidegger's student, H.-G. Gadamer, explains: "There are paths that don't continue and compel us to either climb into virgin territory or turn back. Yet there is no loss in height" (1987, 267; my translation).

For some time, I feared that others might view my path in teacher education as such a logging road. I continued into virgin territory and hope that backtracking will not become a necessary option. The story I present here is a narrative inquiry into narrative inquiry, the very practice that that led me into relatively uncharted territory in one-year teacher preparation program. My students are engaged in narrative inquiry[12]. The meaning of the work I do with students in our rushed shortcut to teacher preparation cannot emerge from a straightforward description of syllabi and class events alone. Although I have done such descriptions in collaboration with my students, (Carola et al 2000), I believe that a good understanding of my work with students must include a narrative of its origins in my own biography.

Alistair MacIntyre drew my attention to the notion that the meaning of practices as well as ideas, lives and traditions is at least in part embodied in their history (1984, 265). If he is right, I should be able to come to a better understanding of my research activities and teaching practices by exploring them narratively. This is not a new task. For instance, self-study by teacher educators is a Special Interest Group at the American Educational Research Association and there are published conference proceedings in this area (e.g. Hamilton 1998).

However, if MacIntyre is right, one should be able to investigate the very practice of narrative inquiry by exploring its manifestation narratively in a particular inquirer's history. This has not been done to my knowledge and I have no resources in this area. However, MacIntyre adds further support to the viability of such an inquiry by suggesting that there are "goods internal to practices" (273) and that these are discoverable through narratives of their histories. Narrative inquiry in teacher education is a practice in MacIntyre's sense (187). By exploring the origins of narrative inquiry in my life and practices, I hope to initiate an investigation of the "internal goods" of narrative inquiry and inspire others to do the same, for as MacIntyre insists, no one can find the goods of a practice alone. Many must engage in the task.

Perhaps I also cherish the possibility to convince my students and myself that on this road, begun from afar, a certain height has been gained, no matter what road blocks have seemed to stop success.

IMMEDIATE CONTEXTS

After completing one of the first narrative theses in 1987, I am at the time I write this, in my seventh year as a teacher of preservice teachers. In my beginning year, in 1992, I was the first and only person who taught a course in Educational Foundations that was called "Teachers' Stories, Teachers' Lives." Over the years, I incorporated narrative components into all my courses, but I even now, as a tenured professor, I am struggling every year to help students understand in what sense their enjoyment of the narrative activities is legitimate teacher preparation.

There have been signs of success. In 1997 I received an award from the American Association of Colleges for Teacher Education for one of my article's contribution to preservice teacher education. Still, I wonder whether I am on a logging road that climbs and climbs, but leads nowhere near a wider institutionalization of narrative approaches in preservice teacher education. I hope that whatever the answer may be to that question, I will be able to say that, even though the journey seems Sisyphus-like, "there is no loss in height." Perhaps when others listen to my journey, the height gained so far may become more visible, especially for those who wish to climb the same mountain.

EARLY BEGINNINGS

To tell my story, I have to begin early, that is, with my own personal narrative and with my own struggles with narrative as a useful mode of inquiry. The episodes below circle around many areas of experience and at times a reader may fear getting lost in the woods. I try to provide some signposts. But essentially, a reader will have to be willing to follow where I lead and experience the journey vicariously, rather than worry about why we are taking a particular path. A surrender to the stories will allow for unexpected connections to a reader's own life. Only after those connections have been made will the legitimacy of narrative inquiry become more apparent.

Facing Difference across a Gap

To mind comes the image of a young teenager standing by a row of windows in a classroom which had become more spacious by open folding doors which usually separate it from the adjoining room. It was gym period in a small Ontario high school in the mid 50's and two grade 10 classes were enjoying a break in routine, a snowball dance. It started with one couple, who then each asked another partner, and so on. The girl by the window was waiting. No one asked her yet. The crowd around her got smaller and smaller. Finally she was the only one left. She stayed until the bell range and everyone filed out. "Perhaps no one noticed," she thought, but a friend remarked, "Oh, you didn't dance!"(Conle 1993,1; 1996, 303).

I was born in 1941 in a small Franconian town in Germany, at the north-western edge of Bavaria. Everybody spoke the local dialect—well, almost everyone. The refugee children who came from the East spoke differently. When I was four years old, two of these children with their mother and aunt were placed to live in our house and later, in primary school, there were several children from the Ostzone (Eastern Zone) and from other territories that had become part of Poland and Russia. Most of the Eastern dialects sounded like "better German" to us in the village. Much later this notion was explained to me: There are certain German dialects which are not considered *salonfähig* or adequate for use by people of "quality". Bavarian, Austrian, north German dialects were sometimes heard in radio plays and had even found their way into print, but certain others were not; like, for example, my Franconian speech.

People often learned to speak a less heavy dialect in situations where it was important to impress someone. At school we were induced to speak Hochdeutsch (High German). I became particularly conscious of this after grade four when I passed an entrance exam into high school at the suggestion of my primary school teacher. I tried for the Humanistische Gymnasium. Later I found that this was the most prestigious kind of high school, oriented towards classical languages. Most of my classmates were sons and daughters of doctors, lawyers, higher civil servants and various academics. The parents of a few of us, like mine, were working class people. I don't remember ever feeling discrimination as such, but when I was invited to my classmates' houses I noticed a difference in language and lifestyle and, I imagine, I tried to adjust my speech.

I was among the best students in my class. I must have been good at the kind of learning predominant in German schools at the time. We studied Latin (beginning in grade 5) and Greek (beginning in grade 8) and I needed to be good at recognizing grammatical patterns; we studied algebra and geometry in grade 7 and 8 and I needed to be good at moving in a world of abstraction; we studied Greek and Roman history, but were never prompted to make sense of the chaos we had all just been through: the war, the hunger, the American occupation, the refugee problems, the destroyed buildings all around us. For example, the original building of my school had been bombed and we were housed in another building, sharing it with an institute of teacher education. We had very few books and materials. I remember a rather thick German reader printed without illustrations in very small font on recycled paper. I don't remember ever engaging in group work. There was a stiff marking system for everything, including religious instruction. I was judged by what I knew intellectually, not interpersonally. Dewey's requirment to, start "from where the child is" and to develop latent interests," I am sure, were not part of anyone's language or thought, just as our roots in our speech community were considered irrelevant or perhaps a disadvantage.

Hochdeutsch or "proper" German also came at us through the media. Books, magazines, and the radio were constant reminders of something other and better. However, I did not learn "proper German" until I got to Canada. Here there was only one other family in our acquaintance who spoke like us; all the other German friends of my family spoke various different dialects: East Prussian, Saxonian, Bohemian, Austrian, Swabian, North German, etc. By the time I married into a formerly upper-class, Austrian family, I was able to speak, not their German, but a very acceptable Hochdeutsch. I had learned the rules in a phonetics course at the University of Toronto and had practiced my proper speech during four years in the Modern Languages and Literatures program. Now, when I go back to visit relatives in Germany, they wonder how I ended up as the only member of my family to speak Hochdeutsch. Back in Franconia though, I can very easily revert to my dialect which I also continued to speak with my parents in Canada.

Those tensions around language in my childhood were linked to self-image, to a feeling of inadequacy and a sense of being different from others more fortunate than I. The remedy for me was a technical one: getting rid of what came spontaneously by forcing my speech into those other patterns, always having to be on guard against slipping back and showing tell-tale signs of the old and more familiar habits. It required cutting myself off from my dialect, from what I had lived, winning a distance from it; and in that distance, living something else, something that was ruled by matters other than experience and familiar habit.

In 1962, I took time out from my Canadian university program to spent two semesters in France at the University of Grenoble. But I shortened my stay in France because I really wanted to get back to Germany. By the time I arrived back in Germany, I had been in Canada for seven years, speaking English; I had studied French in school and at university and had just spent eight months in France, speaking almost only French. I was lonely and quite ecstatic at the prospect of finally being able to study in German at a German university, living with my German relatives in German houses. I took a semester at the University of Mainz, Germany, where I sat in introductory lectures in Philosophy and German Literature.

I remember sitting in a small, very crowded lecture hall, listening intently and trying to take notes: Marx, Hegel, existentialism. I remember not being able to take down one coherent sentence, one sequence of thought that made sense to me. Once again I had come upon a language that was my own, but was also something very different. I had never been introduced to German academic life and the jargon-like abstractions that constituted the intellectual world there. Yes, I could read the literature, the classics, the poetry, but I was a foreigner in the academic atmosphere. That distance I could not bridge. Those abstractions I could not reach, even though I had gone through many instances by then of over-ruling what came natural and of going with a foreign pattern instead. Once again I felt an outsider, as someone excluded from those more fortunate ones who knew and lived something I too wanted, but was not able to be.

The dance episode described at the beginning of this section, I am sure, was not on my mind then, but I see now, why it seemed so significant to me in my conversation with a friend many years later; why it became the symbol, the way to express in one precise, holistic image a series of experiential tensions that had never been consciously formulated as such. I began to see that episode as one point in a long storyline, as one moment in a sequence of clusters of experiences, that I gradually was able to order narratively through certain themes or tensions— tensions between, not only language and person, but also between "me and other," tensions between the need for gaining distance and the need for closeness to lived contexts.

I would not have been able to make these connections without several years of reflective writing in journals and narrative course papers, even though, looking back now, there were signposts everywhere. The dance story became so poignant, not simply because of the language barriers, but because it drew attention, in some quick strokes, to the wider issues of identity and "outsiderness".

Getting on the Road Academically on which I was Traveling Already: Stories of Teaching and Learning

My memory of the dance first appeared in a conversation between me and a colleague at graduate school. We wondered what experiences might have shaped my interest in teaching English as a second language, or in immigrant identity, or in what I then called "alternative narratives". In the excerpt below we explored what I remembered of that time and why I remembered it at all.

C. At the time I did not think it was a crisis. But in retrospect, as I think of it now —(pause). I think that there was a time when I first came to this country that I experienced something of a — uhmm — a kind of schizophrenic position toward myself. I was not able to speak the language very well and I was going to school — (unclear). Except for my family there was no German interaction. I had the feeling that the person English people, usually my classmates, saw was not the person that was actually inside. That there was a difference and that, you know, the me that showed through the language, the English language, when I expressed myself in English, was not the same me as the one that showed when I spoke German. And so I really think -- well, may be this is what triggers the interest in this topic.

B. I sort of want to provoke you to pick a time, a classroom.

C. Oh yeah — OK. — pick a time. It was actually a period of time — there is no incident in my mind right now that I could say: Yes, at that moment I felt this — I cannot think of any incident at the moment
(pause)

B. Tell me how, I'll help you if I can, tell me how old you were at the time.

C. I was 14.

B. So you were in your first year or in Junior High School.

C. I started in grade ten. I skipped grade nine because the principal thought I should go to grade ten.

B. So there you were with a strong academic background, but not the language to back it up. So sometimes you are sitting in class and you can follow things that are written down, but not the things that are being said.

C. Yes, there was a time when I could do that. In class, definitely, I was a student who was quite well prepared. In math, I had studied four years of Latin, I had done Greek, (nobody here was doing Greek). Subject-wise I was very well prepared because I had 4 years of high school and I also knew the grammar of the language, because of the Latin background, although I did not understand the words of the language.

B. Right. So when you are saying that you sometimes felt like two different people, did it make you a quieter, more reserved person?

C. I would think so —

B. More scholarly almost —

C. Well, more reserved. No, I didn't really feel superior to people at all — it is just that I felt that I couldn't show the real me. It was a question of "These people just don't know me really the way I am." The knowledge that I think was remedied pretty soon; because by Christmas, I think, I stood ninth, and by the end of the year I stood third. I mean, I did very well academically. So the knowledge would come through the fastest, but the personality was not coming through.

B. You only had just slivers of yourself on show —

C. And in the interactions, you can't really interact the same way as you do in your own language. You don't show your personality. The personality shows in a very subtle way and when you --- I am trying to think of an incident of when that happened... (Conle 1993, 7).

The notion of language as obstacle comes through very strongly here. I felt an obstacle to the experience of something that needed to, but could not be, expressed. The obstacle was much greater in the area of personality than in the area of things learned at school. Clearly, social relations among teenagers are much more easily shaped by personality than by academic know-how, and for this reason, what I was "good at", the very distancing that helped in academic pursuits, was a hindrance in social encounters. The old tension of not being able to use my language to show and expand who I am, was very likely reinforced by the immigrant experience.

The learning of English in a grade ten Ontario high school environment, where I seemed to be the only immigrant, added another dimension to the language as obstacle issue. Again, as it was lived, the issue did not become conscious as such. But later, actually during graduate work, I could piece it together by telling stories, by remembering flashes of images and episodes here and there, and by exploring the feelings I associated with those incidents.

In grade ten I learned French and English simultaneously, often getting tired of looking words up in dictionaries, and simply substituting English terms for French ones, without bothering to find out their meanings. The bulk of new English words in those first months came from books and from teacher talk: I sat in class for six hours every day, talking to classmates only on the way to and from school or when I was invited into their houses. When I began to think about such things, I realized that English always had for me a certain dryness about it, lacking the warmth and connections to life experiences that stick to words we learn in our mother tongue. Yet my world very quickly became an English world: four years of high school, then four years of university, then eight years of teaching high school. I did not surround myself with German friends, partly because there did not appear to be many German-born teenagers in my town, and partly because I did not look for German speaking people later on.

What has become obvious through hindsight is that the story line of the dance episode did continue into the future and may have been lived out as an inquiry into language, eventually more specifically into the links between language and personal experience.

My highest marks in high school were in languages, in Latin, German and French. I took the Modern Language and Literature program at university. Then I had some thoughts about going into social work, but decided on teaching French and German in secondary school. Later I taught ESL to adults and much later still, I did an MA thesis in second language learning. Such a quick sketch, however, glosses over the motivating impetus behind such a career, its high and low points, and the deeper meanings such activities had for me.

I became a high school teacher, teaching French and German, using the inductive or direct method in vogue at the time, and putting the students through lots of drills, often in the language laboratory. It was not hard to keep my distance, since there was little chance for meaningful personal communication. Teaching was like putting on an interesting act. I learned my role well. I was promoted very quickly. But after eight years I happily stopped teaching altogether, moved to Prince Edward Island (a privince of Canada on the Atlantic coast) to have children and stay at home. It seems that I did not want to continue my story of teaching then. It held not enough promise for me and I let it "run out" without regret.

My enthusiasm for teaching returned with the advent of communicative language methodology, and a chance to teach immigrants in Prince Edward Island their new language. There suddenly was intense communication and almost overwhelming personal contact. I was needed in so many areas of their lives, especially since in that province there were no settlement services available, nor were there many ethnic communities to help integrate the newcomers. The teacher became a kind of lifeline to a lonely Albanian, an Ethiopian, to Iranian Bahai families, or to a young, pregnant Vietnamese woman, who had made that long boat trip to Canada. I was surprised to find I could communicate so well. It seemed I was communicating in spite of language, even without language. What I knew was passed on by a process I did not quite understand. At first I thought it was my knack for making complicated things simple, making grammatical complexities practical. But one day a Polish woman spoke of me to someone and said, "She can communicate and she understands." I knew she was not really talking about my methodology. Was language here now no longer the veil, the obstacle to the transmission of what I knew? It seemed to me I had found a way around language.

And I felt there was authenticity. The person my immigrant students knew, I felt, was "really" me. I was not playing a role. The distance had slipped away and my image of teaching began to change from "teaching as transmission" to "teaching as communication and relationship". Now I think both images and the stories that go with them are both valid for me. One has not replaced the other. The tensions between them are still being played out. But the second one is now predominant in my teaching of education students, especially in graduate programs.

When I place this realization next to other events in my life, I suspect that what emerged out of those conflicting images was a very important theme in my journey, namely, the search for authenticity. I sense this journey is still ongoing, e.g. the tension between the two teaching poles, distancing transmission and communication through relationships, I feel, is still a tacit impetus pushing for resolution, and is somehow connected to authenticity. Writing this chapter is surely part of it.

One day, early in my graduate studies, the experience of being pulled into a story put me onto a narrative road in research and education. It happened that at a time when I wrote many journals for an instructor, Michael Connelly, in a core curriculum course at the Ontario Institute for Studies in Education. I was in the midst of spinning out comments about readings on narrative theory by Schäfer (1981), when I suddenly felt tired and my energy to continue spinning out an idea I had just fervently embraced, suddenly dropped. Instead, I remembered a section from a film I had recently seen: a woman in that film, in a serious predicament, was helped not by analysis of the problem and pertinent advice, but by her friend's empathetic narration of an experience that left room for her to construct her own solution to the problem. For me, a light did not go on suddenly at that point, but writing a journal about that movie was the beginning of a slow turn-around in my journaling: I began to tell many experiential stories. This work became very compelling for me. It drew me in. I loved writing my dissertation, because I could do it through personal narrative. It was emotionally as well as intellectually compelling for me. I told a friend that I could not finish quickly, because I had to "live my dissertation" and that the insights gained came not through reading and writing alone, but emerged in the living I was doing during and in between the writing. Narrative seemed to open up a way of being, academically, that made room for authenticity.

The language as obstacle theme seemed to have changed, or perhaps broadened, to include rich possibilities of inquiry. In my Masters thesis I had explored my work with an adult immigrant from Iran to whom I taught English. The remedy for dry, abstract, distant language was to explore stories which were implicit in the words and sentences he uttered. I found words had histories and experiential contexts. His histories for many words were not the ones I attached to them. Later in my doctoral program, I increasingly saw the potential of recovering stories of lived experiences, bits of life history. The stories then began to stick to one another and align themselves into larger narrative unities. I now recognize that the most striking and energizing quality of this kind of work was the possibility of bringing together inquiry and experience and the potential to develop a language which allowed that coming-together to be expressed.

My early childhood stories were developing further and connected to theoretical writings I encountered. I came to use another metaphor from Heidegger's language when I described my graduate work as "getting onto the road I was traveling already." By this I meant that as I consciously struggled to understand and pursue my educational interests and certain key issues in my life, my chosen curriculum at OISE approached my lived curriculum, the one propelled by those existential tensions. The two became the same road.

Agency through Narrativization: A Merging of Roads

As it was happening, the merging of roads was not a neat, clearly conceptualized event. On the contrary, I often seemed to be moving in several directions at once. Gradually, I searched out the most audible notes that began to sound as I reread and further reflected on the work I had done since 1985. I detected intentions in the stories I was telling: the urge to narrativize abstractions and a great struggle to not experience loss of self within connectedness (Conle 1999). These became the recurring motifs which, in ever new and surprising variations made my curriculum, my "course of life," truly my own. I called these tensions and intentions my "tacit telos" or the tacit ends-in- view that subconsciously propelled my inquiry (Conle 2000).

When I had told my dance story in 1989 to a group of grade eight students in a multicultural school, two girls asked me two questions. One said, "Didn't they play any fast music?" The other asked, "Why didn't you just go and ask someone to dance with you?" In response, I tried to convey a sense of teenage relationships in a small Ontario town in the 50's, where girls only went to a dance if they had a date and, no matter what the music, stayed in couple formation. I also tried to put into words the kind of adolescent I had grown into by then, her reticence, lack of self-confidence and perhaps also her submissiveness to social rules. But the girls were right. Why didn't I cross that dance floor, if only perhaps to break the rules, or to walk out, or to connect and to talk to someone, even the teacher?

My curriculum as a teacher, as a graduate student and as a researcher has been a sequence of steps across that dance floor. There were existential steps taken every day, and as my graduate program allowed me to link intellectual pursuits to experience, the steps were taken more consciously. I gradually "got academically onto the road on which I was already existentially."

One of those steps consisted in many stories of encountering difference.[3] There was my 1945 encounter with the American soldier-enemy-hero-conqueror-rich-man-womanizer-foodgiver; there were stories of the German child born into a hero-worship culture, being constantly faced with images of foreign heroes in the postwar media; there was the child watching, every day, trains filled with hungry city folk off to search the villages for food, giving silver spoons for potatoes; the ten-year-old village girl, going to high school in destroyed urban landscapes; the German teenager in a Canadian high school; the German-speaking girl in a world of English speakers; a woman in relationships with men; a woman/teacher/student facing a world of research and academic language. In all of these stories there were encounters of difference, usually without connections being made; or, if that connection seemed possible, it also seemed to endanger self.

I believe that one can never know for sure what happened in one's life. We can only collect narrative data and interpret them from current vantage points. Nevertheless such interpretive constructions are useful, if for no other reason than that they become incorporated into our ongoing life stories and can shape the future. What I construct in the following paragraphs are personal hypotheses about processes in my life. They are based on many journals, conversations, reflections and the writing of a dissertation.

DEVELOPING HYPOTHESES

I eventually came to hypothesize two modes of meeting difference: an imperceptible taking-in and living of "the other" and, in dialectical opposition, a resolute, intellectual control of it. (I am skipping over many stories here, my stories of married life, stories of a parent, stories of an immigrant, stories of a neophyte academic.) Both modes involved loss or disregard of vital parts of my being. There is both loss of self and one might say with Heidegger and Gadamer, loss of life (Seinsvergessenheit) (Gadamer, 1986). If I imperceptibly began to live and take in an other's identity (e.g. that of Canadian classmates), I did not do it by choice and by consciously changing certain qualities of my old self. Instead, I believe, I disregarded that self and overrode it, so to speak. It was not consulted, one might say, and because of such neglect, there was loss of self. If, on the other hand, I consciously took in "the other"—ideas, languages or ways of life— I began to control and manipulate them intellectually, without actually living them. I began to live and think abstractions, losing out on experience, and on concrete, lively moments of life. In those situation, I suspect, there was loss of life, a loss of fullness of being.

Why did I let this happen over and over again? What was there about "the other" that induced me to act in this way in many different situations? In either mode, in the taking-in and in the controlling mode, I must have endowed the other with a certain power and attraction, as I did in my dance story. Or else, I must have seen the other as given and as rather undifferentiated, as something to be taken in whole, so to speak, so that I did not seem to be able to adopt only certain positive aspects *by choice*, while engaging in real, lived encounters with them.

Gradually, in various life situations, I learned to counter my tendency of responding to difference in these two modes. A "remedy" for this existential problem came to me intellectually, through an understanding of hermeneutics. When I speak of solution and remedy, I still do so hypothetically, for coming to certain perspectives through narrative is not the same as arriving at logical conclusions, at facts; although there seems to be a certain truth-like quality about such insights, especially when they are first recognized!

I fell in love with a German philosopher—well, at least with his ideas. H.-G. Gadamer taught me to think about life as a dialogical relationship between us and our world. Gadamer developed the idea of hermeneutical understanding when he was himself a teacher of university students. In those student/teacher conversations, the one single most important thing for Gadamer, so he tells us in his *Philosophical Apprenticeship,* was to hold himself constantly open to dialogue. It was not a question of arriving at a final understanding, or to deal with something completely and finally. Nor was it a question of taking on something new in its entirety. It was always a question of being constantly ready to revise whatever fixed positions one may have arrived at through constant connection with others in dialogue [Überholbarkeit jeder Fixierung] (1986, 502). Dialogue here is seen as a constant, positive encounter of difference. This particular personal experience of teaching was the basis for Gadamer's theory, as he phrased it: "Actually, the origin of my philosophical hermeneutics is nothing more than my attempt to justify theoretically my learning and teaching style" (1986, 492).

It is easy to see why such an interactive view of understanding was intensely attractive to the kind of person I have portrayed so far. It promised to help bridge those distancing gaps and make those monolithic "others" seem more flexible. My attraction to hermeneutics was intuitive, my understanding of it was intellectual. But I also began to live it in my everyday practice of research with teachers, in my teaching, and in my daily interactions with friends and colleagues, with students and with my children who were becoming young adults. Constant narrative reflection on these events in my life helped make these daily encounters into a new mode of functioning. It was not a completely conscious process, but a process that was indirectly reflected upon through my stories, stories that were about the lived events in which the new way manifested itself (Conle 1993).

And, as I recognized at one point, an increased sense of agency became the key issue. The narrative, reflective activities were to prove themselves as a good road toward personal agency. In 1991, I explained it in the following words:

> As I use narrative forms of language I am a narrator. Even when the story is autobiographical and I am a character in it. As I connect to knowledge via narrative, I insert a space into the connecting process, a space which is created by "I, the narrator." It keeps my voice alive as acculturation into new knowledge proceeds. It keeps my story, my previous biography on the horizon, as something to be connected to, not to be overridden or put aside.

I now notice sooner when I begin to live someone else's ideas, and I begin to change direction; I now dare to use language my way, recognizing the conventions as conventions, but giving myself the right to shape them according to my needs. What previously came at me as something given, as a creation by others, that I somehow had to adopt, I now recognize as something which has a history, has actors and happens in certain settings. I can keep up a dialogue with, at least, certain degrees of freedom, because I can keep my own road in mind (Conle 1993, 90).

Heidegger (1985, 255), quoting the German eighteen-century poet, Hölderlin, said in 1959, "We are a conversation and are able to hear from one another." At this point it became my task to explore hermeneutics in connection with teacher preparation. What I was learning about agency and language needed to connect up with teacher education.

Hermeneutics, Narrative and Cross-cultural Education

Encountering difference, in a sense, is also the essence of education. For me, the hermeneutical, dialogical manner of teaching and inquiring achieves educational significance when I ask, what is, after all, the business of education? Isn't it to a large extent concerned with the process of the taking on of ideas and skills, of how we heed and take on what eventually becomes part of us? Isn't this also what teacher education is all about?

A traditional view of teaching shapes educational encounters into what Gadamer (after Heidegger) would call a process where ideas are merely "in front of us", where they face us abstractly in our minds[4]. Views of teaching as performance, lectures presenting a series of overheads, teachers talking *about* things rather than counting on doing things with students—all these I place into the "traditional view of teaching" basket. What is missing there is our awareness of those ideas and concepts as living, dynamic entities, rooted in existence and coming at us within particular histories. Heidegger (1985) gave a name to the lack of this awareness of time, place and the dynamics of life, calling it *Seinsvergessenhei* (forgetfulness of being). He saw a general forgetfulness of being— an ignoring of connections to concrete existence— as *the* crisis of our times. He saw us live in a world of things of which we do not know the origin or the history. Indeed, as academics and as members of a technically oriented world, we often do use words merely as signs that abstractly point to something without having grown organically in lived contexts as do the words of our childhood

(Conle 1999). We do what I did as child, we override something experiential for the sake of abstraction.

A personal example of *Seinsvergessenheit* was my experience of learning second languages. When I, as a child, faced those German school books, and as a teenager faced all those foreign words, I was not taking on these new things within their lived contexts. An extreme procedure I resorted to, and one which I still remember now, was that practice I invented as a new immigrant student in my grade ten French class. I knew neither English nor French at the time and got very tired and simply refused to look up words in dictionaries. One remedy was to remember in my head both words, English and French, and substitute one for the other without knowing the meaning of either. This was particularly easy for me if the words had some common etymological root as, for example, *le moine* - monk; *la tente* - tent; etc. (Conle 1993). Similarly, because of my knowledge of Latin, which I had studied for four years in Germany, I was able to recognize sentence patterns even though I did not understand the words. I got perfect marks in syntax exercises which many of my Canadian classmates failed miserably. There was great astonishment among my classmates because of this. They probably saw me as a kind of strange puzzle. Since I seemed to have had a mind and training that let me engage in great abstraction, I indulged in such *Seinsvergessenheit*.

The above story I now see as a metaphor for the kind of gigantic feats of abstractions accomplished within academia. The story also, at least in my mind, stands for a cultural (especially women's?) capacity to "live someone else's life"; or for a student's capacity to take up and manipulate somebody else's ideas and then to live with these ideas without really experiencing them as having any "being", any worldly and sensual existence. As teachers and students, do we recognize this capacity within us? Do we know how to counter it?

Heidegger tried to break up the "rock formations" of philosophic language. In doing so, in Gadamer's accounts, he experienced severe *Sprachnot* (language anxiety or dearth of language). He was often no longer understood. Language as obstacle was part of his story as well. In fact, I realized that what I used to live as a personal, mainly private story, was actually a culturally shared one, shared at many levels: by other children who spoke dialects; by social critics who worried about alienation in a technocratic world; by academics who were concerned with reconnecting the life of the mind with the life of everyday experience.

Gadamer tried to counter *Seinsvergessenheit* through dialogue, through developing a sensitivity to our embodied history that is constantly alive in us and affects us every day; and through a hermeneutical encounter of difference. By hermeneutics, Gadamer meant a constant process of mutual interpretation through dialogue, within which a kind of truth and rapprochement is built up gradually. It is not a question of taking in an idea "whole", undifferentiated in its abstractness. Rather, it would be taken in gradually, as it is constructed through dialogue. The conversational exchanges bring at least a partial, lived understanding of what faces us as difference. This kind of taking-in of "the other" promises greater understanding because, in Gadamer's view, we cannot consistently and completely misunderstand one another as long as our dialogue is authentic, that is, as long as we sincerely try to understand one another and do not manipulatively orient our conversation toward success of our own views. In such authentic conversations, our histories are constantly at play, speaking through us at every moment. It is these kinds of conversations I now strongly promote in my classes. I encourage experiential talk, where students exchange stories about their lives.

In trying to understand Gadamer's interpretation of *Seinsvergessenheit,* I realized something about my love/hate relationship with abstraction. I remember telling my advisor at the end of a seminar during my first year of graduate studies that I was often frustrated in my life because I felt I was not "experiencing" things. I am not sure if he understood, but I now know more clearly what I meant: It was the absence of fully experiencing lived contexts that was bothering me. It was what Gadamer (1986, 502) calls the "taking on of ideas at the level of intellect only", taking them on as if they were placed in front of me, so to speak, facing mainly my mind (blosse Vorgestelltheit). They were not thoroughly connected to my lived, everyday existence and I tended to swallow them whole, so to speak. I now suspect this is a danger in authoritarian systems, whether they are systems of education, family upbringing, social ethos or political organization.

Without connections to contexts, even words function merely as signs and the relationship of speaking or thinking becomes an instrumental one, rather than a holistic, lived engagement with the world. But, so Gadamer reminds us, as *Seinsvergessenheit* is happening, all along, an awareness of loss flashes up here and there. In conversation, in our encounters with others, especially with those who are different from us, it can happen that we are shaken up, challenged, and sufficiently engaged, to be able to create language anew and perhaps become aware of who we are in a deeply personal sense. Perhaps, Gadamer suggests, this awareness can come to us through the experience of a work of art. He explains (1986) that this experience is not one of facing an object, not something we can get a hold of by means of a distancing appraisal. It is much more like a world which pulls us in, like true conversations. We do not face art with a measuring, evaluative gaze. We experience it. We are a part of it.

EXPERIENTIAL STORIES IN AN EXPERIENTIAL INQUIRY

I find our relationship to stories has this total immersion quality as well. Not only the stories we hear as children, or the ones we watch in the media, but the ones we write as narrative inquirers and the ones we read in narrative inquiry. When I and my students write our first drafts, or when we listen to each other's stories of experience, we tend not to keep our distance. The stories pull us in. There is even the risk of being swallowed up by the experience of the stories. Luckily the loss of self is temporary. But we do come back changed by the experience. Bertold Brecht, the German playwright and poet, knew this. To make sure that the loss of self would not last too long, even in the relatively short duration of one of his plays, he inserted his *Verfremdungseffekt.* Suddenly two stage hands bring a door on stage when it is time for a character to exit. The audience is jarred into remembering not to get too absorbed, not to forget to think. Stories are teachers of ethos and could become tools of indoctrination. Even a narrative inquirer could fall prey to her own story telling when they take over her person and she begins to define herself in terms of a story, imposing closure on the inquiry. In narrative inquiry, the writer stops to reflect, to hypothesize, to theorize— and then incorporates such reflections into the ongoing story line (Conle 2000). Asking, What does all this mean? What is happening to me in this inquiry? is an important part of the inquiry.

At the other end of the spectrum, of course is "narrativization", narrative's function as a contextualizer of abstractions, of so-called context-free facts, of value-neutral assertions. I now see my narrative work with students in teacher education as a way to counter the Seinsvergessenheit in their academic training. As they take on new ideas about education and as they encounter their multiethnic students, I prompt them to place those experiences within storylines. I want students to link their experiences, both present and past, to their lives in and out of schools. I want them not to ignore their own lived contexts, nor those of the ideas they are encountering. This attitude is far removed from traditional academic practices. It is part of a hermeneutical approach to teaching and learning. But students often fear the risk of such personal engagement.

What an experiential, hermeneutical position offers and demands is the willingness to risk the "I" for the sake of the "we". What hermeneutical interactions offer is not an eventually fixed and final answer, but as Gadamer says, "a constantly changing attempt, or rather a constantly recurring temptation, to get entangled in something and involved with someone" (1986, 335). It means risk of self and an entrusting of ourselves to language, a putting into play of what we know through previous experience and offering it up to others, to language, and putting it at the mercy of our own doubts. We constantly cross gaps in this way—we step across dance floors. We risk self, but we do not get lost. We emerge with a new experience that has taught us something.

NARRATIVE INQUIRY IN TEACHER PREPARATION

I believe I owe my readers a clearer view of the work I do with students in order to convey a stronger sense of how the personal narrative I am presenting led to something interesting in teacher preparation. Essentially, in our classes we work with experiences. We attempt to function in academically unaccustomed ways, both rhetorically and with regard to goals and tasks. Narrative is our vehicle and our outcome. When we develop ways of communicating with each other narratively rather than argumentatively, we are finding out about the importance of not neglecting contexts, histories and feelings. This has become important in studying schools, in cross-cultural education, in remembering instructional strategies, and in becoming aware of practical knowledge acquired during years of schooling. The chapters in this book present examples. There are others.

In some of my courses, teaching candidates, in pairs, negotiated entry to a school they wish to study because they found it particularly interesting in some way. When they then talked or wrote about what they found there, I ask them to "own their perceptions," that is to say, to attempt to convey who said or saw what, where and when, rather than convey generalizations and fact-like truths (Conle 1997). This is not as easy as it may sound, because we seem to be trained in our academic culture to sound as if we really know what we are talking about, to convey facts and conclusions. I ask my students to speak hermeneutically, that is to keep in mind that those facts are interpretations and should invite dialogue rather than defend conclusions.

My teaching candidates also write "is-when" stories about a particular teaching strategy or technique which they experienced in their practicum. (See ch. 9). Here they need to account for the characters involved, the mood of participants, feelings experienced, the plot of events, milieux, etc. The resulting stories, once collated, are intended to contribute to a very lively knowledge base developed by the students themselves (Conle and Sakamoto 2002; and ch. 9 in this volume).

The major assignments presented in chapters 2, 3, 4, and 5 combine and expand various smaller assignments into a grand Personal Narrative, that consists of a complex set of personal stories of teaching and learning. Such a chapter can also be seen as a comprehensive set of data on the chapter writer that can help in decisions about whether or not to continue certain stories in one's professional life. Similarly, when we discover a fragile story of teaching and learning, we may decide to strengthen it (Beattie and Conle 1996).

Finally, when I ask students to write a Personal Cultural Narrative (Conle et al 2000), I ask them to focus on their cultural histories. The greatest benefit here comes from mutual listening to each other's stories in culturally heterogeneous classrooms. Immigrant students may find commonalities with mainstream students, while the latter discover that they too have a culture, even though it seems submerged in the commonplace. Stories of difference make it more visible. When it becomes recognized as something constructed within a particular history, it also comes to be recognized as susceptible to change. This may bring relief or anxiety. In either case, listening to difference across the gaps created by ethnicity, religion, gender, class, or ability can be exhilarating.

I will stop my story here. There are signposts elsewhere of things to come. Kieran Egan (1997) urges educators to reshape curricula in schools so that teachers and students can explore various kinds of understanding. Narrative plays a major role in his vision. Narrative has also found more general legitimization as a mode of inquiry (Fenstermacher 1994, Connelly and Clandinin 1994, Conle 2001) in teacher development. Teacher educators are beginning to share accounts of their practices (Hamilton 1998). We may not yet be accustomed to the notion that a researcher's life and his or her professional work are intimately connected (Conle 1999), but well established researchers are beginning to link their research to their personal lives (Newmann and Peterson 1997). Finally, it seems not unlikely that narrative inquiry in teacher preparation will begin to step from the margins toward center stage, filling the gap left in the spectrum of offerings at preparatory institutions that seem so far have ignored the need for teaching candidates to become better acquainted with themselves and to use forms of inquiry that are congenial to the experiential and contextual nature of their work. Perhaps I am after all on a good road, not on one that leads nowhere. I may not have to back track after all.

REFERENCES

Beattie, M. and C. Conle. 1996. Teachers' narratives, fragile stories and change. *Asia Pacific Journal of Teacher Education* 24(3): 309-326.

Conle, C. 1993. Learning culture and embracing countries: narrative inquiry through stories of acculturation. Unpublished doctoral thesis. OISE/UT.

Conle, C. 1997. Between fact and fiction: Dialogue within encounters of difference. *Educational Theory* 47(2): 181 -201.

Conle, C. 1999. Why narrative? Which narrative? Struggling with time and place in life and research. *Curriculum Inquiry* 29 (1): 7 -33.

Conle, C. et al. 2000. The asset of cultural pluralism: an account of cross-cultural learning in pre-service teacher education. *Teaching and Teacher Education* 16(3): 365-387.

Conle, C. 2000. Thesis as narrative: What is the inquiry in narrative inquiry? *Curriculum Inquiry* 30(2): 189-213.

Conle, C. 2001. The rationality of narrative inquiry in research and professional development. *European Journal of Teacher Education* 23(1): 49-63.

Connelly, F. M. and D. J. Clandinin. 1988. *Teachers as Curriculum Planners: Narratives of Experience.* New York: Teachers College Press.

Connelly, M. and J. Clandinin. 1994. Personal Experience Methods. In N. Denzin and Y. Lincoln (Eds.) *Handbook of Qualitative Research.* London: Sage Publications.

Dewey, J. 1897. My Pedagogic Creed. In *School Journal.* Chicago: A. Flanagan Co.

Dewey, J. 1904. Relation of Theory to Practice in Education. In R. Archambault (ed. 1974)*John Dewey on Education.* Chicago: University of Chicago Press.

Egan, K. 1997. *The Educated Mind. How Cognitive Tools Shape Our Understanding.* Chicago and London: University of Chicago Press.

Fenstermacher, G. 1994. The knower and the known: The nature of knowledge in research on teaching. *Review of Research in Education* 20: 3 - 56.

Gadamer, H.-G.1985. *Philosophical apprenticeships.* Cambridge, Mass.: MIT Press.

Gadamer, H-G. 1986. *Gesammelte Werke [Collected works],* vol. II. Tübingen: J. C. B. Mohr (Paul Siebeck).

Gadamer, H-G. 1987. *Gesammelte Werke [Collected works],* vol. III. Tübingen: J. C. B. Mohr (Paul Siebeck).

Hamilton, M.L. (ed.) 1998. *Reconceptualizing teaching practice. Self-study in teacher education.* London: Falmer Press.

Heidegger, M. 1950. *Holzwege.* Frankfurt: Klostermann.

Neuman, A. & Peterson, L.P. 1997. *Learning from our lives: women, research and autobiograph in education.* New York, Teachers College Press.

Schafer, R. 1981. *Narration in the psychoanalytic dialogue.* In W.J.T. Mitchell (Ed.) *On Narrative,* 25-50.

ENDNOTES

[1] This paper contains many excerpts from Conle 1993.

[2] Connelly and Clandinin (1988) have described narrative inquiry for teachers. However their advice of what teachers can do as curriculum planners does not encompass what my preservice students are doing. The demands of a one-year teacher education program are quite different from the context I believe Connelly and Clandinin assumed when they wrote their book, i.e. graduate studies and a concurrent teacher education program.

[3] The following paragraphs are modified sections from Conle et al 2000.

[4] *Blosse Vorgestelltheit* is Gadamer's name for this encounter of abstractions (1986, 502).

In: Teacher's Stories, Teacher's Lives
Editor: Carola Conle, pp. 171-182

ISBN 1-59454-472-7
© 2006 Nova Science Publishers, Inc.

Chapter 7

REFLECTIVE SESSION (EXCERPT ONLY)

Carola Conle

Now that we have written our stories, what do we make of them? How have they helped us think of ourselves as teachers? How they have helped us clarify what we bring to our teaching and become more aware of how we understand our students? It is difficult to answer these questions individually, by each of us looking at his or her own work. But through our many conversations we found that we can help each other look, that another pair of eyes perceives patterns, subconscious question marks or subtle tensions. These are often so much part of our regular way of talking and acting that we are blind to them. Often we did not see them when asked directly, but as we listened to each other's stories, we began to see these habitual patterns. Carola suggested we have a conversation to reflect on our stories and she started us off by formulating some more specific questions which we could ask each other for that purpose:

Questions

- Are there, implicit in our stories, questions we seem to be asking ourselves?
- What are they?
- How have we found out what they are?
- How have these shaped our approach to, and our interest in, teaching?

- Do they shape our interactions with students?
- What have we found out through the personal narratives about our particular way of understanding students?

We met to ask each other these questions and recorded our answers by way of concluding our work at this point.

Conversation: June 29, 1995

Present: Joe, Michele, Robin and Carola (Loreen was looking after her baby and sent in some questions and comments)

Michele

I started to think about the things that you were a bit concerned about because you thought perhaps it might be material that others would misinterpret and work against me within my career as a teacher. We talked about different ways of dealing with that by putting some context around it. I finally came to the conclusion that perhaps I would start with a bit of an apologia. We started to write these stories; they were personal stories. I think that reading your story about the subway, Carola, was something that allowed me to open up and be vulnerable with regard to different experiences that I had had, because you explored that in yourself, facing the idea of your own prejudices. I thought I could do that too, that I could open up and deal with sensitive subject matter without ever thinking that it was going to be read or experienced by anybody else other than our small class. And I felt comfortable sharing those things with the people within the classroom. When we started to go beyond the classroom in our head, the idea that perhaps we were actually exploring some material that might be of interest and value to other people, other teachers, perhaps even students, hadn't real dawned on me. I thought mmh, I wonder. When I went to your office a month or two a go and looked at the stuff, I felt quite comfortable with what you underlined and suggested for edits. We took some stuff out.

At that point of editing, I started to realize who I was, and for me the context for this writing is that I'm a person who remembers those things that are a little bit off the wall. I'm a theatrical person, so what intrigues me in terms of literature, within terms of drama, are those things that are theatrical, they're the dramatic. Those are the things that I want to explore, that I will remember, that I will write down as a part of my memories. It might be just a very small percentage of my experience of who and what I am, and just because I find that part interesting, it doesn't mean that I am bizzarre. It's just what I like to explore as an artist and that I will reflect on, as opposed to the mundane. So it has been an interesting reflection to suddenly say: Well, as a teacher, do I dare to talk about these things that are a little bit different or to a certain extent taboo? Do people want teachers who experienced this, or feel that, teaching their children? As an artist, I hadn't thought of that.

Joe

I've never felt that I wanted to take back anything that I've written. What has happened though, is the process of observing and chronicling with the purpose of putting it together into this kind of a format has made me stand in a frame an awful lot when I'm in a classroom situation.

Carola

What do you mean by frame?

Joe

A frame of — every once in a while, I will remember, hah, I have to observe and remember today. It's a good thing because it makes me personally much more aware of nuance in students' behaviors and meanings of behaviors which I might have just have glossed over: "Oh, it's a crazy day today, for me, for the kids, for the school." I began to see the interconnectedness of a tremendous amount and number of events.

Carola

You don't have an example by any chance?

Joe

Well, the example that immediately comes to mind, is reading your story about language, and how in one way you were ashamed of, or made to feel ashamed of the language that you speak, and that really hit me very powerfully, because I've come up against a series of events in my life — I've come up against feeling enormously inadequate in the way I speak, the sound of the way I speak, or the accent of the way I speak.

When we were five years old, my father purchased a home in suburban Philadelphia at a sheriff's sale, so he bought a home, I think it was $1,300.00 on a street where homes were selling for $50,000.00 then. It was run down, he had to build it up; but he wanted to live in his own home; the church, (he is a minister), had always given him a home to live in. But what that meant was that suddenly I went to a different school district, rather than Philadelphia school district. It was a different milieu. And the first thing I noticed was I didn't talk the way the rest of the kids talked, I certainly didn't wear the same kind of clothes.

And — to jump ahead a little bit — when I got to Africa, and I was speaking French, I was particularly aware of the fact I was being judged all the time on my French, and the best thing that happened to me was when in the middle of a conversation after I'd been there for a year, some Frenchman said, "Where were you born?" I said, "the United States" and they'd go crazy.

Coming back from Africa, I immediately went into the professional actor training program, where the way you speak was immediately challenged, and it had to be changed, and an awful lot of actor training is changing your speech to make it more flexible to make it adaptable, to enable you to invent the unique speech of a character that you are portraying, tone, intonation, rhythm, all of that. You have to give up your language in order to become something else.

Now this year, I'm working with Grade 9 students who are in the literacy and numeracy program, half of whom are from Guyana or Jamaica, half of whom they think they speak English and can communicate in English, but it's not standard; and so every time I would say to John, "You know, John, you can't say *he go store*". "Why, sir?" "Because we say, *he goes to the store*." "*He goes store* we say in my island. Everyone knows." "Yes, you are communicating, but we are trying to get you to communicate in a different way." So I was acutely aware of the fact that I was challenging this kid's language, his being, his philosophical background. Actually, one of them said to me, "I don't want to change the way I speak!" He really took my breath away. I didn't know how to respond to him. Finally I recovered and said "Well look, Jim, I'm not saying you have to give it up, I'm asking you to acquire another way of speaking and using language which is going to help you in other situations. When you're with your friends, when you're at home, when you go back to Guyana, of course, that's the way you are going to speak. But this is not going to be helpful in this situation." "What do you mean?" "Well, you're not going to get your grade 9 credits, let's start with that." So I was thinking of those kinds of resonances.

Michele

Professor S. called it, I think, the language of your nurture and he dealt with that issue in class. He said that the argument you had to present was, no, this was a part of your soul; you don't give up the language of your nurture, but you maintain it in certain environments. Exactly as you said, Joe, you have to understand, if you want to succeed within the context of the rest of the world, if you want to get a good job, you will be judged by how you speak. You will be judged as being uneducated or incapable because of the way that you are speaking. It might not have anything to do with the reality of who and what you are, but unfortunately, there are prejudices within our society and within the work place, and they will expect that you communicate in a certain way.

Carola

Hold on for a second. I sidetracked you by asking for an example. You were saying that you felt there was a frame, and you are now more aware of how various things now hang together, and I asked you for an example. I just don't want to leave that point as it is. Are you saying with this example of language that there is a whole storied world? Or some baggage that comes to mind as things are happening? Or what do you mean?

Joe

Around this table, you all know, I've been teaching for 15 years training actors. During that time, I didn't have the tools of narrative reflection under my belt, they were there obviously, but I never got them out.

I can honestly say that I taught for 15 years looking at the students and their problems in a detached way: I'm figuring this out; we're figuring these problems out together; and we're finding a way through the text; we're finding a way through this technical problem; we're finding a way through this play. What has happened to me since I've started this narrative recording, is that I am much more aware of myself in the student — myself in that student; or that student in me when I was at that age or at that level of vulnerability. I am much more aware of things that happen to me, that have shaped me, that are influencing my values. I've become more aware of where I came from and how I acquired these values, and what they mean to me. Whereas before I just assumed that all we needed to deal with was: we've got these 'higher' problems to tackle. I just find myself much more empathetic with the needs of the kids. I mean for 15 years I went on teaching students — I'm sure some of them were having problems with money, and didn't have enough food to eat, as graduate students, or as undergraduate students. I think I was vaguely aware of some of them being on food stamps. But now I know when Anthony comes to school and he hasn't had breakfast.

Carola

What isn't quite clear to me is how this emphathy is linked to the narrative activity that we've done together.

Joe

The narrative activity has made me understand where I come from as a teacher, what I have gone through, why I believe what I believe. Through the narrative exercises, I am more attuned to some of those needs in my students.

Michele

I think I have become more thoughtful about how I function in the classroom, and how the students respond to me. I think that through my reflections I've become more sensitive and aware of the impact that I have as a teacher . As Joe said, I've seen where I've come from and how my values were established. I think I do things thoughtlessly less often now. And if I do, I tend to suddenly pull myself back and begin to realize the impact of what I've done; and then I've got to deal with it and don't let things go away. I've become more sensitive of how much you affect a child. Part of it is because I think back to how I was impacted by things that perhaps others would not have been impacted by — such little things!

Joe

Remember we read an article by Brightman?

Carola

Britzman?

Joe

Britzman: when you come into the classroom you are the sum total of every teacher that has ever affected you.

Carola

That could be Britzman. I don't remember. Yes, that makes sense. So now you know that in an experiential way, because you've remembered your experiences and may be that's what you still do when you're standing in front of your kids?

Robin

It's how others hear what I say, and then you become a part of their story too. It's not just your story anymore.

Michele

But then does the process allow a positive conclusion? They say, you parent as you have parented, unless you struggle against that. Many people say, I'm sounding just like my mother! Do we teach as we were taught? I'm struggling against being a teacher like many of the ones that taught me. Does this process help us to reflect and go against that ?—You do what has been done to you. Though that doesn't make intellectual sense to us, emotionally that's what happens to people. But we have gone through a process which I think has brought us to a positive conclusion, we've become more sensitive or empathetic in a way that is going to move us forward as teachers. I think that's a beautiful image: yes, we become a part of their stories, we become sensitive to the fact that we are becoming a part of their stories.

Carola

Do you want to make any comments about the writing process?

Robin

It's nice having had a bit of distance to re-read it now. Just when I finished it, I was so happy I had gotten it done! And then I started being critical: Oh, I hate this! Oh no, oh no! Now that there's been some time and space, it is interesting, because even reading that first chapter of yours, Carola, now the course really makes sense!

Carola

That's interesting! I want to explore that a little bit more, because I've had that experience this year with my students. The people in the narrative course this year, some of them when they read the paper that I wrote *Between fact and fiction*, they said, now I understand what you're saying. I'm intrigued by what you said, Robin, because I think if I gave people the paper first, they would not understand it. There's a certain process.

Robin

It's just different when you're in the course, in the writing of it, than when you're looking at it. Now I'm reflecting about the writing and about the course. It's a different kind of reflecting when you're in it. I guess that's it. It was kind of a neat feeling now.

Carola

You mean now you can explain it?

Robin

Yes.

Carola

Yes, while you're experiencing it, and you're trying to puzzle out what's happening to you, you don't have the distance to really try and understand. I'm wondering if I should explain more about what we're trying to do; I probably don't do enough of explaining?

Robin

But sometimes too, it's nice if you come to your own realization without someone else's vocabulary. Now it makes sense and now I can agree or disagree with what you say. But it's funny. Even—I'm just thinking about the whole issue of getting permission for certain sections from people, the issue of informed consent. Talking to N. about that issue with the little girl. I said, "Can you just read it? What do you think? Is it okay? — It turns out they were wanting to get her IPRC'd at her school because she had a horrible year with the teacher. I showed N. little bit of this; she read my letter to Joe, and she read a bit of Joe's piece. And then, "Maybe I shouldn't get her tested," she said, "Oh, all this labeling!" Wow, it was just perfect timing! I did ask her, whose agenda, whose benefit is it to have the girl labeled? If she's had a really crummy teacher? And so N. decided she's going to wait another year, and if she still feels the need to go through the review, then she will. She was saying, how can I put that in the girl's file? How does that affect the future teachers?

How does that affect her: she's got that label! So, it was a really good example of her resonance with Joe's piece and how that resonance helped her to come to her own conclusions.

Carola

I think you raised another issue just now with that example: what we hope our audience will get from the stories. People will read our stories, and as they read them, they will sometimes question what they are doing, thinking of their own classrooms as they read the stories.

Robin

It was especially neat with her, because she's someone that is concerned with what the experts say: What does the study say? —really not, What do people say? So it was great to have her respond that way, saying, "Wow, what an interesting story!" and just sort of pull it in and apply it to her own situation.

Carola

So it had an impact. This is what I hope our audience will get from our work. In a way, this is a very practical consequence, that the readers might draw from it. Practical in that it will directly affect their practice because the story will evoke an issue in someone's practice today, and she'll want to do something about it. A reader might get an idea, what he can do because he hears a story about it.

Robin

It's just now all coming to me how people do react to a story—with either a "me too" or a "not me" reaction. Instead of being defensive, it creates another story and a whole resonance. N. was really able to see the issue from what I said and from what she read. She seemed really interested in it. "Oh, that's really interesting! Can I read your piece too?" Before, it was just something I was working on, but once she had seen one little application of it ...

Michele

I don't know if this connects up, but I discovered something about myself as a writer, about when I could write, and the way that I did write. I was surprised. I didn't know really— I mean, I knew I could write, but I'd done more academically oriented things and to suddenly be thrown into the whole narrative process — I felt very relaxed and good about it, and everthing just sort of flowed out of me, and it fell together in a natural way. You know how I agonize over writing, its terrible for me! But here I found my time to write. I found that there were certain things that I could do easily, that felt comfortable, that I enjoyed writing.

Carola

You found that form right in the course, it didn't take you very long. I've used one of your journals in one of my papers, and I'm just getting reviewers' responses back. One of the reviewers said about your journal, "Is this edited, did it come in this form? If it's edited, you should say why you reshaped it and how you reshaped it." I wrote back NO, it was the way it is. I guess, they didn't think that somebody would write a journal in this form. I think that's very true for you, that sense of writing.

Michele

That's why the dialogue that I use in this writing is interesting. I guess my background has influenced my writing. I never thought of myself as being able to write dialogue, and perhaps I thought of poetry of being more formally structured and that kind of thing.

Carola

Part of your practical knowledge. Because you have been in the theatre, you've heard people do dialogues, and so that when you started to write your narratives, that became your style.

Michele

The shape of it was very natural. I think it was these whole little encapsulated incidents that were perfectly shaped in and of themselves. And that's why it felt so good.

Carola

You didn't agonize. I was going to ask you, Robin, about the writing process because it took you quite a while to put your pieces together. I remember at one point you said, "I think I've got it!" It was something somebody had said: about kitchen and smells — and you said, yeah, that's going to be the way I'll put it together.

Robin

I remember you said at one point: It seems like you're very rushed; it seems like you are on a very fast train ride through somewhere. I was just panicking because I was thinking, try to make it into a long narrative, and instead of letting it go with the little small images — like little smells. You know how different smells remind you of something else in a different place? So when I was finally able to go with that, it did feel finished. Joe helped a lot; he made an interesting observation, just saying, "very traditional settings, very traditional teachers," and I was thinking, it's interesting that that came across because it is not what I remember. Like Michele, I remember the little quirky details, so then I was developing an awareness of how I listen and how I see. What do I really see? It's neat to have somebody else say, this is what it said to me. It just help so much to look at it in that slightly different way.

Carola

I think that's an interesting process, one I want to remember more when I respond to students. How do we respond to a piece that's given to us? We can critique it, we can analyze it, we can do all kinds of things. What you just pointed out was that Joe said: Well, this is what I make of your writing, this is how it comes across to me.

Robin

Just like the narrative letter we wrote in class as a hypothetical response to an associate, like the one in my piece: Let me say these ideas back to you, this is how it came across to me.

Carola

So he gave it back to you in the way it came across to him, and you then were able to say: well, yes, but not quite! And then you elaborated to change your writing. I think that's a really important process for dealing with associates as well as with students.

Robin

To respond: *Yes, but not quite.* It was just a little in-between situation. The timing when he said it was just righ, so that I could say to myself: "Oh yeah, it was not clear." I tried so make it clearer and now I feel okay with it.

Joe

I'm listening, and I agree with much of what I'm hearing, except my antenna goes up when I hear: it's good for all students. I don't know. I think it's great for us at this level, or the level we were two years ago. I mean we're still students, but we are advanced level students. I don't know that I could really respond that way to the papers my grade 9 students turned in. They need to know acceptable or unacceptable: this is good, this is bad. I don't know.

Carola

To me, what Robin said resonated with an experience I had as a graduate student with one of the people on my thesis committee who dealt with me that way, and I found that wonderful. Joe, I think you're right, it's one kind of response and it may very well be that at another time, you better give a different response. I mean if I have the chapter full of typos, somebody's got to say so. But as far as developing content, as far as actually working out my ideas, the "this is what I make of it" response is helpful. Final edits, that's something else. But the actual creative part, the part when you have to come up with more and more, it helps when somebody says this is how it comes across in my experience.

Joe

What I found with students is that you have to be a broken record, you've got to repeat, repeat, and then repeat again.

Carola

I have to do that with you too, Joe!

Joe

You never had to do that with me! *(Lots of laughter!!)* It's very true, it's the broken record syndrome.

Robin

It would be neat to compare though how they respond at that stage, when they're just starting to become aware of the power of their voice. As adults it's different because you just have more of an awareness of that, but when they're just realizing "oh, that's the way my idea came across to you?" I don't know.

Carola

The power of voice, I think that's what does it. You see, if the professor — even at the graduate level with me — comes with a judgment, saying: this is really good stuff, then it is the authority who said okay, it's good stuff. I may accept the judgment or rebel. But if it comes with a qualifier of "This is how I understand your ideas," then my voice is still there. It's less of an authoritative relationship. I can say, okay, that's his reaction. This is how he is able to take it. But I didn't really mean that. What I really mean is something else. And I have to rewrite it to get that meaning across more clearly. But I stay in charge, my voice is in the foreground and his reply was more of a personal reaction to it than a fact. It therefore lets my voice stay in the foreground. Voice is an issue at any level. So, we'll see how it works. In our sequel, you can let us know how these things turn out for you and your kids!

Michele

I wonder how the mini-series will go?! (Laughter)

Carola

Loreen asked about whether this work has made you more self-aware about the way you teach and relate to your students. Do you see yourself continuing to write about your teaching? How about a sequel? Are you writing still?

In: Teacher's Stories, Teacher's Lives
Editor: Carola Conle, pp. 183-192

ISBN 1-59454-472-7

Chapter 8

GAINING OUR WORLD WITHOUT LOSING OUR SOUL

*Carola Conle**

We believe that through this work we have gained a particular understanding of curriculum as well as of ourselves. We have come to a better understanding about what has been our curriculum, our course of life, as it evolved in schools and other places of education. We have also caught glimpses of an important dynamic in curriculum (Conle 2000), one that is carried along by what Dewey calls "interest," Garrison calls "Eros," and MacIntyre describes as a "quest." Carola has called it (after the philosopher Heidegger) "getting on the road on which we are already (Conle 2000)."

Dewey explains "interest" as "an unconscious but organic bias toward certain aspects and values of the complex and variegated universe in which we live" (1934, 95). In our narratives, especially when we began our work, we intuitively followed this "organic bias." As we decided what to talk about and to what among the myriad aspects of our universe we want to give our attention, we went by feeling, we attended to whatever felt right at the moment. Desire, Dewey suggests, "converts mere emotion into interest in objects as conditions of realization of harmony " (15). We want those things that seem to promise solutions to tensions in our lives. In the stream of things that pass by us, we subconsciously give our attention and interest to those objects that might restore harmony. Such objects

---

* With input from Robin Hoffman, Michele Pinet, Joseph Totaro and Loreen Teoli.

become the contents of our stories. In our case, we also often had the sense that we wished to set something right, to work something through that was not quite in balance. This sense was no more than a feeling, a favouring of certain issues and storylines.

At times there also were certain passionate desires. As preservice candidates we have strong desires: I want to be the best teacher I can be; I want to make a difference; I do not want to be like the teachers I had; I want to help my students the way Mrs. A. helped me. I want to overcome my fears --- . Such desires also served as an impetus to gather narrative data on our lives and thus constitute our curriculum in the course. Carola would encourage us to write out our ideas and , importantly, our experiences connected to those ideas. We should focus on what we wished most to talk about; or one might say in Deweyan terms, to let our interests and desire guide us. Garrison (1995a, 408) reminds us that "the ancient Greek word *Eros* meant 'passionate desire', [...] a passion for the good, or at least what we perceive as the good, either for ourselves or others." Feelings, morality and education come together when Garrison recommends an education of Eros, an education for wisdom. "A good education brings out the best in us by holistically unifying our character in knowledge, emotion and action in service of desires directed toward the good—that is, those persons, things, and ideals that are deemed to be of most value" (409). A good education seems to put us onto a quest for wisdom; for what is most wisefor us as tgeachers and of the greatest good in out practice.

MacIntyre (1981 [1984]) suggested, first, that we best perform such a search for the good narratively; and secondly, that it is important to realize that the good in a practice is not defined ahead of time, but comes into view during a narrative quest. It is therefore advisable that we investigate our interests and desires narratively and collaboratively, taking those initial desires and interests only as starting points to find implicit goods in the practice of teaching.

An open-ended searching for what is the right and good thing to do in our teaching is of paramount importance in the curriculum we describe. There are very few specific, preset outcomes for our course. In our narrative curriculum we tap into Eros because our storytelling is not constrained by directives: We tell whatever seems compelling at the time, moving in whatever direction our desires move us, towards whatever seems of most value at the time. We soon experience our narrative activity as a kind of quest for something not yet known. Often there are dilemmas and existential tensions that direct our storytelling. Often contradictions and tensions move the telling along so that lived experience becomes a launching pad for inquiry. Input from others who hear our stories is important and often shapes the direction our stories take.

We experienced the motivation and excitement that comes when school curricula begin to coincide with what we call our "lived curriculum" (Conle 2000); that is, when we in our academic environment can follow the subconscious question marks that our lives have assigned us.

This reconstruction of experience in our curriculum has had several important consequences for our professional development. First, by getting to know those lived stories within us, we feel we now have greater choice vis-a-vis our predispositions. Secondly, we feel ourselves to be part of processes of change because the storytelling itself produces change. Finally, we believe that autobiographical narrative as a methodology facilitates our decisions and indirectly represents a social critique. Let us speak of these consequences in turn.

GAINING CHOICE

Elements of choice arose through the concrete and more differentiated understanding that we feel we now have about what seemed normal and given in teaching. What at first glance seemed normal behavior for us in our classrooms ("That is just me; that is just the way I teach"), we came to see as the result of the sedimented history of many lived experiences. Dewey knew this a long time ago and explained it in *The child and the curriculum* (1902). We read his article in our course, but it entered our practical understanding only through our narrative activities. Having seen the history in our own and our friends' behaviour, we no longer take our student's performance as a factual condition. We are now looking for the stories behind it. We have lifted the heavy veil of the taken-for-granted that hides choice. No longer do we believe that "things just are," that schools are a certain way and that we need good techniques that work in all circumstances to fit ourselves most appropriately into the way things are. Every taken-for-granted is a construction and has a history.

We know that we have become the way we are as teachers in part because of experiences we had as students. The sedimentations of these experiences are limitations to choice. However, new experiences are still constantly modifying our identities and our professional knowledge. With them, elements of choice enter. A new experiential understanding achieved through the telling of a story will change, we believe, our existing pool of experiential knowledge. As we begin to understand "the student in us," as Loreen says, the stories we tell in the process of this understanding become, for our listeners and often for us, new experiences, albeit vicarious ones. They reconstruct what we believed and experienced before. TThrough this reconstruction, they will change who we are and what we bring into our classrooms (Conle, Li and Tan 2002). Let us look at this process of change more closely.

ENACTING CHANGE

The telling of an experiential story is an act of change (Crites 1971, Conle 1997). It changes the standpoint for any future telling of the same story, if only ever so slightly, because it incorporates contextual material such as the current context, mood, commentaries from listeners, and so forth. Because of these incorporations we can usually never tell the same story twice, for the standpoint from which it is told the second time will have shifted through the telling— even ever so slightly.

It is also in connection to this standpoint of telling— or now-perspective, as Carola calls it — that is present in every act of storytelling, that the opportunity for conscious input into a change process arises. We decide what we are going to produce as our next story. We decide what to place next to what and what to leave out. (Again, the element of choice is important). We can decide to bolster fragile subplots or pay less attention to storylines we wish to let run out. Carola and Michele both recognized such storylines. Carola moved to counter the power of abstractions over her; Michele moved to escape the power of negative expectations.

Any choice, once enacted, will change the standpoint from which we view the general stock of our lived narratives in the future. It will change the stories we are able to tell in the future, for a new story will have been added and by its presence will have shifted the standpoint from which any of the previous stories can be retold. If the standpoint changes, the story changes.

We need colleagues and partners in the storytelling to help us in these moments of decision and discernment. Their input and their resonating stories change our now-perspectives. Their input, as much as new circumstances, is part of our learning.

A QUEST FOR THE GOOD

Along with those elements of choice and change, moral dimensions starkly arise before us, for we know that, just as our teachers years ago, we are now the ones that help construct crucial experiences for our students. We know that our moral responsibility is very great. Michele sums it up well in that quote from Haim Ginott she remembered :

> I've come to a frightening conclusion that I am the decisive element in the classroom. It's my approach that creates the climate. It's my daily mood that makes the weather.

We also know that the responsibility is not all ours — many other factors besides the teachers in our lives contributed to the quality of educational experiences we had. We are not completely responsible as individuals for the social world we live in. We are neither all powerful, nor simply passing on a given. We are part of settings we did not create and of plots we did not write.[1] But we do contribute to those settings and plots through the writing and living we do now.

Often our stories have to do with what is morally defensible. How do we ensure that what we do for our students is good for their intellect as well as for their hearts and spirits? This issue of moral goods in teaching needs much attention, more than we can give it here. But we nevertheless want to explain the perspective which now, at this point in our work, has come to inform our convictions and therefore, we hope, will also show in our practice.

As teachers we often ask ourselves what is the right thing to do. By right we mean not only what is intellectually defensible, but what is the morally right thing to do in a particular situation. In search of answers to such questions, we do not have at our disposal a given set of rules or obligations, nor a list of virtues.[2] A postmodern, pluralistic society has made these unavailable. With MacIntyre (1981/1984) we want to place ourselves, narratively, on a quest for the good, in which the good is not already defined, but should be continually sought at the level of practice and in the sphere of living one's life.

The quest for the good, for "what am I to do" coincides with the question, "Of what stories do I [and my students] find myself [ourselves] part?" (MacIntyre 1984). By making narrative sense of our lives, of our actions, and of our institutions, we gathered data on moral issues; for when we told our stories, they almost invariably featured moral dilemmas. Narrative representation seemed to sharpen our ability to perceive those dilemmas in a very concrete, personalized way. We are continually on the road to define, for ourselves and for each other, what might be the good of our personal and cultural history in the long run and what , on short notice, might be the right thing to do.

Issues raised through autobiography are very intimately tied to a teacher's daily practice. Abstract readings and arguments may or may not be. Oser (1994,

92) laments that "deliberate values education [...] is not directed sufficiently to the action of the teacher;" that ethical theories and case studies "will probably not enhance professional morality; rather, [they] will enhance only analytical knowledge about moral issues." Although we do not have easy answers to this very complicated area in education, we believe that we have found a way around the problem Oser refers to. We feel that our narrative efforts very intimately connected to our morality and our practice as teachers.

The good we seek for ourselves professionally and for our students is inextricably interwoven with the circumstances of a situations. Once told in story form, those circumstances and their moral dimensions become part of our efforts to decide on a suitable course of action. The stories stay with us. A story may be lengthy and intricate, revolving around eternal question marks, or it may be relatively short, coming to mind as we act, as it was the case for Loreen when she deliberated about her drama lesson. The memories of those stories stay with us as we face our students. They influence our instructional decisions, just as Michele's memory of Mark Twain's story had a direct impact on her teaching that same day during her practicum (Conle 1996). Memories from our own experiences perform in this way, as much as the stories that we hear from each other and process through resonance. Focusing on these memories gives us a chance to expand their meanings and link them more consciously to the longer narratives of our lives and the moral issues we face.

We obviously do not see ourselves mainly as transmitters of information or trainers of skills. Nor is our emphasis on values clarification as such. We know that through our interactions we do transmit moral values. The kind of people we are matters. The kind of values we consciously or tacitly transmit matter. Through inquiry into our schooling histories we feel we have begun what will be a perpetual narrative task. We inquire into the circumstances that have made us people with particular values which we now bring into classrooms along with pedagogical and subject matter knowledge. A collaborative quest for understanding our embodied values and their history will be beneficial in a world that for the most part has lost conscious connections to its moral history (MaIntyre 1984 [1981]).

In our course we restricted ourselves to stories about learning and teaching in and out of school. We realize now that such autobiographical efforts have not just been a quest for the recognition of educational identities and educational baggage, but have also been a critique. In the process of determining what features of a context have significance and by describing connections and influences, autobiographers necessarily engage in a form of critique (Steedman 1986, 14; cited in Franzosa 1992, 396). The critique arises through the temporality of the narrative and through the choice of contents. Let us look at this process more specifically.

IMPLICIT CRITIQUE

When we tell events from our youth, we try to truthfully represent them as we find them in our memory. But that truthfulness does not represent a true event or the true child in school as it was at the time of the event. We, from our now-perspective, with the language we speak now, see continuities that were invisible to the child; we see social perspectives that were invisible at the time, not only to the child, but also to the teacher. In the telling, now, we construct a social perspective, one that shapes us now, as we tell our stories.

We no longer think of schools as just schools, we think of schools in our lives as places where specific learning experiences were constructed by specific actions and circumstances. This tells us that we have a part in the construction and in the authorship of the social perspective presented in our stories. When Michele tells how she triumphed over her nun/teachers by her wickedness; when Joe tells how the practice of assigning IQs became a curse to his learning — these are not faithful representations of the child's view, but constructions of a social analysis that is implicit in the story as it is told now. An educational autobiography, says Franzosa, "requires the writer to develop a social analysis that consciously proceeds from the memories of the past rather than concealing them, and honours the personal significance of living experience, rather than repressing it. While the lost voice of a child as student cannot be recovered as it 'really' was, that voice can be reconstructed to tell a convincing story that makes the landscape of schooling recognizable and coherent " (410). It gives it a coherence that it probably did not have at the time, but one that modifies actions now in our new positions as teachers. It is therefore a critique of the circumstances then and, potentially, also a critique of the current situation. Both critiques are evident in all of our five narratives.

Our personal narratives gave us a new way of seeing. Through our autobiographies we seize the right to construct our selves and our education. In Franzosa's (1992) words, we enact the right to author an educated self. We learn because we construct experiences as we tell them. The changes that each construction and reconstruction bring about in our view of self and of the past are part of our learning. We can never tell the same story twice, if the now-perspective has changed ever so slightly. The reactions of our audience, the questions of our colleagues, the happenings in our lives — all these we see as constant input into our now-perspectives and as sources of change that will be evident in any potential future telling of events, no matter how often they may have been told in the past. Any new telling will be a reconstruction of "old" knowledge and previous experiences. With Dewey we believe that this is the essence of education. We hope that the narrative reactions of our audience will continue that reconstructive, experiential process.

REFERENCES

Carr, D. 1991. *Educating the virtues*. London and New York: Routledge.

Conle, C. 1996 . Resonance in student teacher inquiry. *American Educational Research Journal* (in press).

Conle, C. 1997. Images of change in narrative inquiry. Teachers and Teaching 3(2): 205-219.

Conle, C. 2000. Thesis as narrative or "What is the inquiry in narrative inquiry?" *Curriculum Inquiry* 30 (2): 189-214.

Conle, C. , Li, X. and J. Tan. 2002. Connecting vicarious experience to practice. *Curriculum Inquiry* 34 (4): 429-452

Crites, S. 1971.The narrative quality of experience. *Journal of the American Academy of Religion.* 39 (3): 391-411.

Dewey, J. 1902. *The child and the curriculum*. Chicago: University of Chicago Press.

Dewey, J. 1934. *Art as experience*. New York: Capricorn Books.

Franzosa, S. 1992. Authoring the educated self: Educational autobiography and resistance. *Educational Theory.* 42 (4): 395-412.

Garrison, J. 1995a. Deweyan prophetic pragmatism, and the education of Eros. *American Journal of Education.* 103 (4): 406-431.

Garrison, J. 1995b. Deweyan progmatism and the epistemology of contemporary social constructivism. *American Educational Research Journal* 32 (4): 710-740.

MacIntyre, A. 1984 [1981]. *After virtue: A study in moral theory*. Notre Dame, Indiana: University of Notre Dame Press.

Oser, F. 1994. Moral perspective on teaching. *Review of Research in Education.* 20 : 57 - 127.

Steedman,C. 1986. *Landscape of a good woman: A story of two lives*. London: Virago Press.

ENDNOTES

[1] Carola took this lesson from the German philosopher Martin Heidegger as well as Alistair MacIntyre (1984).

[2] Carr 1991 (Chapter 4) speaks of an *Ethics of Obligation* and an *Ethics of Virtues*.

In: Teacher's Stories, Teacher's Lives   ISBN 1-59454-472-7
Editor: Carola Conle, pp. 193-221   © 2006 Nova Science Publishers, Inc.

Chapter 9

"Is-When Stories": Practical Repertoires and Theories about the Practical[*]

Carola Conle[†] and Mitsuyo Sakamoto[‡]

Abstract

The issue of being practical presents a continuous challenge, because student teachers' meanings for that word tend to be in sharp contrast to meanings that allow inquiry and are connected to personal and cultural histories. Instructor and student perspectives elucidate the struggle to find a compromise within this tension in the form of a particular narrative exercise assigned in a foundations course of a one-year consecutive teacher-training programme. Investment of identity and performative language were required in order to construct collaboratively a narrative repertoire of techniques and strategies that was practical in a non-technical sense.

---

[*] This chapter is an adaptation of an article formerly published by *Journal of Curriculum Studies*.

[†] Carola Conle is an associate professor at OISE/UT where she teaches in pre-service as well as in the graduate programmes. Her current research focuses on social imagination and on the impact of interpretive views of knowledge on curriculum. 252 Bloor St. West, 10th Floor , Toronto, ON M5S 1V6 Canada. Tel: 416-923-6641 X 7505; Fax: 416-926-4744; Email: cconle@oise.utoronto.ca

[‡] Mitsuyo Sakamoto recently obtained her doctorate from the Department of Curriculum, Teaching and Learning at OISE/UT. She is interested in the social formation and sharing of knowledge.

IS-WHEN STORIES: PRACTICAL REPERTOIRES
AND THEORIES ABOUT THE PRACTICAL

Student teacher: Tell me how to teach!

Instructor (thinking): '[Student teachers] flock to those persons who give them clear-cut and definite instructions as to just how to teach this and that' (Dewey 1974: 321).

Student teacher: I need to be taught how to survive in the classroom.

Instructor (thinking): 'Immediate skill may be got at the cost of power to go on growing' (Dewey 1974: 320).

Student teacher: I want to develop a repertoire of techniques and strategies.

Instructor (thinking): 'Such persons seem to know how to teach, but they are not students of teaching... the root of the matter is not in them' (Dewey 1974: 321).

As a teacher educator (Carola Conle) and former student teacher (Mitsuyo Sakamoto) in the foundations section of a one-year teacher-education programme, we live these dichotomies and conflicting aims almost daily. The issue highlighted in the imaginary dialogue prompted us to reflect on a particular exercise Carola used in her courses. Drawing on both student and instructor perspectives, we began our reflection three years after the exercise was first introduced. Carola acts as first-person narrator through most of the article and is later joined by Mitsuyo's voice.

The issue of being practical, in the sense I interpret my students' meaning of the word 'practical', presents a continuous challenge, because their meaning tends to be in sharp contrast to the meaning of the word that allows inquiry and is connected to personal and cultural histories (Gadamer 1960, 1987a, 1987b, Dewey 1974, Schwab 1971, 1978). My students seem to understand the word as the opposite of impractical, as providing helpful hints for action, whereas the writers I mentioned seem to distinguish this sense from one that refers to what asserts itself in action as a result of prior experience. One has to do with planning and specified desired outcomes, the other has to do with inquiry and with what is difficult to specify. Consequently, as we describe below, the sense of repertoires in relation to the two meanings is entirely different as well. Below, my former student, Mitsuyo Sakamoto, and I attempt to elucidate that difference and describe some teacher-education curriculum content that struggles to accommodate both meanings.

We present a compromise created within conflicting aims and purposes. We do not present this as an instructional technique to be copied. We simply describe our experience in as much narrative detail as we can and offer this account as an inquiry on our part, not as a new proposal for teacher education. We hope the issues around its inception and development will prompt our readers to reflect on similar compromises they experience in their programme. Alongside the account of an activity I devised, we present its rationale, and the deliberations surrounding its development. I frame the presentation of our work within the issue of what might be meant by the word 'practical'. Anyone involved in teacher education today knows how confounding this little word can be in decisions and evaluations of what is offered in pre-service programs.

WHAT DOES IT MEAN TO BE PRACTICAL?

The sense made of the words 'practical' or 'practice' covers a wide range of meanings that quickly reveal two major, very different orientations and attitudes toward knowledge and contributes to the dichotomies felt by instructors and teaching candidates.

What is 'practical'? Is it just the opposite of what is generally called 'impractical'? Is it what works, what is least complicated and most likely to achieve a desired result? What is practical to a student of teaching in a one-year teacher education programme? Is it what helps him or her give an acceptable, or even splendid, performance in the teaching practicum? Is it what is useful to the improvement of various aspects of schools and schooling (Wraga 1999)? What do we as teacher educators have in mind when we speak of the 'practice' of 'practitioners' or when we design courses to influence or perfect such practice? Do we have the skilled application of theoretical knowledge in mind?[1] Does our meaning refer to what expert teachers do (Shulman 1987)? Is our focus on what actually happens in classrooms or on what researchers, policy makers or teachers believe will happen? Do we hold that there is a body of practical knowledge that can become the knowledge base for pre-service teachers and do we conceive of this as techniques and strategies, performed by, or at the disposal of, a teacher? Or could it be that we mean none of these interpretations when we use the word 'practical' or 'practice'? What might be such an additional view?

Out of the many interpretations implied in the questions above, I select two main orientations. One is being practical in the sense of applying theory, and a second, often called a technical or instrumental views (e.g. Schön 1983), assigns being practical to those who use known means to create equally known outcomes.

Both of these orientations lie at the heart of decision- making in teacher education, particularly today, at least in the context in which I find myself working. Viewing practice as the application of theory still dominates much of teacher education, but I shall not discuss this orientation here.[2] However the second interpretation of *practical* concerns me because it is predominant among my pre-service students and has been, in my experience, extremely hard to dislodge, for students at our Faculty need to have an eye on proficiency. They go out to schools to be evaluated very soon after they enter the programme. I, on the other hand, cannot help thinking of John Dewey who 100 years ago warned against a misplaced emphasis on technical expertise and proficiency early in a teacher's career:

> To place the emphasis upon the securing of proficiency in teaching and discipline puts the attention of the student teacher in the wrong place, and tends to fix it in the wrong direction (1974: 317).

Dewey (1974) believed that proficiency should not be stressed until certain processes have taken place: '[O]nly where the would-be teacher has become fairly saturated with his subject-matter, and with his psychological and ethical philosophy of education' (p. 320); only after having learned to observe 'interactions of mind' and 'how teacher and pupils react upon each other – how mind answers to mind' (p. 324); and finally, only after having gained some sense of 'the attitudes and habits which his own modes of being, saying, and doing are fostering and discouraging in [students]' (p. 326). In other words, before settling into preferred teaching strategies and before having their own proficiency judged, teaching candidates need to not only to become well acquainted with subject matter and foundational knowledge about all aspects of schooling, but to practice observing students closely and to begin to get better acquainted with themselves and their own educational histories. Specifically, Dewey suggests, early teacher education should be a process of 'turning back upon one's own experiences and turning them over to see how they were developed, what helped and hindered, the stimuli and inhibitions both within and without' (p. 324).

Dewey seemed to indicate that what has been learned through prior experiences will emerge and be reenacted in the practice of teachers. 'Practical', in this third view, seems to refer to what asserts itself in various types of action, shaping them as a result of having been embodied through prior personal and cultural experience. This meaning of practical predominates in Connelly and Clandinin's (1988) term 'personal practical knowledge'. They base their work on Polanyi (1958), Schwab (1971) and Elbaz (1983).

Polanyi (1958: vii) explained that such personal, practical knowledge is largely tacit and not consciously held in an actor's awareness at the time of action. Knowing, Polanyi contends, is an action in which 'sets of particulars' are subordinated as 'clues or tools' in the active comprehension of something. In teaching, those clues may be anything learned earlier through experience. An actor in a classroom, such as perhaps a teaching candidate in a practicum class, does not focus on such subsidiary clues or tools when involved in a particular act of comprehension. 'Clues and tools are things used...and not observed in themselves' (p. viii). The use of tacit know-how makes knowing a practical affair in the sense that it emerges out of prior action and contributes to future action. Past acts of knowing furnish the clues and tools for present action, which in turn shapes actions to come. This process of course occurs tacitly, outside any planning activity and outside the conscious awareness of the knower.

This tacit use of the past in the present is a very personal process, is irreversible and exhibits two important characteristics. One, it changes everyone who performs it; two, it is non-critical. No one can decide after the fact, after an event of comprehension took place, not to understand and not to be influenced. Everyone is shaped by it. An event of comprehension, understanding and interpretation, as Polanyi (1958: viii) points out, is therefore 'inherently hazardous'. We risk ourselves in the process. This subsidiary involvement of the past in the present is no mere imperfection of practical knowledge, but a vital component of it and cannot be eliminated.

Such practical knowledge evolves through the knower's involvement in specific situations. This link to the specific and the particular has of course been well explained by Schwab in a set of articles published in the 1970s. Schwab (1978: 289) saw the connection to particulars as another aspect of the practical. 'The subject matter of the practical... is always something taken as concrete and particular and treated as indefinitely susceptible to circumstance'. The practical refers to this student in that school, with those people at that particular point in their lives and in that specific situation. It cannot be generalized and turned into helpful hints for teaching candidates.

Practical problems are just as specific. 'Theoretical problems' for Schwab (1978: 289) reminds us, 'are states of mind. Practical problems, on the other hand arise from states of affairs in relation to ourselves'. They are personal problems. Although they may have systemic causes and may be shared by large numbers of people through some common features, it is unlikely for such shared problems to be exactly alike. One personal solution can therefore not simply be transferred to other cases, either in one's own career or in the lives of others. 'Applications to other cases proceed only from analogy and turn out to be good ones mainly by chance' (p. 288).[3]

In what sense, then, can there be professional repertoires? How could such repertoires be taught or shared? How may one even know the problems and solutions that demand a particular repertoire? How can we, as a teacher educators, create courses for people who, I believe, largely depend on clues and tools of which they are not aware, who understand things that are ineluctably particular, and who face problems that are predominantly and specifically theirs? What is the status of a solution to a problem encountered in the way Schwab describes? Can it be a recipe for action or requirement in teacher training? If not, how can it become part of a teaching candidate's practical repertoire? If instructors or students find a solution to one such problem, it can only help others by analogy. There must be constant inquiry.

Pondering these questions, I decided that my courses should be courses characterized by inquiry, not by the passing on of solutions. If Schwab is right, candidates may only sense that a practical problem exists, but not know its exact nature. This latter point led most directly to the kind of inquiry that I came to consider useful to student teachers:

> We may be conscious that a practical problem exists, but we do not know what the problem is. We cannot be sure even of its subjective side— what is it we want or need. There is still less clarity on the objective side— what portions of the state of affairs is awry. These matters begin to emerge only as we examine the situation.... At some indeterminate point along the way, as the problem assumes shape,.... It becomes more of a search for solutions and less of a search for the problem (Schwab 1978: 290).

My candidates therefore were to examine situations and experiences and search for problems as much as they were to search for solutions.

I connected Dewey's (1938) emphasis on experience in education, Polanyi's (1958) characterization of subsidiary tool and Schwab's (1978) idea of inquiry to Gadamer's (1960) notion that prior experience, both individual and socio-cultural, provides particular lenses to recognize and deal with present situations.[4] In that view, people and places have histories, each practical action or situation has a history and these are intertwined with a person's identity. Gadamer (1960), in his philosophical hermeneutics, spoke of *Wirkungsgeschichte*, or 'effective history', that is, of the personal and cultural history that shapes all of our practices, perceptions and actions all of the time. Wenger (1998) points out how effects of history link up with identity, teacher identities not excluded, and sees the practical as 'doing in a social and historical context' (p. 47), and as entering into experience without ever being discussed or stated (p. 84), while demanding an 'investment of one's identity' (p. 97). The personal risk Polanyi (1958) mentions seems to be the risk of one's personal history and the identity shaped by the latter. All of us risk our lives, so to speak; we offer them up to change, each and every moment we encounter problems, find solutions or simply engage in action. And we are generally not even aware of what is happening to us.

I, therefore, tend to ask my students to look for problems that initially are only vaguely sensed, to find solutions that cannot be solutions for all times or all people, and to invest part of themselves, of their life history, in such inquiry. The risk of self is required. When students of teaching inquire into the practical in the sense Polanyi, Schwab and Gadamer have described it, what is needed at the very least, is the investment of their personal identity, together with their personal and cultural history, in an inquiry process that is unavoidably concrete and particular and does not depend on pre-defined problems. Nor can it rely on transferable solutions.

In the 8-months pre-service programme at the University of Toronto, I offered an optional course entitled 'Teachers stories, teachers lives: the place of narrative in personal-professional development'. The major assignment in this course was the composing of a 10-20-page 'personal, cultural narrative of teaching and learning' in which candidates explored their practical knowledge; 'practical' meaning here as referring to what is learned through experience over time and what exerts itself in action, as Dewey, Polanyi, Gadamer, Schwab and others have described. Students did various exercises in preparation for this grand narrative, such as journal writing, and the reading and responding to literary narratives about teaching and learning experiences.

There was also one exercise in which I tried to accommodate my students' yearning for activities they see as immediately useful to their current teaching performance. However, I also did not want to lose sight of Dewey, Schwab and the others and my third interpretation of being practical described earlier. Below I present a sample of an assignment devised as a compromise between these two orientations to the practical. I also present parts of the reflection Mitsuyo Sakamoto and I engaged in several years later, trying to understand this exercise in connection to issues and theories of the practical. I made it a regular component of one of the three foundation courses I taught in the pre-service programme. It is an exercise that requires inquiry into experience and is also meant to be helpful in repertoire building. Neither focus should move into a purely technical or instrumental realm.

STUDENT TEACHERS' INQUIRIES INTO THE PRACTICAL

As I mentioned above, in devising student teachers' inquiry, I rely on Dewey's (1974: 322) interaction of minds and 'the large capital of an exceedingly practical sort', available to students from their own prior teaching and learning experiences. In addition, I rely on narrative forms of expression in a mode of inquiry that may have a direct link to the acquisition of a teacher's practical repertoire. The possibility that teachers' repertoires may have a narrative base has been pointed out:

> [A] reflective teacher builds her repertoire or teaching experiences, holding examples ... not as methods or principles to be applied like a template to new situations, but as stories that function like metaphors, projective models to be transformed and validated through on-the-spot experiment in the next situation (Schön 1988: 26).

Schön seems to envision this projection and validation of story models as a deliberate activity, carried out as a consciously directed experiment-like inquiry in which the content of the model is consciously manipulated and used in solving problems and in building a practical repertoire. The realm of the practical directed by the personal, practical knowledge I just described, I fear, does not readily fit such conscious deliberations, because the content of the practical in this sense may not be readily available to the student's awareness and may not be inquired into directly, as Schwab (1978) pointed out, and as Connelly and Clandinin (1988) have explained.

Because of the extent to which Schön's work has been debated in the literature on reflection (Grimmett and Erickson 1988, Russell and Munby 1992), it is important for the discussion here not to assert that projective and validating activity could never rise to a conscious level, but to maintain that it is unlikely to do so during the hustle and bustle of teaching, and that, if it does, it can never be final, definitive or complete. Some of the metaphoric activity Schön describes must remain at the tacit level and would not be readily available to conscious inspection during teaching. Moreover, once something does becomes available in someone's awareness through what has been called reflection-on-action, it is highly questionable whether such items actually correspond to, or represent accurately, either the actual contents of the actor's consciousness, or what happened at a particular event. Here Schwab's doubts coincide with those expressed by Habermas (1984) when the latter cautions against 'philosophies of consciousness' attitudes that prompt confusion between interpretations of one's own consciousness and direct truths. Habermas warns that one's consciousness can never be completely transparent to one's introspection. As teacher educators and as student teachers, we should therefore not fool ourselves into believing that what we actually do in classrooms corresponds to what we think we are doing, and that what we know can be equated with what we think we know. 'To *think* one is obeying a rule is not to obey a rule. Hence it is not possible to obey a rule "privately": otherwise thinking one was obeying a rule would be the same thing as obeying it.' (Newman 1996: 300, citing Wittgenstein 1953).[5]

This epistemological doubt could be extremely debilitating in teacher education: teachers cannot trust their own beliefs about their practice. My solution to the dilemma resulting from this 'untrustworthiness' was to let students work narratively. It has been my conviction that personal narratives about one's actions and knowledge implicitly carry along practical knowledge that is not named directly (Conle 1992, 2000; Conle, Blanchard, Burton, Higgins, Kelly, Sullivan & Tan 2000). Moreover, such knowledge need not be named directly for it to change (Conle 1997b). In other words, as an instructor, I may prompt students to engage in activities that 'work on' their practical knowledge even if they are not able to name it precisely. The emphasis would be on the description of preliminary and ever-changing phenomena and on the avoidance of 'conclusive evidence'.

I also believe teachers need time for inquiry that momentarily interrupts, or at least slows down, the flow of activity experienced. Although interpretations of events and abilities may begin in class, they will take place outside of class during the part of teacher work that Carlgren (1999: 54) characterizes as 'design practice', a part of teachers' work that takes place in the planning stages of classroom activities and is essential to the development of practical knowledge or practical repertoires. The inquiry I envisage is a narrative exercise in which students are asked to narrate, in as much detail as possible, a specific technique or strategy as they remember it being enacted in the practicum. It may be that the choice of a particular technique is based on a sense of puzzlement, but more often it may emerge out of a sense of satisfaction. To what degree, then, is such a narrative description an inquiry? It complies with Schwab's (1978) criteria mentioned earlier. It makes concrete particular circumstances and deliberations; it throws light on hitherto neglected observations of students and self; it gives rise to questions and problems as the writing proceeds or as a story is heard or read by others. The narration is not done for strategic purposes. It is not to produce a generalizable case; it is not produced to be critiqued.[6] The primary purpose is not to pass on a knowledge base, but to throw an indirect light on someone's practical knowledge by narratively scanning someone's experience of a particular situation, without the assurance that 'true' practical knowledge is being named.

The inquiry can become collaborative, even though parts of it are very self-centered. The connection from one inquiry to another happens by analogy, as Schwab (1978) suggested, when the inquirer shares the products of his or her efforts. I have elsewhere described this process as "resonance" (Conle 1996). Reading or listening to each others' experiences, students usually think of sets of images and situations from their own life that are similar, but not identical, to an instance encountered in the other's story. I specified the processes of connection involved in this analogical activity, by suggesting that elements in one person's story correspond metaphorically to elements in another person's story. If such resonance in collaborative narrative inquiry occurs within experiences of techniques and strategies, it is likely to help build practical repertoires through metaphorical connections. Here Schön's (1988) point on the link between metaphor and repertoire is helpful. Inquiry and repertoire building come together, even though epistemological warrant is not available. Inquiry and professional development, reflection on the past and planning for the future, become one in such work.

I named the exercise I devised along these lines 'is-when stories' because most often, when I ask a teacher to describe a particular strategy, he or she might begin to do so with the words, 'That *is when* you (do such and such) and (this or that) happens'. *Is-when* is the temporal marker for a story about the practical, about actions experienced in the classroom. The answer to the question: 'What is [the name of a technique]?' is presented in temporal form, not in the form of a set of prescriptions or commands. Is-when stories arise out of specific settings, events, actions, moods and moral values. They are open-ended and do not provide any epistemological certainty as to what actually happened or what the author actually knows. Nevertheless, as narrative products, these stories are part of both student-teacher inquiry and student-teacher professional development.[7]

IS-WHEN STORIES

I used the method of narrative inquiry, the idea that a repertoire may exist in narrative form and the notion of resonance, to develop an exercise in which my student teachers examine their practicum experiences, reconstruct them narratively, and build a shared repertoire of teaching techniques and strategies among themselves. Presenting the following sample gives me the opportunity to convey the importance of narrative detail and structure in the exploration of the practical. Many 'cases' presented in teacher education manuals do not have the narrative detail or the experiential quality of our 'is-when stories'. Rather than searching for obviously didactic material, my students try to represent experiences with as much contextual information as possible, even if it seems almost irrelevant at first. In this sense, the exercise resembles narrative field texts (Connelly and Clandinin 1994). One of the instructions I give my students is to make sure their inquiry of the technique or strategy has a narrative quality. By this I mean that there need to be a plot, mood, milieu, identifiable characters (including that of the narrator), and an explicit or implicit moral. The language needs to be performative, not evaluative (Conle 1997a). The following is an actual sample from a former student. It is not an exemplar, but exhibits some of these criteria.

Is-When Story: 'Teaching a Short Story to a Difficult Class'.
Elena Falvo (Pseudonym)

Having[8] observed this rambunctious group of grade twelve English students at the general level for just one period, I knew full well that I had to nab their attention and interest when I 'took over' the next day. My associate had explained that this class was most definitely a challenge for any teacher, particularly a student-teacher. 'Thanks,' I thought, 'just what I need to hear to relax me for the upcoming lesson!' Mr. Jacko (pseudonym) went on and on about the virtually non-existent attention span of these students; in fact, it was so low, he said, that even performing intricate backflips in neon spandex while playing the kazoo and juggling tea cups would only intrigue them for about fifteen whole seconds. No pressure here! What was I going to do? My acrobatic skills weren't all that wonderful, to say the least. Here I was, ready and eager to teach English, and the prospects of imparting any knowledge to my audience of students seemed quite bleak. Nonetheless, I was determined to try. If nothing else, I would at least attempt to reach these students -- student who weren't willing to do much, yet who weren't expected to do much either. These were to be *my* students for the next nine days and although they would probably hiss and cackle when I would introduce their new short story, I was determined to prove my associate wrong. I suddenly felt like Jill Solnicki (Solnicki 1992) -- the reality of this profession was starting to feel quite shocking.

That night, I thought long and hard on how to entice these students -- how to approach the short story in a way which they might find interesting. I didn't want them to keep thinking that this literary genre, like all others, was a nemesis, but a friend of sorts. No easy task. How was a short story going to appeal to them -- youngsters who seemed so uninterested and unwilling. I had watched them closely: There was Carlos, for instance, who I'm still convinced actually believed he could learn from osmosis -- that is, lying his head on his shut binder for the whole seventy-five minute period. There was Helga, who was consumed with issues of sex -- she wanted to know how one contracted herpes and how it could be treated -- not how the setting of a story enhances the theme! There was John, who had this inexplicable need to yell at the top of his lungs, at the most inopportune time, for no apparent reason. There was Scott, who had this incredible talent for buzzing the office without ever being noticed -- not to mention his flair at sneaking out of the class long before it was over. These were some of the students to whom I would present the short story.

With these faces and behaviours imprinted on my mind, I leafed through countless short story anthologies. I couldn't find one that was good enough: some too boring, some too difficult, some too infantile, most outdated. I finally decided on 'The Sniper,' a short story about the civil war in Ireland where a soldier unwittingly kills his own brother, thinking him an enemy. The story had suspense. It was touching. It was real. I felt confident that it would work. Great. The story was selected, but how was it to be taught? I decided I would take a risk. If I didn't try, I would never know. I would scrap the teacher-directed Socratic lesson that my associate adhered to. According to me and these students, it simply did not work -- at least not in this particular classroom: 'Hey Miss, are you gonna bore us to death like he does?' I responded to that student that night in my head with a resounding 'NO.' My evolving teaching style told me that lecturing for the whole period did not work for me; that this student's question made me realize it didn't work for the kids either. And, weren't we in this for them? I knew I was.

So, on Tuesday I went in, after a lot of contemplation and anxiety the evening before, and gave a lesson (that spilled over into the remainder of the week) that neither the students or I will soon forget. What I had decided to do was let the students learn this short story in an interactive, fun, creative, collaborative, and dynamic way. My associate would probably raise an eyebrow or two, but I wanted to approach the story in a different way than what they were accustomed to. A slogan for a running shoe came to mind: JUST DO IT. My idea could work. I had to try it out. After all, if I didn't take risks now in practice teaching, when would I?

I knew that it was a good idea for teachers to try and cater to the various learning styles of students -- to try and appeal to as many of the seven intelligences as possible; to dare to use music and video and movement in the lessons; to make the learning experience as interdisciplinary as possible. This is what I did. I started the class that day by having them listen to a powerful contemporary song by an Irish rockband. Why? Because the song, with its stinging lyrics and intense rhythms, was about the ongoing war in Ireland. They listened attentively, burning holes with their eyes into the lyric sheets I had provided. Why is she making us listen to this?, they undoubtedly wondered. When I explained that the song painted the backdrop for our new short story, I could see in their eager faces that I had broken through. I was making some kind of impression on them, and I think it was good. The students were listening and contributing. My associate looked on in shock. Most of them knew about the horrors of war all too well. Most of them came from South American countries where the politics of fear and injustice were familiar to them.

Something wonderful happened then. Something completely unexpected. They began sharing their stories. Painful stories about the realities of war. They could related to the anguish in the singer's wailing voice. They wanted to read the story: it wasn't about their particular experiences, but it appealed to their common experience.

We read the story together, in a circle, each taking turns. Some of their thick accents made the comprehension difficult. That didn't matter now. What did matter was that they no longer were preoccupied with how to plan their next escape from this class or how to pass a note to a classmate. They were sincerely interested in the story, and needless to say, I was elated with their responsiveness. Even Carlos opted to detach his head from the comfort of his binder and participated.

After the story was read, I had them do something collaborative and new to them. I made these students, the very ones who were notorious for sitting in their seats unmotivated and unchallenged, teach ME the story -- for them to teach each other the story. And they did. And they did so exceptionally well. In groups of four, they worked together on the elements of the short story. One group tackled plot, another theme, another character, and so on.

After this process was completed (which took two periods), each group made a presentation. They were all prepared and excited to relay their findings. I was overjoyed at their effort.

I then decided to incorporate some drama. They created and role played a dialogue before the class. They worked in pairs. I asked them to perform a skit depicting the conversation that would ensue between the sniper and his mother or father -- the very night that the soldier had killed his own brother. The students took this very seriously. They performed emotional and gripping mini-plays. I was so impressed and my disbelieving associate was awestruck [...].

I concluded the analysis of this story by showing the class parts from the movie 'In the Name of the Father.' Here they saw the song, the story, and their skits come alive on the screen. Many of the students thanked me for an excellent week. But I didn't need their thank you's -- the interest in their eyes was all the thanks I needed.

The narrative elements I mentioned earlier are in evidence. There are characters, including the teacher; there is a plot; readers are made aware of a certain atmosphere and context and an underlying moral agenda. Elena describes the awareness of herself as character in the story in great detail. Some of the students are vividly portrayed. However the character of the associate is rather vague and one-dimensional. Mitsuyo and I thought perhaps the student teacher/associate teacher relationship was tinged by an judgmental-evaluative rather than an inquiry attitude on Elena's part. Student teachers' rush to judgment is well known (Conle 1997a). Pushing teaching candidates to describe what they saw, heard, felt, etc., rather than present comments that seem to fix or harden a character was one attempt by me to counter this rush to judgment and promote inquiry. I asked Elena in the margins of her story to omit several comments about her associate unless she wanted to specify more clearly how she came to form these judgments.

In a recent interview, Elena told me about her differences with Mr. Jacko. In fact, she said that they were now both working in the same district and some time ago she came upon Mr. Jacko at a meeting. They heatedly argued about ways of teaching. Later, at still another meeting, Mr. Jacko apologized for 'raking her over the coals' and admitted that what she was trying to do with students was 'threatening' to him.

In m y response to the exercise, I also questioned Elena's characterization of the four students as too conclusive, given that she had just observed them for one period prior to the class she is describing. This applies if I take what she says at face value. Perhaps she added some descriptive detail to enhance her story? I had told students that such embellishments were not forbidden; after all I had no way of checking the truthfulness of their stories. In my recent interview with her, she pointed out that she does not remember embellishing the details about students, but she believes that her report of Mr. Jacko's warning very likely was done for narrative affect. I was something she herself might say. Indeed, she said, she tends to throw such outrageous imagery at students to get their attention.

Truth and truthfulness however are issues in narrative inquiry (Conle 2001) and rhetorical moves that would enhance fictional writing may take away from the inquiry quality of this exercise. On the one hand, an is-when story is an experiential account, written within the dynamics of life and experience. It should never become a fixed, prototypical case. The 'truth' of its detail although assumed during the telling, may very well change as an inquiry proceeds and a story is retold in light of new insights or reflection. To avoid a kind of hardening or fossilization, as it were, I am always careful to warn students not to conceive of what comes to mind about the situation as 'the truth' about an event. But they have to be as truthful as they can be in the telling if the story is to count as inquiry (Conle 2001). Otherwise the narration becomes fiction, still of some use in repertoire-building, but no longer an inquiry in the sense I described earlier. At the same time, students are asked to keep in mind that the story is a construction. A month from now, a year from now, they may tell it differently.

This is a very complicated agenda, only some of which I explained to the students at the time. The evaluative comments I received at the end of term reflected the difficulties some students' experience in trying to understand the rationale for the 'rules' of the exercise. 'A useful exercise, but somewhat confusing in terms of the rules', was one year-end comment; 'explanation was unclear; how can you do "is-when" without making conclusions?' was another. Students often saw the exercise as merely a reflection on what happened without realizing that the telling was likely to affect their practice. 'Again-- only a reflective exercise', one student commented. Mitsuyo and I now believe that if Dewey's, Polanyi's, Schwab's, and Connelly and Clandinin's notion of the 'the practical' became clearer to them, their understanding of the exercise would likely change.[9] Such clarification is unlikely to occur, regardless of an individual instructor's efforts, if the program as a whole, both philosophically and structurally, is predominantly given in the technical -rational mode that almost inevitably surfaces when proficiency is expected early and the need for how-to blocks anything else.

However, my course as a whole pointed into another direction and was likely regarded as an oddity. In this exercise, I did not encourage discussion or debate on related issues. I did not ask students to classify the contents of some one's story. The narrative engagement was key.With hindsight additional questions for Elena occur to me now, questions that did not come to the fore at the time when I dealt with about 36 exercises in the middle of an eight–week course, in a section of the course that was only worth 20% of a student's final mark. What decisions were likely made 'in-action', at the spur of the moment? What was recognized while writing the story? These questions may have been asked by fellow students in small groups at the time, but at the time they were not asked by me. It is these narrative elaborations themselves that promote the collaborative nature of the inquiry. Having to think of the narrative details in and of itself is the inquiry goal.[10]

Listening to the stories of others usually creates more 'data' on one's own experiences. Such 'data' did not always come easily. Not all of my teaching candidates write narratively on their first try and I give them time in class to practice. I prompt them to tell me more about their feelings, about what they remember their students doing, comments from associate teachers, as well as their own reactions. I ask them to tell about the situations they walked into as student teachers, the atmosphere in the school, the mood of the class, before, during and after the events, and so forth. Many of these comments also come from their classmates who sometimes ask for more specifics on the plot, that is to say the technique or strategy, or for more of the narrator's thoughts. This is done for the purpose of obtaining more 'data' for the narrator, but it is also done for the sake of the audience. Resonance-type responses have a greater chance, the more concrete, narrative details is available in a story offered to listeners.

The listeners are in fact both the beneficiaries and the co-constructors of an is-when story. For example, requests for clarification through more narrative detail help the writer to get more 'data' on the events, but also help the listeners connect the story to their own experience in an effortless way, through resonance. In order to function optimally as collaborative inquiry, resonance has to be heeded and allowed into the listener's set of responses; it should not be passed over as inconsequential or unacademic. I often ask, 'what came to mind as you listened to [so and so's] story?'

As an aside: I could ask you, the reader of Elena's story, what came to mind, what memories were stirred as you read the story. In a 'me-too' reaction, listeners and readers may recall some of their own situations and can begin to turn these over in their minds, as Dewey suggests. In this way, they begin to modify their own histories because, by being drawn into someone else's story, they go through a vicarious experience— the next best thing to real experience, as some of my students tell me. In a similar fashion, repertoires can be modified. This assertion emerges as part of the inquiry Mitsuyo and I engaged in several years after she was a student in the class Elena also attended.

INQUIRY INTO THE USE OF 'IS-WHEN STORIES'

In 1998, three years after I first tried out the exercise, my former student, Mitsuyo Sakamoto, and I began to study many is-when stories and reflect on their particular qualities and the circumstances surrounding their production. Mitsuyo will describe what she remembers of her experience with the exercise in 1995, outlining its context.

Mitsuyo (written in 1998)

> The 'Is-when' Stories [...] were given as an assignment before our class left for one of our practicums, were collected when we returned, marked by Carola and returned to the students, who then shared them with others in the class on a voluntary basis. Sharing occurred orally or by exchanging the written texts, either in the large group or among two or three partners who gave each other mutual feedback.
>
> Being admitted to a Faculty of Education was not easy. Our Faculty at that time normally received approximately 6000 applications annually, and only about 1000 students were accepted each year. These students were academically successful individuals who already had to some extent a

teaching-related experience before entering the Faculty and were highly motivated to become good teachers. They stumbled on harsh reality when they were placed in learning situations very different from what they were accustomed to. In my case, I had gone through years of 'traditional' schooling in Japan that rewarded regurgitation of knowledge and devalued my own experiences or 'stories'. I came to underestimate the knowledge I already brought with me and did not expect to have it validated. What seemed to be praised in the past was my ability to listen and to follow teacher's instructions. I did not realize my own strengths, weaknesses and potential as a professional. The 'is-when' exercise began to foreground some of this ignored knowledge.

It was particularly difficult for me as a novice teacher who had not yet established a repertoire of teaching techniques to deal with numerous, different teaching situations. Many new situations, which might not seem overly difficult to deal with for an expert teacher, seemed like unmanageable obstacles because of my lack of experience. Because our teacher training was to last for only eight months, I felt I needed to gain and expand my knowledge about teaching quickly and efficiently. I had to deal with the everyday reality of a school: unpredictable questions from the students, public announcements interrupting class, last-minute school assemblies, the principal visiting my classroom, students forgetting to bring their text books—teachers must be prepared for anything. It was so easy to feel at a loss with what was expected of us: apparently simple things such as knowing how to act or what to say in a classroom. There were numerous choices we could make, yet we knew that we had to be aware of possible consequences. Our actions were being evaluated. It became very important for me to be introduced to, and acquainted with, as many in-class situations as possible, so that I could have diverse expectations as to what my decisions might be in a classroom. Is-when stories provided this opportunity.

The complexity of our situation was heightened in another way. Toronto schools are often highly multicultural environments, where people come from various ethnic background, speak over 80 different languages and bring with them very different kinds of schooling experiences. There are reports that in 1996 close to the majority of children came from homes where language other than English was spoken. The increasing influx of immigrants from different parts of the world requires educators to be more sensitive, to and knowledgeable about, their students' needs and concerns. We had to observe carefully as well as listen attentively in order to tailor curriculum and teaching style to the students' needs and interests. We could not simply recycle what we were used to. We needed to inquire and reflect.

I found our is-when stories especially exciting and unique. On an individual level, I was given an opportunity to realize and voice my teaching experiences and celebrate successes. This, I believe, led to self-empowerment and critical self-evaluation. By sharing our stories with one another, we exposed each other to many teaching situations which we had not encountered during our practicum. The story telling helped us think further.

I also believe that if such story activity could become institutionalized in connection with the practicum, the teacher educators and associate teachers could gain a better understanding of what their teacher candidates go through by identifying events where important learning had occurred. They could better identify our moments of difficulty, anxiety and frustration, and we could seek solutions together.

We documented an experience so that it could be shared and scrutinized by us and others. Through the narration, we reconstructed our experiences in our heads, giving the experience a plot with climax and denouement, characters, and milieu. This re-organization of one experience into a story allowed us to make meaning out of an indistinct background of experiences. As our audience listened to the stories, their own stories struck a chord with the story they were listening to.

The exercise of writing an 'is-when' story was student-driven. Our instructor did not provide a teaching template to all students for them to simply follow. I am now convinced that 'teaching effectiveness, to my mind, is not a context-free and fixed property of a teaching behavior. It is, rather, a local achievement constructed under immediate and particular circumstances' (Doyle 1997: 97).

Carola

Mitsuyo's account confirmed my concerns about the perceived needs of my pre-service students and their conception of the practical as 'how-to'. Mitsuyo highlights students' desire to develop proficiency quickly, as well as their expectations of a process that seems to ask for the efficient application of theory provided at the faculty. However, she also leaves an opening for the acquisition of professional expertise in a potentially non-technical way.

Mitsuyo also notes that it became very important for her to be introduced to, and to be acquainted with as many in-class situations as possible, so that she could have diverse expectations as to what her decisions might be in the classroom. This increased acquaintance with class situations, I suggest, can come through vicarious experience, can be inquiry-based, and can constitute or modify narrative repertoires.

THE NARRATIVE CONSTRUCTION OF A
REPERTOIRE AND ITS RELATION TO THEORY

In the set of stories Mitsuyo and Carola have collected from students, the following are among the titles: Storytelling; Class debate; Strategy for visual learners; Cooperative learning at its best; Guest speaker; 'Naval Combat'; 'Le Passé Composé'; Role-play; The day Neil Diamond came to class; Star system; Name that dignitary; Song, stories, and satisfaction; Bingo; This is jig-saw jeopardy; Tableau: Marriage-as-I-see-it. These is-when exercises are often about teaching techniques that have a theoretical base. For example, much has been written about cooperative learning, jigsaw exercises, role-plays and simulations. In this sense, the practical in the is-when exercise contains the application of theory or of previously defined technical knowledge. But that is not all it is. The theory or the technical knowledge has to fit into, and is expressed as a part of, each student's history and therefore involves risk of the very stuff that constitutes our identity.

For instance, Elena more or less unconsciously put her personal practical knowledge (Connelly and Clandinin 1988) at risk. She was very aware that she as a person was at risk and used the word more than once: 'I decided I would take a risk'; 'if I didn't take risks now'. But besides this deliberate risk, there was very likely a more involuntary risk. Knowledge acquired through previous experience, personal knowledge (Polanyi 1958, Connelly and Clandinin 1988), provides subsidiary tools in Polanyi's sense of that term, tools that are used in present intentions, efforts and actions. Polanyi (1958: viii) suggests that 'personal knowledge is an intellectual commitment and as such inherently hazardous'. Having become part of one's sense of oneself as a person, it is constantly put at risk. Her personal knowledge shaped what Elena did that day in class. Whatever she may have read -- she mentions Solnicki's narrative she read earlier in the term in another experiential exercise -- and whatever she believed about teaching short stories or managing difficult students was at risk and could change at any moment. This mode of change is quite unavoidable. In order to act authentically, the actions that day had to 'fit' with her personal practical knowledge and her personal identity. She might have attempted to enact something else, try out something new, but making changes in those areas is not simply a matter of technique, but a matter of profound personal change.

Did the exercise also contribute to buiding her practical repertoire? Elena reports that she now consistently uses story-telling in her teaching of Secondary English and even more so in her teaching of Theology. Her students always write journals because she values working with their experiences. She asks them to write 'exactly what they feel and think.' If a section is too personal, they should mark it 'DNR' (do not read). Students in turn react to Elena's own, personal stories that she brings into the classroom because she wants to convey to her class that teachers are 'living, flesh-and-blood persons'. Parents in her last parent -teacher meeting reported to her that her students appreciate her personal approach.

JOINT REFLECTION

Adding our own hypothetical thoughts about the process of repertoire building as we imagine and experienced it, we see the process evolve largely within the realm of the practical that has been the focus in Carola's courses. She intended it to produce repertoires that were practical in a non-technical sense. Most practical from this point of view would be any new experience—vicarious or real—that shines some light onto prior, experiential knowledge and helps to extend and revise it. The two are not conceivable one without the other. The new becomes integrated, very likely not as a piece of additional expertise, but as an intimate, hard-to-specify modification of the old and therefore involving personal risk. Such modification can happen automatically within practicum situations and can be promoted through narrative inquiry, individual and collaborative, when some more conscious observation, perhaps even choice, may be inserted. However, deliberate decisions are only part of such a process.

The repertoire acquired narratively may be more valuable as a subsidiary tool than as a piece of technical expertise, deliberately kept at hand for further use. Carola's earlier accounts of her work with pre-service candidates (Conle 1996) explain how this may be so. Her student, Michelle Pinet, related a sudden memory that came to her rescue at a crucial, difficult moment in class. It came unexpectedly and she used it as an analogue for action she needed to take at a particular instance. The memory and the action correspond metaphorically one to the other, a correspondence that is characteristic in resonance-type responses. Also, in one of Carola's cross-cultural education classes (Conle et al. 2000), Dan Blanchard described something similar: He was happy that he had heard many narrative experiences of his immigrant colleagues in Carola's classes. Reliably, the memory of those stories suddenly appear at certain critical moments when he needs help in relating to the predominantly multiethnic students he now teaches. In this way, the stories of his former colleagues have become part of his practical repertoire to appear in times of need. They are not silent instructions he keeps in mind; they are not identical to the situations he encounters. But Dan finds them useful because they seem to automatically guide his actions analogically. The connection between the stories and the situations can be seen as a metaphorical connection that springs up by way of resonance. The repertoire is practical in a non-technical sense. Linda hints at a narrative repertoire when she linkens her dilemma with unruly students to that of Jill Solnicki parytly autobiographical work. Linda had recently read her book for another exercise in our class and apparently some sort of narrative repertoire building was at work.

Yet there is no doubt that Carola's initial phrasing of the request to write up a technique or strategy, to name it, and to provide sufficient detail to elaborate the components of a technique, moves the is-when exercise into the direction of the technical-rational. She is giving in to the need for how-to. Still, the request for a narrative execution of the task adds non-technical dimensions. When teachers and students create a collection of such stories, available for repertoire expansion to anyone who reads them and experiences them vicariously, the acquisition of this repertoire is non-technical. It will be created through resonance (Conle 1996). Resonance-type responses are set off by an image, feeling, or descriptive detail in a story and evoke a similar, but not identical, set of details in another set of experiences. This kind of reaction is as unpredictable, as are responses in everyday interactions, or responses to works of art. Connections create similarity while preserving difference. They are automatic, not consciously directed. They are not necessarily logical. A reader of this article does not have to take our word for this, but might think back to what went through his or her mind while reading Elena's story. Did readers not think of events in their own lives as they read? Was the kind of response they had to the story not quite different to how they responded, for example, to the last two paragraphs? How much more intense and relevant might resonance be, if they read a narrative about a practice in a current field of interest, containing descriptions and possible solutions to their own tasks and challenges?

Carola's dilemma about a combination of the two meanings of 'practical' in the work she offered to her students in the is-when story exercise has not disappeared. It reappeared, for instance, when she read Mitsuyo 1998 reflection on her own is-when story done in 1995. We present our reflection on this issue as a dialogue containing the original 1995 document:

Mitsuyo

I was a bit uncomfortable in taking on the task [assigned by Carola in 1995]. Of the four practice teaching sessions that I had, the third one was by far the worst experience for me. Although (fortunately) I passed it, my associate teacher did not seem to like what I was doing in my classroom. The practice-teaching report I got from her was full of criticisms. After such a miserable experience, I was at a loss as to what I could write about. I did not know what my other classmates were writing, but I suspected that they were writing about a game they had played in class or activities they had designed themselves. For me, I could not write about any of those things. I ended up contemplating for days and finally wrote about a few sporadic incidents which occurred between me and my students. I titled my paper 'Mutual respect'. It consisted of a few examples where I managed to build a good rapport with my students.

You collected our papers on the due date and returned them to us with some written feedback. It turned out that I did not get an 'A+' because I did not name a specific teaching technique or strategy.

Carola

I penalized you for not providing a specific technique because this was what the marking scheme that I had previously negotiated with the class required.[11] Yet, now with hindsight, I realize that you were the student who demonstrated a more Deweyan practice than many other students who described games or other activities that Dewey (1974) would name 'sugar-coating'. The following excerpt from your 1995 is-when story made me realize this point.

Mitsuyo (1995)

The last practice teaching was not particularly an easy one for me. My associate teacher was an extremely busy person, being actively involved in school activities. In other words, she had very little time for me, and therefore I was basically on my own. However, this experience was not a totally unpleasant one, largely because of my students.

It was my first time dealing with senior students, as well as with students with so many different ethnic backgrounds, but it was truly a rewarding experience. I found them to be mature and intelligent, as well as articulate and responsive.

During my two-week stay, I was determined not to be condescending to my students. I realized that by now, they all have a good grasp of what is expected of them, so I never made a big deal in regards to discipline. That is, if the student was absent from class, I assumed that he or she had a good reason to be absent. The same principle applied when students were late.

I had several adult students in my class. One of them, Irina (pseudonym) ... had four children. She occasionally had to miss my class for obvious reasons; one day, her son forgot his lunch so she had to deliver it to school; another day her daughter was sick, and so on. However, when she was able to attend my class, I quietly handed her the material she had missed from the previous class, and quickly explained what she was expected to do for the next class. She just nodded quietly, but she looked grateful. Later my associate teacher commented on the way I handled Irina. She said that if I had been more authoritative, Irina might have walked out of the classroom. [...] She had only come to Canada three-and-a-half years ago [...] with her four children. She is determined to finish high school, but said that at times it is very difficult for her to come in on time or hand in her assignments on the due date. She [once] mentioned that every time she goes to the office to get a late slip, she hears sarcastic remarks which are very discouraging and frustrating for her. [...][12] [It] was a big class with close to 30 students, and they frequently asked me if they may be excused to go to the washroom. I did let them leave if they were the first ones to ask; but if someone had already left the room and hadn't come back, I politely asked the second student to wait until the other person returned. The students had no problems with this arrangement, and politely obliged.

Another thing I did was always to say 'thank you' to my students. Not 'thanks', but 'thank you'. I wanted to show that I was treating them with courtesy and respect. Whenever I had a student present something, or read aloud a passage, I always showed my appreciation. Then they always cheerfully said, 'You're welcome!' A response I wasn't really expecting back from them. However, this proved to me that politeness on my part encourages polite response from them.

JOINT REFLECTION

Mitsuyo attended to the feelings and reactions of her students, as Dewey recommended. She also acted in a way that would not alienate her from her own heritage. Respect is important in Japanese culture. As Wenger (1998) suggested, personal and cultural identities are put at risk in teaching practice. We are not at all sure if Mitsuyo made this link consciously. She does not portray it so. But we believe she acted with her 'identity invested', (using Wenger's words again), and did not want to become alien to herself by foregoing respect in the classroom, even though it was not modeled by the teachers around her. She found this issue important enough to write about and was hesitant and confused by the technical orientation of the exercise. Her attention was, in Dewey's (1974) terms, with the minds and hearts of her students. She reflected on experience to see what helped and hindered. And Carola penalized her for not portraying a recognized technique or strategy.

The dilemma of the practical in pre-service teacher education continues, but so does the conviction, hope and effort to keep practice dialectically connected to theories about 'the practical', as well as to the needs of students who are engulfed in a culture that seems enamored with the certainty technical knowledge offers. We would like to help teaching candidates to become students of teaching. We would like them to acquire a sense of inquiry that will shape their careers. The difficulty lies in convincing them of the importance of inquiry and of viewing inquiry-oriented settings as useful in an institutional context pervaded by the need for rapid development of teaching proficiency. What is seen as practical from the view of gaining proficiency and technical expertise is vastly different from what 'practical' means if inquiry into experience is the aim.

As a final step in our effort to understand the exercise, we consulted two sets of evaluations Carola solicited from students at the end of each term. They were done anonymously, both in 1997 and 1998. Carola asked for reactions to each major course component including the is-when exercise. In 1997, several students commented that the assignment was not clear or easily understood. Some comments: expectations/instructions were not clear; examples would have helped; hard to understand the focus/theme. We interpreted this only partly as Carola not having prepared her students sufficiently. In part, we believe, the confusion resulted from the discomfort narrative expression generates in our non-narrative academic culture, as one candidate commented: 'A bit confusing, didn't really find it that useful. .... I just have a hard time writing and talking about myself, which made this course very difficult for me'. Responding to some of the 1997 comments, Carola in 1998 asked groups of students to evaluate previous samples of is-when stories according to the criteria she would use in her own evaluation, namely: detailed presentation of a technique or strategy; narrative, non-evaluative, open-ended languages; and overall narrative quality, such as evidence of characters, settings, mood and implicit or explicit moral. There seemed to be less confusion, but she did not notice a marked improvement in the quality of the work handed in by a students at the lower end of the marking spectrum. Again, most students commented positively on the exercise in the year-end evaluations.

The actual, practical value of the exercise in repertoire building would of course not be evident at that time, but would only emerge experientially once students were in their own classrooms.[13] However it is interesting to note the sense of usefulness attributed to the exercise by many of the students. It leads us to believe that our meaning of practical had been picked up by these students. The following were comments that suggested this:

- I liked this assignment. It was effective in getting me to think about my practicum experience. In keeping this assignment in mind, I went through the practicum with a heightened awareness of what I was doing.
- *Very* useful. ... Thank you for the most useful course I had at the Faculty. If I'm a more thoughtful and caring and responsive teacher, it's because of you!
- Fun project—thought about times in my life I hadn't thought about.
- Made me more reflective about what I'm teaching and I see that you really need to take the time to do this.
- I hope these will be collected. I think they are a great resource for students. In the future, don't make collecting them to be put in the library an afterthought.
- This has been a course very unlike the traditional, but it has changed or broadened my thinking processes. Thank you.

What advice can we give to those who would like to try the assignment with their students? It was done by us in a narrative context: the entire course orientation was on narrative inquiry. We are not at all sure how it might work outside such a context. Certainly, if the stories were used as cases for discussion and critique, the whole dynamic of the work would change and students would likely write in an evaluative tone, rather than narratively. They would likely offer opinions rather than experiences. Even within a narrative perspective, if the contents of such stories came to be seen as 'facts about myself', the danger might arise of students painting fixed pictures of themselves, something to be avoided in professional development. The sense of inquiry would be lost. The same danger arises if non-evaluative, open-ended language that students' struggle with gives way to factual, conclusive statements. But current academic traditions are based on the latter and the acceptance of narrative expression is new for most university students. For the exercise to really flourish, our pre-service teacher education culture generally would need to have a greater orientation toward both narrative expression and narrative inquiry. There would have to be greater general awareness of the meaning of 'practical' that has defined the location of the work we present. From that vantage point, our exercise is a step into a new academic culture that brings its own dangers and advantages.[14] The reflection we presented here is a personal, practical inquiry into this territory. We hope our readers find in our narration connections to their own practices and to the dilemmas they face.

REFERENCES

Carlgren, I. (1999) Professionalism and teachers as designers. *Journal of Curriculum Studies,* 31 (1), 43--56.

Conle, C. (1992) Language, experience, and negotiation. *Curriculum Inquiry,* 22 (2), 165—190.

Conle, C. (1996) Resonance in pre-service teacher inquiry. *American Educational Research Journal,* 33 (2), 297–325.

Conle, C. (1997a) Between fact and fiction: dialogue within encounters of difference. *Educational Theory,* 47 (2), 181–201.

Conle, C. (1997b) Images of change in narrative inquiry. *Teachers and Teaching,* 3 (2), 205–219.

Conle, C. (1999) Why narrative? Which narrative? Struggling with time and place in life and research. *Curriculum Inquiry,* 29 (1), 7–33.

Conle, C. (2000) Thesis as narrative or, what is the inquiry in narrative inquiry? *Curriculum Inquiry,* 30 (2), 189–214.

Conle, C. (2001) the rationality of narrative inquiry in research and professional development. *European Journal of Teacher Education.* 24 (1).

Conle, C., Blanchard, D., Burton, K., Higgins, A., Kelly, M., Sullivan, L. and Tan, J. (2000) The asset of cultural pluralism: an account of cross-cultural learning in pre-service teacher education. *Teaching and Teacher Education,* 16 (3), 365–387.

Connelly, M. and Clandinin, J. (1988) *Teachers as Curriculum Planners: Narratives of Experience* (New York: Teachers College Press).

Connelly, M. and Clandinin, J. (1994) Personal experience methods. In N. K. Denzin and Y. S. Lincoln (Eds.) *Handbook of Qualitative Research* (London: Sage), 413–427.

Dewey, J. (1938) *Experience and Education* New York: Collier.

Dewey, J. (1974 [1904]) The relation of theory to practice in education. In R. D. Archambault (ed.), *John Dewey on Education: Selected writings* (Chicago: University of Chicago Press), 313–338.

Doyle, W. (1997) Heard any really good stories lately? A critique of the critics of narrative in educational research. *Teaching and Teacher Education.* 13 (1), 93–99.

Elbaz, F. (1983) *Teacher Thinking: A Study of Practical Knowledge.* (London: Croom Helm).

Fenstermacher, G. D (1994) The knower and the known: The nature of knowledge in research on teaching. In *Review of Research in Education* 20, 3–56.

Gadamer, H-G. (1960, 1975) *Wahrheit und Methode.* (Tübingen: J. C. B. Mohr).

Gadamer, H.G. (1972) Theorie, Technik, Praxis. In H.G. *Gadamer, Gesammelte Werke*, vol. IV, (1987) pp. 243–266. (Tübingen: J.C.B. Mohr).

Gadamer, H.G. (1974) Was is Praxis? Die Bedingungen gesellschaftlicher Vernunft. In H.G. Gadamer, *Gesammelte Werke*, vol. IV, (1987) pp. 216–228. (Tübingen: J.C.B. Mohr).

Grimmett, P..P. and Erickson, G. L. (Eds.) (1988) *Reflection in Teacher Education* (New York: Teachers College Press).

Habermas, J. (1984 [1981]) *The Theory of Communicative Action, Vol. 1. Reason and the Rationalization of Society*, trans. T. McCarthy (Boston, Beacon Press).

Kagan, D. M. (1993) Contexts for the use of classroom cases. *American Educational Research Journal*, 30 (4), 703–723.

McKeon, R. (1952) Philosophy and action. *Ethics*, 62 (2), 79–100.

Newman, S. J (1996) Reflection and teacher education. *Journal of Education for Teaching*, 22 (3), 297–310.

Polanyi, M. (1958) *Personal Knowledge: Towards a Post-critical Philosophy* (Chicago: University of Chicago Press).

Russell, T., and MUNBY, H. (1992) (eds.) *Teachers and Teaching: From classroom to Reflection* (London: Falmer Press).

Schön, D. A. (1983) *The Reflective Practitioner: How Professionals Think in Action* (New York: Basic Books).

Schön, D. A. (1988) Coaching reflective teaching. In P. P. Grimmett and G. L. Erickson (eds.), *Reflection in Teacher Education* (New York: Teachers College Press), 19–29.

Schwab, J. (1971) The practical: arts of the eclectic. *School Review* 79 (4), 493–542.

Schwab, J. (1978) The practical: a language for curriculum. In I. Westbury and N. J. Wilkof (eds.), *Science, Curriculum, and Liberal Education: Selected Essays* (Chicago: University of Chicago Press), 287–321.

Shulman, L. S. (1987) The wisdom of practice: managing complexity in medicine and teaching. In D. C. Berliner and B. V. Rosenshine (eds.), *Talks to teachers: A Festschrift for N. L. Gage* (New York: Random House), 369–386.

Shulman, L. S. (1992) Toward a pedagogy of cases. In J. Shulman (ed.), *Case Methods in Teacher Education* (New York: Teachers College Press), 1—30.

Solnicki, J. (1992). *The Real Me Is Gonna be a Shock: A Year in the Life of a Front-Line Teacher* (Toronto: Lester Publishing).

Wraga, W.G. (1999) "Extracting sunbeams out of cucumbers": The retreat from practice in reconceptualized curriculum studies. *Educational Researcher*, 28 (1), 4–13.

Wenger, E. (1998) *Communities of practice: Learning, Meaning and Identity* (Cambridge UK: Cambridge University Press).

Wittgenstein, L. (1953) *Philosophical investigations,* 3rd edn, trans. G. E. M. Anscomb (Oxford: Basil Blackwell).

ENDNOTES

[1] Carlgren (1999, 51) debates this issue.

[2] For a detailed discussion of this orientation see McKeon's (1952) description of what he calls the "logistic" approach to theory and practice.

[3] To the extent that what we present below is practical in Schwab's sense, it is not offered as a proposal to be implemented by others.

[4] This is by now a familiar stance to take. Here I comment only on its importance for teacher education curricula.

[5] Newman (1996: 302) calls Schön's depiction of reflection-in-action "supposed inner reflection" and misleading.

[6] The lack of the general validity of such stories as exemplary cases and the lack of critical evaluation distinguishes the exercise I describe from much of what is printed in the literature on cases (e.g., Shulman, 1992; Kagan, 1993).

[7] The exercise described in this article is therefore very different from the general use of cases, as, for example, described in Kagan (1993) or Shulman (1992).

[8] Pseudonyms are used throughout this story. Some small editorial changes have been made, including the title of the story which was 'Songs, Stories and Satisfaction'.

[9] Some of the students comments from the year-end evaluation in 1997 and 1998 are given throughout this paper.

[10] See also note 6

[11] Mitsuyo also lost marks for frequently using the present tense instead of the past, thus lessening the narrative quality of her account in favour of generalizing remarks. She still found Carola's drawing attention to this tendency useful in the graduate work she finished in 1999.

[12] Some details are omitted to preserve privacy.

[13] We have no follow-up data, in part because there was a hiring freeze at the time and many students took positions elsewhere.

[14] For a discussion of these dangers and advantages see Conle (1999).

In: Teacher's Stories, Teacher's Lives
Editor: Carola Conle, pp. 221-254

ISBN 1-59454-472-7
© 2006 Nova Science Publishers, Inc.

Chapter 10

AN ANATOMY OF NARRATIVE CURRICULA*

Carola Conle

ABSTRACT

As narrative curricula become more diverse and widely established, a clearer understanding of their particular nature and function should accompany their use. I review rather far-flung practices in relation to the particular narrative functions they rely on. I use Schwab's commonplaces as common denominators that cut across all these practices to determine different locations for curricular gain. Then, without wanting to tear apart what is essentially a holistic phenomenon, I find it useful to look at narrative curricula through three different lenses, named by Genette (1980) "narrative", "story" and "narrating." These facets of narrative are highlighted in different ways in various curricula, prompting different forms of narrative engagement. They help me locate and distinguish different outcomes.

AN ANATOMY OF NARRATIVE CURRICULA

Narrative curricula outside the field of language arts and literary education as such are no longer marginal experiments. They have become established in graduate and preservice teacher education and professional development. There

---

* This chapter is an adaptation of an article formerly published by *Educational Researcher*.

have been classifications of educational narratives as well as critiques; there have
been defining statements and prominent reviews. However, specific curricular
elements in these areas have rarely been described and are not at all obvious.[1]

This rather extensive field of narrative activity becomes even more diverse—
and also more traditionally curricular—if proposals for narrative learning in
schools are included. The use of story has been recommended for the primary and
for intermediate education, in the field of art education as well as moral and
environmental education. It has been discussed as an important, though often
neglected, feature of teaching.[2]

Yet within this astonishing proliferation of a field that was in its infancy 15
years ago, there has been no comprehensive delineation of its various
components, no differentiation in the educational functions of these various
components, and no extensive proposals on how one might see the connection
between narrative and curricular learning outside the traditional use of narrative in
literary education.

As narrative curricula become more diverse and widely established, a clearer
understanding of their particular nature and function should accompany their use.
I would like to begin to contribute to this understanding by offering what I call an
anatomy of narrative curricula, that is to say, by reviewing rather far-flung
practices in relation to the particular narrative functions they rely on and how
those functions point to potential curricular results.

Such a review cannot be all-inclusive. The field is too large. However there
are major orientations with regard to intent and curricular use. Specifically,
didactic and instrumental intentions differ from practices where the emphasis is
on experience and inquiry. I intend to select sufficient examples from both of
these orientations to make more subtle differentiations in curricular practices.
Major space will be given to clarify those practices that view narrative research
activities as curricular activities, simply because this overlap is not generally
acknowledged. Examples in this area will come chiefly from my own work and
describe individual and group learning involving personal, experiential encounters
with oral and written narrative texts. These encounters of course are not
necessarily outside the field of literary studies, but they are generally outside of
educational activities aimed at aesthetic appreciation for its own sake or for the
sake of enculturation into the world of literature. Instead, the purpose of such
narrative curricula is to serve in the field of teacher development and in certain
forms of moral education. A notion of curriculum that accommodates such uses
needs to encompass not only planned curricular events, but also informal learning
experiences. It encompasses not only what is explicitly learned, but also what is

learned practically, at a more tacit level, touching not only the intellect, but the moral, practical. imaginative realm.

The curricula-cum-narrative map I intend to provide will be constructed with the aid of two analytic frames, both originating from work done in the sixties and seventies. One derives from the French literary critic, Gerard Genette; the other from the Chicago curriculum theorist, Joseph Schwab's, Aristotle-based "topics" that helped him sort through a field of curriculum in disarray at the time. I use Schwab's commonplaces as common denominators that cut across various practices to determine different locations for curricular gain. Then, without wanting to tear apart what is essentially a holistic phenomenon, I differentiate various possibilities of narrative engagement by looking at narrative curricula through three different lenses, named by Genette (1980) "narrative", "story" and "narrating." These three facets of narrative are highlighted in different ways in various narrative curricula, prompting different forms of narrative engagement. They help me locate sources of curricular learning and serve to distinguish among different outcomes.

In order to proceed with these tasks, I first briefly describe some of the practices from which I will select examples for my analysis. They range from various forms of narrative inquiry in teacher development to case-based instruction, to non-literary uses of narrative in schools.

NARRATIVE CURRICULAR PRACTICES
IN TEACHER EDUCATION AND IN SCHOOLS

It must be assumed that, in teacher education, narrative curricular practices have their roots in, and are historically linked to, narrative research (Conle 2000). In the early eighties, participant observation projects—for example, by Connelly, Clandinin and Fullan (1993)—focused on teacher knowledge and teacher thinking. Researchers, acting as teacher aids, wrote narrative field notes on teachers' activities (Conle 1997b). Listening to teachers, researchers reflected with them about the meaning of their everyday lives in and out of schools. It was assumed that such joint reflection was a form of professional development for the teacher involved. In other words, there was an informal teacher development curriculum enacted in such research activities.

In the eighties, in some graduate teacher education seminars in some institutions, narrative inquiry served as a vehicle in formal graduate curricula (Grumet 1988; Connelly and Clandinin 1988; Nicholson and Conle 1991). When the inquiry in these settings was autobiographical, it was often seen as part of feminist agendas, where women teachers and teacher educators found a particular curricular discourse to reflect on their own experiences. Graduate students began to use narrative language to investigate thesis interests (Conle et al. 1998 [1988]), or to discern and improve particular problems they perceived in their own teaching practices (Hamilton 1998). As specific forms of action research and self-study, such practices have now firmly established themselves in graduate programs when, alongside the research function, curricular functions are intended. Experiences are being investigated narratively, including inquiry experiences They become curricular experiences for the inquirer—and possibly also for the audience, if the experiential narratives are read or listened to by others.

To the extent that the more recent arts-based inquiry (Barone and Eisner 1997) differs from the narrative inquiry described above, its curricular function seems to be particularly aimed at an audience's reception of data presented through performances, images or artistically conceived texts. Creators of such works hope to change members of the audience through the experience of data crafted into various art forms, for example, into plays (Goldstein 2001, Cole and McIntyre 2001). Curricular and research functions are still closely connected.

One might say that almost at the opposite end of the narrative practices spectrum, narrative cases have perhaps the largest and most widely accepted history in narratively oriented teacher education, usually preservice teacher education.[3] Here the curricular function is easily discerned: Cases are used by teacher educators, also educators of nurses and physicians (Shulman 1992, Kagan 1993), to induct neophytes into their profession. They serve as vehicles for discussion of important issues and as means of acquisition of key concepts and practices.

The use of narrative in schools ranges from a proposed need for meta-narratives (Postman 1995) and stories-to-live-by, to moral education (Oser 1994, Puka 1990) to important components of general re-orientations in education (Egan 1997)[4]. Most of these practices are primarily didactic and intend to teach specific, pre-determined things in formal ways. The use of narrative is outside literary education as such, but shares its traditional reliance on powerful cultural functions of narrative: Stories open possibilities to our imagination. The quality of those possibilities is vital to the quality of our future. A person without access to certain stories is a person without hope, without social vision. In Frye's words: "We choose in accordance with our vision of society. The essential thing is the power of choice" (1963, 63). The narratives available to us delimit our areas of choice. It is the narrative repertoire of our imagination that helps us distinguish the world we live in from the world we want to live in. Non-literary uses of narrative in schools still rely on this traditional role of narrative.

In the various uses of narrative curricula in schools and in the teacher education practices, the meaning of curriculum is not the same. Notions of curriculum are diffuse and an inordinately large number of definitions exist (Jackson 1992). I need to specify some common denominators that cut across all of them before I can determine different potential locations for curricular gain in different narrative practices. These locations will be significant when I finally attempt to sort through narrative curricular functions, using Genette's three categories.

LOCATIONS FOR CURRICULAR GAINS: THE FOUR COMMONPLACES OF CURRICULUM IN NARRATIVE PRACTICES

One way of characterizing specific curricula is to examine them through the lenses of the four commonplaces: student, teacher, subject matter and milieu (Schwab 1977, Connelly and Clandinin 1988). These commonplaces combine in different ways, becoming more or less prominent, and more or less salient, in teaching and learning situations. The way they come together in a particular situation has much to do with the quality of teaching and learning in that situation and with particular results. I shall present specific samples of the narrative practices to which I referred above and describe them in terms of the four commonplaces, before distinguishing various narrative curricula according to different narrative functions and point out potential locations for curricular gain. The curricular practices I select range from teacher education to professional development to school practices. It will be important to remember that I do not restrict the term curriculum to the delivery of a syllabus, nor do I see curriculum as always taking place under the guidance of a teacher in formal teaching and learning situations.

The Commonplaces in Narrative Teacher Education Curricula and Non-literary Narrative Practices in Schools

I briefly exemplify various combinations of the four commonplaces (teacher, student, subject matter and milieu) in some of the narrative practices and activities mentioned above.

If the narrative activity tends to have autobiographical learner inquiry as its key component (e.g. Conle et al. 2000), the object of the inquiry is the learner himself or herself; that is to say, the "student" and the "subject matter" commonplaces are hardly distinguishable, even though the student may be examining particular issues or topics in order to get data on his or her own life. If, on the other hand, the narrative activity occurs informally, for example, as part of a participant-observation project in a teacher's classroom (e.g. Connelly, Clandinin and Fullan 1993), the researcher as well as observed teacher—who is also functioning as "subject matter" or object-of-inquiry—are "students" in an informal narrative curriculum, each benefiting in a different way. Moreover, the researcher-student who is setting up this learning situation, assumes a teaching role of sorts—granted very much in the guise of a facilitator and prompter for inquiry. "Teacher" and "student" are co-inquirers and co-learners, each with their own crucial expertise contributing to the process.

The "subject matter" in such teacher education projects is the teacher/student's practical knowledge. It is not taught, but sought out, while the immediate focus is on making sense of lived events. The "milieu" varies greatly, from the helter-skelter of a classroom, to the intimacy of conversation, to the isolation of an inquirer facing her text. All of these are embedded in the research environment of the study. Such settings, the curricular aspects of which are very complex, were prevalent in bringing about major advances in the field of teacher knowledge and teacher thinking (Elbaz 1983, 1991), but were also seen as vehicles for professional development by the participants and therefore had curricular value.

Another narrative curriculum occurs in certain types of action research undertaken by teachers. Here a convergence of the commonplaces "teacher", "subject-matter" and "student" obtains as well, even though the subject matter is usually a specific aspect of the teacher's practice, rather than his or her life more generally, as it is in autobiographical inquiries as such. A better understanding of his or her practice is a personal learning outcome for the teacher involved in action research and may bring about major changes in his or her knowledge. Consequences of that curricular gain may be improvements in the daily practice of teaching.

In preservice case-based instruction, the commonplaces are more clearly evident: the teacher educator clearly fulfills the teaching function, the teaching candidates are clearly the students and the subject matter may vary from philosophical issues (Hare and Portelli 1993), psychological principles (Jackson and Ormrod 1998) to classroom management (Silverman et al. 1992). Perhaps this clarity with regard to the commonplaces of curriculum contributes to the ready appreciation of the use of cases in teacher education and teacher testing, while other narrative methods meet a certain resistance from teaching candidates and administrators who do not see, for example, candidates' self-study on their immediate agenda (Ontario College of Teachers 1999, 2001; Conle and Sakamoto 2002).

The commonplaces in non-literary narrative practices in schools are also quite complex. For example, Egan's (1997) reform proposal to base schooling on achieving various kinds of understanding—some of which heavily rely on narrative practices— involves "students" and "teachers" in a conventional way, while the subject matter is narratively shaped. A similarly straightforward functioning of the commonplaces occurs in Hutchinson's (1998) suggestion to return to narrative's traditional use as a strategy for transmitting ecological and cultural understandings to children. On the other hand, in the moral models approach described by Oser (1994), practiced by Puka (1990) and researched by Conle (2002), the teaching function is in part taken over by the narrating "heroes" and the subject matter may not be easily defined, since, although the stories told may have a specific subject, the curricular aim is a contribution to the moral education of each particular student. The outcome is likely to vary from student to student and may not be detectable at the time of instruction, because it is not likely to happen within the conceptual, but within the moral-practical-imaginative realm, and may only become evident much later in the student's life.

"Milieu" as a curricular commonplace tends to be very similar in narrative curricula as in other teaching and learning situations, except for the requirement that in some of the practices described, the learning environment has to be such that it tolerates and facilitates narrative interactions and these are quite different from the traditional interactions expected in classrooms, especially at higher levels of education. Narrative interactions tend not to accommodate argumentative discussion, but require an atmosphere that promotes personal experiential reactions (Conle 1996), contextual statements and expressive language (Conle 1997b).

Milieu and the other three commonplaces point to the areas in which different functions of narrative produce different curricular effects. Effects are likely to differ to the extent that particular commonplaces function more or less prominently and unambiguously in particular narrative curriculum situations. They point to the locations where learning may take place. For example, if the teacher and student commonplaces merge in narrative preservice teacher education, the candidate will undergo certain experiences (Dewey 1934, 1938) that may tacitly affect his or her personal practical knowledge (Connelly and Clandinin 1988). Whereas in practices where the commonplaces function more separately, we can locate some of what was learned more easily and in more traditional ways of assessing conceptual and performative knowledge[5].

Not only are commonplaces emphasized in different ways, but different narrative curricula require different kinds of narrative engagement. In order to distinguish among these engagements and describe them, I present Genette's categorizations and definitions of narrative functions.

THREE DEFINING FACETS OF NARRATIVE

Definitions of narrative become analytical tools. I use them heuristically in order to get a clearer idea about where one might look if one wanted to point to curricular results. Alongside a tremendous amount of work by narratologists and others (Scholes and Kellogg 1966; Carr 1986; White 1981; Sarbin 1986; Ricoeur 1984, 1985, 1988; Connelly and Clandinin 1990), the word narrative seems straightforward and is understood in its everyday usage. It involves temporal sequence, a plot, characters, a context, and as Kermode (1967) pointed out, a teleological quality or the sense of an ending. For my purposes, Genette's (1980 [French 1972]) seminal analysis becomes most useful. Aimed at distinctions in literary works, it is sufficiently basic and at the same time general that it seems applicable to all the types of narrative materials and activities at issue for the purpose of curricular analysis. Genette prompts me to look at narrative from three perspectives, each affording me a different view: I may focus on events and situations that are being described, that is, on the "story" that is being told, given that the same events can be told in different ways; I may also focus on rhetorical moves that create a particular "narrative" or "narrative statement"; and of course there has to be the actual "telling", without which there would be no statement, and perhaps not even a story to tell.

Without wanting to tear apart what is essentially a holistic phenomenon, I find it useful to look at narrative curricula through these three different lenses. Genette (1980, 25) named them as follows: "Narrative" or "narrative statement" refers to the narrative statement, that is, "the oral or written discourse that undertakes to tell of an event or a series of events." It becomes available for textual analysis and, as a product, it is marked by teachers or gets published in research. In what follows I use the term "narrative statement" for this facet of narrative. For example, the oral account given by a Holocaust survivor to high school students (Conle and deBeyer 2002) will be labeled as a narrative statement. Secondly, what Genette calls "story", he defines as "the succession of events" that are the subject of the discourse or statement. Story is the "totality of actions and situations, taken in themselves, without regard to the medium, linguistic or other, through which knowledge of the totality comes to us." When I feel I have something to tell, it is likely that I have in mind such a set of events and that this "story" prompts me to produce a narrative statement. A survivor of the Holocaust has such a story, but is unlikely to be willing or able to tell it all. On the other hand, the felt obligation or urge to speak is motivated by that story. In very different circumstances, teachers too may feel that motivation, if only in very casual staff room chats with colleagues. There is a certain content that wants to be told, so to speak. Below I use "story" in this sense. Finally, for Genette, there is the act of "narrating", the act of telling (also perhaps writing or filming). It includes the situation in which such acts take place. The "act of narrating" is tremendously important for we create different narrative statements about a particular story in different situations. The curricular milieu in which a telling takes place is likely to have a great influence on the way of "narrating" and on the resulting narrative statement.

Genette's conceptualizations provide me with a framework that serves to discuss various uses and effects of narrative in education. As I begin to work with this framework, it soon becomes evident that different narrative curricula rely on different facets of narrative for their potential curricular usefulness. Without wanting to restrict this reliance to one of the categories in each case, I nevertheless find it useful to explore how various relationships to the three facets of narrative highlight different learning dynamics.

IMPORTANT DISTINCTIONS IN NARRATIVE ENGAGEMENT

The crux of the matter has to do with definitions of narrative and with functions of narrative that are different in different curricular situations. Narrative makes particular practical demands and achieves particular results in different curricular situations. These particularities are of key importance when I attempt to locate sources of learning and possible sites where we could search for curricular results. Let us look at some specific examples of narrative curricula to see how they highlight "narrative statement," "story" and "narrating" in different ways[6].

I begin with a sample from the didactic/instrumental orientation and then move to various samples chosen from the experiential/inquiry use of narrative. Examples of the latter will largely be taken from my own work, since I can understand them as an insider and report on them in a performative rather than an observer attitude.

Cases Used in Teacher Training

William Hare's distinctions about the nature of cases (Hare and Portelli 1993, 19ff) are important. All cases in case-based instruction, he contends, are written for a didactic purpose. Either they serve as vehicles for conveying propositional knowledge and as examplars for ideas that the authors of the cases deem educationally important. (Such cases therefore need to be memorable.) Or, as open-ended case studies, they are designed to raise issues for discussion, and therefore have to "scintillate with some credibility" and "appeal to the teacher," so that the issues come alive. To pinpoint the nature of the narrative engagement in case-based instruction, let us use the following excerpt from Jackson and Ormrod (1998):

> Although thirteen-year-old Connor arrives at Kennedy Middle School each day clean and well groomed, his threadbare clothes set him apart from the other students. After two months, he hasn't found a single friend—a single classmate who will accept him as he is. Connor's impoverished circumstances are called to everyone's attention at the beginning of third-hour history class one day. When Mr. DeVenney is temporarily distracted by a message from the main office, Zach calls out, "Hey, Mickey, what's with wearing the same two pairs of pants all the time? Haven't ya noticed that they're way too short for you and are, like, fallin' apart?" "I can't help it if my family doesn't have much money," Connor replies sullenly. "Like, how poor *are* you? I see you eatin' a peanut butter sandwich and drinkin' Koolaid everyday at lunch. Don't you know that they have free lunches for people like you?" (Jackson & Ormrod 1998, 117)

In this text, the narrating act is played down. We don't know who the narrator is. The focus is on a character and a setting that may or may not be taken from some one's actual experience. If it is "real," we do not get the impression that one of the characters wants to tell his story. Characters and narrator are different people and the story is told because it needs telling in the view of the unknown narrator, although perhaps the narrator is the real life author who wants to present a vehicle for classroom discourse. The details given in the narrative statement are seen to be there for a pre-designed purpose.

In a case such as this, it is the story, in Genette's sense, that is important in a curricular way. It is more important perhaps than the narrative statement, because the aim is to have teaching candidates discuss the situation presented, rather than give, for example, a textual analysis of the narrative statement. However, at the same time, the importance of the story is also diminished, because we suspect that it is made up and we are not as intensely drawn into it as we might be if we were, for example, presented with a colleague's experience,[7] or if the narrative statement were written with all the rhetorical devices fictional writing can muster. Since most cases are relatively short narrative statements written in a summarizing fashion, they do not allow in-depth engagement during the actual reading.

Cases are meant to prompt engagement during follow-up discussion or reflection. Candidates will consider the story and the narrative statement important, if they each illustrate points that they consider significant for their future professional life. Teacher educators using the text hope that it leads the candidates to reflect about professional possibilities. They also know that the narrator/author wants them to handle the material in a certain way. Often there are specific questions at the end of the case and particular outcomes are intended, not for the story as much as for the students who read it. In addition, educators may have their own agendas for the use of cases. As narrative statement, therefore, a case has predominantly instrumental value.

Experiential Teaching Stories in Teacher Preparation

An experiential story of a teaching activity used in pre-service teacher preparation is rhetorically and practically quite different from the cases referred to above. For example, the narrator is one of the characters in the story; the story is not intentionally fictional; and the major curricular function is tied to the act of telling the story.

In one of my pre-service courses, candidates were asked to tell a story of a teaching strategy or technique they experienced and used in their recent practicum. Elena (pseudonym) begins with her worries about her first lesson to a particularly difficult class. She remembers details about some of the students, her associate teacher's comments, and that "the prospects of imparting any knowledge to [her] audience of students seemed quite bleak." The excerpt below begins with her preparation the night before. It so happened that the strategy Elena chose is a narrative one. Other students did not, but it was important that the experience of the strategy was reported narratively. I need to give an excerpt of some length so that the particular experiential narrative quality becomes evident.

With these faces and behaviours imprinted on my mind, I leafed through countless short story anthologies. I couldn't find one that was good enough: some too boring, some too difficult, some too infantile, most outdated. I finally decided on 'The Sniper,' a short story about the civil war in Ireland where a soldier unwittingly kills his own brother, thinking him an enemy. The story had suspense. It was touching. It was real. I felt confident that it would work. Great. The story was selected, but how was it to be taught? I decided I would take a risk. If I didn't try, I would never know. I would scrap the teacher-directed Socratic lesson that my associate adhered to. According to me and these students, it simply did not work -- at least not in this particular classroom: "Hey Miss, are you gonna bore us to death like he does?" I responded to that student that night in my head with a resounding 'NO.' [...]

> I knew that it was a good idea for teachers to try and cater to the various learning styles of students -- to try and appeal to as many of [Gardner's] seven intelligences as possible; to dare to use music and video and movement in the lessons; to make the learning experience as interdisciplinary as possible. This is what I did. I started the class that day by having them listen to a powerful contemporary song by an Irish rock band. Why? Because the song, with its stinging lyrics and intense rhythms, was about the ongoing war in Ireland. They listened attentively, burning holes with their eyes into the lyric sheets I had provided. Why is she making us listen to this?, they undoubtedly wondered. When I explained that the song painted the backdrop for our new short story, I could see in their eager faces that I had broken through. [...]. Most of them knew about the horrors of war all too well [and came from] countries where the politics of fear and injustice were familiar to them.
>
> Something wonderful happened then. Something completely unexpected. They began sharing their stories. Painful stories about the realities of war. They could relate to the anguish in the singer's wailing voice. They wanted to read the story: It wasn't about their particular experiences, but it appealed to their common experience.
>
> We read the story together, in a circle, each taking turns. Some of their thick accents made the comprehension difficult. That didn't matter now. What did matter was that they no longer were preoccupied with how to plan their next escape from this class or how to pass a note to a classmate [...].

Elena then proceeded to have the students teach her and each other the story, in groups, working together on plot, theme, character, and so on. She reported on the presentations and her feelings of joy at the students' success.

I asked them to perform a skit depicting the conversation that would ensue between the sniper and his mother or father -- the very night that the soldier had killed his own brother. The students took this very seriously [...].

I concluded the analysis of this story by showing the class parts from the movie 'In the Name of the Father.' Here they saw the song, the story, and their skits come alive on the screen (Excerpt from Conle et al. 2002).

Taken from real life situations, this piece is used to explore the narrator's own experience, and is also presented to colleagues as an experiential-repertoire-building exercise. Here narrating, the act of telling, is particularly important because the narrator/student-teacher tries to tell/write all s/he remembers of a particular teaching sequence. During this act of telling, he or she is likely to remember or discover incidents and details not held in mind at the outset of the telling. The telling is intended as an act of inquiry and is assigned by the teacher educator for the purpose of having teaching candidates collect some 'data' on their experiences, in order to become better acquainted with their own, often tacit practical knowledge of teaching and learning. As these experiences are shared, listening to a colleague's narrative statement will elicit more 'data' from one's own life. At the same time, a vicariously obtained experiential teaching repertoire is being shaped for each candidate.[8]

The story in such an exercise is important since it usually is one that 'wants' to be told, either because it was at the time a particularly successful professional moment or a very tense and challenging one. The story is also important because it may become part of an experiential repertoire for the author/narrator and perhaps (vicariously) for members of the audience. One might say that in this way it resembles the cases discussed above. However, unlike what happens in cases, an experiential story like Elena's likely enters a colleague's practical repertoire at the very moment of encounter, when the narrative statement and narrating draw the audience into a story that is by them experienced vicariously (Conle, Li and Tan 2002).

Finally, the narrative statement is significant because it—not the lived events or the subsequent discussion—becomes an object of evaluation. In the segment offered above, the student/author received marks according to whether the chosen technique or strategy was described and named in the statement and whether the narrative aspects of plot, characters involved, mood and context were sufficiently evident.

Journal Writing

In journal writing, the extent to which the "student" becomes his or her own "teacher" depends on the "milieu,"[9] which varies from research project environments, to preservice classrooms, to primary or secondary classrooms. Within these contexts, the role of the teacher again varies, e.g. the teacher as audience for a journal may be very much in the student's mind and may be directing a response to a particular issue. Often, however, the teacher image fades as a student writes more and more for him/herself and the act of narrating takes on a teaching function: the student takes on the responsibility for the direction his or her curriculum takes as the narrating progresses. The following sample is one of Christina West's (pseudonym) journals, done early in a project that took three years of data gathering (Conle 1993). As part of a preservice assignment, Christina was asked to write a journal about anything at all, anything that was on her mind:

A friend of mine died last year. She was a very dear friend. Her death still bothers me. Every time I think of her, I think of my past, growing up. She certainly influenced my life.

She lived next door to us, in my old neighbourhood. She was living there when my parents moved there. I got to know her better when I was about nine and offered to cut her grass for her. She was in her sixties at the time and still worked.

In our conversations she found out that my birthday was a day after hers. She would talk to me about the different zodiac signs and what each meant. She described the prominent characteristics that us Aries possessed.

My parents told me that her husband had died a month before I was born. She was an Anglo-Saxon. She was living in the house that her mother and grandparents had owned. The house had probably been built in 1913. I'm sure she had seen many changes in her neighbourhood.

When my parents moved there, it was the time that Italians were immigrating to Canada, especially to this area of Toronto. My parents had no knowledge of English and so were unable to converse with her. [In] my conversations with her, she seemed to be a very prejudiced woman. I think that this stemmed from the fact that she was unwilling to try to understand our culture.

As the years passed, our relationship developed. She was my resource for many areas that my parents were not familiar with in the Canadian way of life. She helped me get started on my stamp collection, she taught me how to type on her antique typewriter and she showed me how to make crepe flowers.

I, on the other hand, was able to interpret my Italian culture and ways to her so she could better understand. I was also the person that was able to do chores for her that she was unable to do. We both learned from one another. We each had a lot to give each other (1989 in Conle 1993).

If this story had a purpose at the time of telling, it was not known to the student teacher/author at the time. Rather, Christina simply felt that this was something she was willing and ready to talk about. How do journals such as these fit into Genette's scheme? Christina created a narrative statement shaped by a story she constructed from events in her life. The story had never been told before and it is very likely that it only came together as a story through the act of narrating provoked by the journal writing exercise. Christina picked these events, out of the blue, so to speak. They were not part of any larger picture, such as a set of stories; they were not part of any task she had consciously set herself. Later, the resulting narrative statement was put alongside of other such narrative statements and became part of a much larger story that gradually emerged and became recognized as an important story of Christina's understanding of herself as an Italian-Canadian woman who had wanted to study Science to prove her father wrong—her father whom she remembered as always putting down women and the value of human relationships.

Christina's curriculum at the moment of journal writing hinged on her readiness and ability to allow herself to scan her life and pick out something she intuitively felt was important, to select "a story" that was created largely by the narrating act itself. In this way, an awareness was created that was to lead her to a particular understanding about her life, her choice of career and about was important for her professionally. The "teacher" commonplace here is ambiguous. I as the teacher-educator/researcher had a teaching function, but Christina's act of writing itself took on some of this role. I of course also took on a student/inquirer role when I tried to understand Christina's narrative statements and the stories implied. This was my function as a participant observer in a research project that did not ignore the curriculum of the researcher.

Narrative Curricula Connected to Narrative Participant-observation Projects

Narrative research that is based on participant observation often has a curricular function alongside its inquiry function when certain narrative curricular practices are incorporated into participant-observer research. When narrative accounts are constructed from field texts and shared with participants as means for the latter's professional development, the researcher and the participant are both experiencing curricular changes. The story in a "narrative account" (Clandinin and Connelly 1991) is predominantly lived by the main character, while the account as narrative statement is chiefly constructed by the narrator-researcher who is generally a minor character in it. The curricular effect is aimed at the main character, although the narrator of course is also in a learning situation. The location for this learning is connected to the spaces created by the writing of field notes and the writing of narrative accounts directed to the participant. I will expand on this notion below.

The following two excerpts (a and b) are taken from a research project where I observed Christina West, as a High School Science teacher, during her first two years of teaching. She had been my research participant during her pre-service preparation year and had written many journals about her personal background (including the one presented earlier). We had met often and there had been many conversations. By the time the following excerpts were written, we had begun to build some trust in our relationship and there was already a large data base of narrative field notes. I focus on these now (excerpts "a" and "b"), even though there were of course taped conversations and journals in that data base as well. What is most striking about these two samples is the fascinating relationship between the potential power of the researcher's narrative statement in a participant's story.

Narrative Field Notes—The Potential Curricular Power of "Narrative Statements" in Christina's "Story"

After presenting a short excerpt from my field notes, I take up the function of narrative statements, of the act of narrating, and of the story in turn. Their relationship is noteworthy in regard to curriculum elements potentially present in such narrative research activities.

Excerpt (a)
    I asked Christina how the two kids that she had had difficulties with in grade ten were, and she just gave a bit of a groan and said, actually, there had been another problem. A girl was attacked in the hall by three female students. The girl apparently said that she was at the wrong place at the wrong time. But she had told Christina that she was now afraid to come to school and she also told her she had thought of committing suicide. When she did return to school, she was doing her work in the psychologist's office the whole day because she was afraid to come to class. Teachers were helping her to do her work there. Christina said there was no room for

Science being done that way. She thought that maybe the girl would have to repeat Science next term. I asked about the other three girls and Christina said that they were suspended (Conle 1993, 247).

There are in this excerpt, of course, two stories: the story of Christina's teaching [minimally present above] and the disturbing story Christina told about the students. She spoke to me between classes, making time in her busy teaching day. As the narrator in the field notes, I rephrased what Christina told me. My language is sparse, there are few details and the plot seems rushed, in strange contrast to the educational and emotional impact the story about the students obviously had on Christina. It was a nugget placed into the flow of field notes covering a day of teaching. I did not add details in my narrative statement to make that emotional story rhetorically more appealing. Still, I believed it to be a faithful rendering of our conversation. Amidst the onslaught of events a beginning teacher faces everyday, my sparse narrative statement merely salvaged something that might eventually become part of an important curricular story in Christina's life.

My field notes were written to be used for further reflection by both the researcher and the participant. As narrative statements they were important because they provided pieces in an extensive 'puzzle' to be reread, analyzed and linked to other such pieces that would eventually form a comprehensive narrative of Christina's teaching and the practical knowledge she had at her disposal. I, the narrator only had a side role to play as a character. But, while Christina was indeed the main character, her story is told through my voice. The narrative statement of Christina's teaching was largely created through my, the narrator's, perceptions and was shaped largely through my consciousness and the details I was able to perceive and chose to put on paper. There always are constraints of course, for the teaching story is lived by Christina, while it is manipulated by me. The rhetorical shape I give it critically influences the narrative statement my participant receives. A 'final' narrative statement [it is never final, but can always be retold] will emerge only gradually as the large database gets reworked, mainly by me, but also through the feedback Christina gives, once she sees the accounts I construct out of my field notes for her approval and reflection.

The act of telling, the narrating in Genette's terms, is very significant in the task of writing field notes. The situation in which they are noted down is key. Are they written from comments scribbled down during the observation? Are they entirely written from memory after the participant observation of the day is complete? Perhaps a day or two later? What does the writer tell herself about the activity?

During the narrating of my field notes, I generally told myself to recover anything from my memory, without filtering for relevance, consulting brief notes taken during the session. I could not decide at the point of writing the field notes what might eventually be significant. I did keep to narrative language, but did not aim the language at Christina as audience. Narrative accounts would be written later to her for that purpose. These accounts could contain sections from my field notes, as, for example, the above piece. The spaces created between the scribbled comments during participant observation, the writing of the notes and the eventual narrative account or analysis are curriculum spaces for me: they are my learning opportunities. Christina's curricular opportunities on the other hand depend on what happens in the spaces created between the lived story of her teaching and the narrative statements presented to her.

The relationship between the narrative statements and the story in such fieldwork is interesting. The story is lived by Christina, and in a small part also by me, as I experience her teaching day. There may be times when the story wants to be told, just as it was the case in the experiential teaching story given above by Elena. Christina's mini-story about her student that day may be one of these moments when a story 'wanted' to be told. Much of the time, however, a story is so much part of ordinary school life that the main character feels no urgency to tell it. Instead, I as the narrator/researcher, noting down details, begin to see a story that should be told. I tell it and give it as narrative statement to the teacher to consider. It is a possible interpretation of her story and I hope that Christina too may recognize it as an interesting part of her life. If that is the case, and if the statement in some way affects the story of her life as she might have tended to tell it, this effect is a curricular event in her professional development.

One cannot over-emphasize the tenuous quality of the story and the major influence of the narrative statement on how a story may develop or even be recognized. The opposite of course is also true, namely that a story may be overly powerful in the life of a participant and that it may not allow in any other, more fragile stories about certain aspects of the participant's life. To make this point more strongly in view of its potential curricular significance, I add still another section of field notes from the same project. Christina's fragile story (recognized by me before it was accepted by her as such) centered on valuing orientations toward learning, nurturing and relationships. These were alive enough in her pre-service year, but became swamped in her first year of teaching (grade nine and ten Science). In that year, school structures and values embedded in high school curricula had fused with Christina's love of Science and her valuing of conceptual content. This combination threatened her compassion, gentleness and willingness to give attention to emotional needs. The following excerpt from my field notes are indicative. In a sense, this excerpt points to a crisis in Christina's teaching stories. It was the day before exams and students would not pay attention to the Science work she wanted them to do:

> Excerpt b.
> The class became extremely noisy. Christina found her own solution to the tumultuous situation. She refused to become an ogre and come down hard on the students; she refused to yell or to send people to the office. She also refused to punish everyone for the inattention of some. Things came to a head on this last day before exams. Christina ended up speaking to only a few interested students and left the rest joking and yelling on the far side of the room. When the students had left, she told me how upset and how discouraged she was. She said that she 'just couldn't talk to them' (Conle 1993, 240).

Christina valued her relationship with students. She also valued the importance of Science. Both had been compromised. Would the narrative statement, the narrative play-back of her situation, help her reflect and recognize how the episode fitted into her private and professional life? Would she accept my rendition of it? In addition to these uncertainties, that are nevertheless the essence of a narrative curriculum here, there are uncertainties tied to interpretation. Without contextual information, and even with such information, the relationship between narrative statement and story is not at all obvious. Does the above narrative statement tell a story about an uncaring, incompetent teacher? Or are these notes misinterpretations by an unsympathetic, untrustworthy observer? Are they both? Or neither? At the time, I believed I wrote about a beginning teacher who experienced serious tensions between two opposing teaching dispositions and teaching aims. But the story behind the narrative statement is not obvious. This, I believe, should be considered a truism with regard to all narratives. But in such tenuousness of story also lies great curricular potential, for the story of one's life is not fixed. One narrative statement does not tell so very much. It can be retold and one's story, even about past events, can become quite different from the way it was once portrayed, by others or by oneself. The intervening narrative statements are key. In taking field notes as narrative statements, the essential point is that the curricular power of the narrator is not to be overlooked.

Arts-Based Inquiry

I include a few observations on art-based research because it overlaps with the narrative inquiry situations I have been describing. However there are some sharp differences. Arts-based researchers do not see themselves limited by the rationality requirement ascribed to the social sciences (Conle 2001). This , in my view, changes locations for curricular gains. Arts-based researchers use artistic means both to prompt inquiry and to represent their findings.[10] For example, Finley (2001) restored and covered with collage a store mannequin to explore her own life history. Nevertheless, arts-based researchers tend to supplement their artwork with narrative statements to convey meaning to an audience and to describe processes of inquiry. These statements that accompany creative acts further reflection and fix the story of the research in discourse.

Unlike other experience-based narrative research with a curricular intent, arts-based researchers do not feel limited by the rationality requirements of narrative inquiry (Conle 2001) in the elicitation and representation of data. The story of the object of inquiry when fictionalized becomes secondary to what researchers and participant consider the most important elements to convey . What counts is the impact on the audience. Also the act of narrating seems less important; not unimportant, but losing in curricular significance to aesthetic doing/making (Barone and Eisner 1997) and to the creative act of engaging in an artistic activity. The presentation of findings to an audience becomes the main curricular event, the curricular significance of which is tied to the stories it evokes in the reader/perceiver/audience. Goldstein (2001) squarely envisages this curricular aim as one of the main purposes of her project. The play she and her participants created from the data of her research is being performed as an artistic as well as an educational exercise. The narrative statement of her work, in the form of a play, takes on a significance that resembles case-based teaching. The case, of course, has been very differently created, being the result of participant observation and being an artistic representation of data. Goldstein revises her play, her narrative statement, to incorporate feedback from various audiences. It is thus never final. When arts-based inquiry is used with such curricular intentions, it seems to recreate the narrating act over and over again, each time in a different curricular situation.

Experiential Narratives in Holocaust Education and Moral Modeling

Elsewhere I describe a four-year funded study (Conle 1997-2001) that allowed me to monitor the telling of experiential narratives to school children by persons who recount some unusual, perhaps heroic, events, or who are leading extraordinary lives that could inform the moral imagination of children. Michael Englishman was one of our speakers. A survivor of the Holocaust, he now tries to help today's students keep in memory something that should never be repeated and is essentially incomprehensible—the persecution and degradation of Jews under Nazi rule. His are narratives of death and survival, and of trying to make a new life.

He told me he would not even try to remember and tell all of the "story," even if he could. It is imperative for his ongoing educational efforts that he finds a balance between the three facets of narrative: between remembering his story and putting together his narrative statements so that the narrating does not stir up too much of the story and bring him nightmares or traumatize his audience.

Each telling somehow adds and changes the story he remembers. The narrating act, Michael told me, was extremely difficult in the beginning; it became less so with experience. It is never easy. It is never exactly the same. Since his audience in part shapes his narrative statements, the act of telling his stories continues to be a learning experience for him. It is part of Michael Englishman's ongoing curriculum as a survivor. On the other hand, he consciously forms narrative statements that can be taken in by young people and have curricular value. They have a definite teaching function and enter students' lives in a curricular way.

Students bring their own constructions to their understanding of his experiences. For example, when Michael described his work at an underground Nazi factory that was built into a mountain, one student reported having imagined this in a desert, another connected it to TV images, a third to the film *Schindler's List*. Like all of us, children connect narratives of the unimaginable to what they can imagine, given the imaginative repertoire they have. It is very likely that each narrative statement widens that repertoire in some way, because new connections are constantly being made, creating substantial extensions of previous images and ideas. Assuming this narrative impact to be a fact, I've made it my task to find a language that allows me to recognize and describe the moral quality of our moral models' offers to children (Conle 2001). I need to ask myself, why are Michael Englishman's narrative statements particularly effective in a particular student's curriculum? What would endanger such effectiveness? How do they differ from well-taught literary stories? Can we know anything about how they become part of children's stories and help them think and act in particular ways? Where might we look for curricular results? These questions I explore elsewhere. Only the last one fits into the scope of this review and is dealt with below. Having given an overall sketch of different qualities of narrative engagement, I need to speak more directly of what I mean when I speak of curricular results.

OUTCOMES OF NARRATIVE CURRICULA

Taking into account the definitions and provisos about narrative curricula given earlier, I am about to consider where one might look for curricular results. Before doing so, I need to say something about what might count as a curricular result.[11] I envisage five outcomes:

Advances in Understanding

Questions may be generated and there may be productive meaning-making as the result of narrative encounters. An example may be the Holocaust education curriculum I just described. Students/inquirers/audiences may come away with a deeper comprehension of particular issues or phenomena . They may understand something differently from the way it was understood before. There may be a deeper appreciation of complexities. Frames of references may become more trustworthy (Barone and Eisner 1997).

Increased Interpretive Competence

Enhanced competence in finding multiple interpretations of a particular event or phenomenon is an avowed aim of narrative activity (MacIntyre 1984, Conle 1997c). Barone and Eisner (1997, 89) believe that narrative should help us notice what had not been seen before and help us know what to neglect in our efforts of interpretation. Student teachers like Elena and her classmates may more readily be able to distinguish and value subtle teaching events once they have narrated and vicariously experienced a great many stories of teaching and learning.

Richer Practical Repertoires

It is hoped that one result of narrative practices will be the development of useful repertoires of both an imaginative and practical nature. While practical repertoires that are readily available for recall are among the aims of case-based instruction, educators using more experiential narratives hope for tacit repertoires acquired through the vicarious experience these practices can provide. These repertoires may not be readily available for conscious recall at, say, a testing question. Instead they become part of some one's personal practical knowledge (Connelly and Clandinin 1988) and appear when the need arises in performance, e.g. during teaching (Conle 1996; Conle, Li and Tan 2002).

Changes in Life

Clandinin and Connelly (2000) have insisted that through narrative inquiry new stories will be told and lived. Autobiographical narrative inquirers have reported specific changes in their personal and professional lives (Lindsay 2001, Conle 1999) or in the lives of their students (Conle, Li and Tan 2002). Others ask educators to avail themselves of the traditional power of narrative to make students' lives more meaningful (Postman 1995) and their actions more socially informed and ecologically sound (Hutchinson 1999).

Visions Gained

One of the greatest curricular results to keep an eye on is the capacity of narrative to bring before our consciousness what might be. Visions of what can be—or of what should not be—are important factors in decision making, and narratives put those visions before our eyes and ears. Moral modeling agendas are shaped by such possibilities. In this respect, it does not matter to what extent the narrative is fictional or experience-based, the offer of what might be is made in both. Arts-based instructors hope for powerful prototypes and canonical images (Barone and Eisner 1997, 86) that may at times elude linguistic description, but tacitly guide action.

WHERE SHOULD WE LOOK FOR NARRATIVE OUTCOMES?

I've tried to show that narrative statement, story and the act of narrating perform very different functions in the various curricula I've selected. The importance of Genette's facets of narrative varies as each facet becomes highlighted or recedes into background in different ways. This variety allows some 'educational guessing' about where to look for curricular results.

Moments of Encounter

In those activities where curricular results depend on the effect of the narrative statement on an audience's own stories, the moments of encounter are obviously key. The chief curricular impact is likely to happen during moments of experience as a narrative is read or heard (Booth 1983, 1988). Examples would be student teachers' encounter with Elena's experiential accounts of teaching strategies, or grade ten students listening to Michael Englishman's presentation. Post-experience reflection and conversational exchange may give direction to this first impact, but could not be significant without it. Narrative moments of encounter are characterized by what Conle (1996) calls "resonance," i.e. the spontaneous metaphorical connection of parts of one's own life to the parts of the narrative statement one is hearing or reading. Feelings and images described elicit "me too" reactions and memories from one's own experience. Narrative encounters that bring about a great many of such connections are particularly productive curricular events, since they facilitate a potential reshaping of one's prior experiences in light of the current encounter (Gerrig 1993).

To a certain extent, such connections, at a continuous but less conscious level, must occur in any effort to understand any narrative that is presented to us. We bring to the words and images given to us our prior experiences with those words and images and the meanings we have associated with them in our imaginative repertoires. This constant evocation of prior knowledge through association contributes to vicarious experience. Gerrig (1993) points to experimental evidence in psychology that suggests that the changes associated with such vicarious experience are less a matter of new images and ideas added to prior repertoires, but are changes of substance, of the old by the new.

Checking for Acquired Content

The curricular emphasis on the moment of experience of a narrative statement is likely to be important in all of the activities described in this article with the exception of case-based instruction, where intellectual follow-up, and subsequent reflective effort is more important than the encounter of some one's story with someone else's narrative statement. In the use of cases in preservice teacher education, for example, it is not the experiential encounter with a narrative statement, but the latter's instrumental usefulness in conveying important content or provoke discussion on such content, that carries curricular results.

These results can be determined more easily than results in experiential narratives, because we know how to probe for the acquisition of content in a student's propositional knowledge. This certainly applies in case-based instruction. It may also be partly useful in more experiential curricula whenever narrative statements convey interesting content. The Holocaust education described above is a case in point. Important propositional content is conveyed. It could be found out what contents were actually remembered. Similarly, Elena's classmates could be asked questions about the contents of the strategy-stories they heard, although Conle and Sakamoto suggest that repertoire-building in that exercise was chiefly experiential and therefore not entirely available for cognitive analysis.

Changes in Life

In activities where the narrating act is particularly important because it potentially changes the story of the narrator during the telling of the story, we might look for curricular results in the narrator's life. We should look for these kind of results in autobiographical theses, as for example in Lindsay's (2001) dissertation, referred to below. We might examine Goldstein's (2001) repeated narrating of her research. One might look for the impact of narrating when a narrator such as Elena writes about her practicum strategies or Christina writes her journals.

Sometimes narrators flatly state that in their view—with hindsight of course—curricular changes have taken place in their personal and professional lives. Lindsay (2001, 198), a nurse educator, who just recently completed a narrative, autobiographical and collaborative thesis, stated: "I can see movement in my life from a frozen, passive position to involvement and awareness." She recognized an old story: "I waited for the perfect nursing opportunity to come along—I watched the parade and waved at the people going by, but kept myself apart at the roadside curb" (198). In Lindsay's view, recognition of an old story is not without practical consequences for current actions: "The stories we reveal as we tell each other of our experiences have meaning in terms of what we do with other people" (195).

Lindsay feels she is now on her way to becoming the author of her own life. The assumption is that our identity and practical knowledge are at least in part constituted by narrative statements and stories we tell and hear, and that it is important to author the stories, not just live them. This is a painstaking, long-term effort: "It has taken me years to look at what happened and even longer to discern meaning from that experience" (79-80). The suggestion is that such reconstructions of experience frees us to be more useful to ourselves and others. Lindsay asks, "How can a nurse be present to a patient, if the situation calls up an experience that has not been reflected on or reconstructed for learning?" (209).

As I already pointed out, it is of course notoriously difficult to ascertain whether such curricular change has indeed taken place. Often teachers or students can tell only with time and with hindsight. These assertions of learning are part of their "story", rather then being statements of fact. Narrative processes of change are diverse and difficult to detect (Conle 1997a). Moreover, one can never be sure of exactly what has taken place, especially in one's own experience.[12] Still, the intuitive sense of change announced in autobiographical research should not be categorically mistrusted or easily dismissed. There are ways of going beyond intuition. They have to do with an examination of sets of narrative statements over time.

Sets of narrative statements created by autobiographers or narrative researchers working with participants can be scanned for evidence of elements of tacit inquiry. Where there is inquiry, there likely is learning going on that can be confirmed by others. For example, as a researcher of Christina's professional development, I had accumulated sets of field texts and they were examined in the construction of narrative unities (Connelly and Clandinin 1986). When I detected changes, they could be confirmed by Christina's sense of what was going on in her life. Or else, an examination of my narrative statements could corroborate her intuitive sense that her story was changing.

Sets of autobiographical statements were also available to me as an autobiographical researcher and I did examine them to detect my inquiry process and the changes it brought. Heeding a participant's, or an inquirer's, intuitive certainty that good things are happening can be useful. I examined how what seemed to be an intuitive realization of change could be corroborated by linking and comparing sets of narrative statements. I picked out key sets and found they were connected by what I called the *third term* in metaphorical processes that linked them (Conle 2000). A particular third term had generated more and more narrative statements because there was something in my story that produced tension and 'asked for' resolution. I called this dynamic that seemed to have pushed along my inquiry, my *tacit telos*. Not being able to name straight off this telos, nor the potential resolution, I had to wait until the inquiry had produced many narrative statements over months and years and until I had an intuitive sense that something had changed in my story of myself. At that point my intuitive descriptions could be corroborated by textual analysis of prior narrative statements. It seems that changes in one's life will be reflected in changed stories one is able to tell about one's life, and in one's own recognition that one's stories have indeed changed, as well as the recognition of others, that these changes became evident through textual analysis.

CONCLUDING COMMENTS

In my attempt to clarify curricular qualities of various narrative practices, I have emphasized the need not to get lost in deliberations, assertions and education recommendations that treat students, teachers, subject matter and social contexts as separate, unrelated entities when curricular matters are discussed. When these four commonplaces are grasped together, yes, notions of curriculum become more complex; but they also potentially become more personally meaningful and socially relevant. Curricular complexity and meaningfulness result from connections to life and quest-like inquiry experiences.

In order to prevent teachers from being viewed as mere technicians, and students as mere receptacles, elements of inquiry and experience in curricular situations need attention. Narrative practices easily comply when they are not completely subsumed under purposes outside themselves: narrative is not merely a good means toward a predetermined end; it does not only serve as useful illustration or to provide telling examples. It is a very complex phenomenon. Because it is pervasive in everyday life, it can create the bridges between the everyday and the academic world that, e.g., John Dewey (1938) had in mind. Hopkins (1994, 146-147) describes what schooling can be like when it stays close to experience, inquiry and narrative. The narrative curriculum, he suggests, if it becomes a main orientation in schools, is "a process propelled by the imperatives of individual self- development," where students routinely ask : What does this subject mean to my life? How does it help me make sense of my life or give it direction? Students might examine economics "from the perspective of the self as an economic actor" or look to the social sciences in search of understanding his or her ethnicity, race, or conditions of life as a social-political being" (147).

When inquiry connects to issues intimately connected to one's life, learning becomes all-important, as important as practicing their art is to committed musicians, painters or poets. As these endeavors, narrative curricula highlight the importance of the moment—the experience of the moment and what happens in encounters with people and things, moment by moment. But how often are teachers and students preoccupied with consequences and ignore how the curriculum is experienced, moment by moment? The quality of the moment can shape motivation and the experience of the moment eventually becomes what we understand by experience when we speak of gaining experience or being experienced.

Yet the close association to art, in my view, must not abandon reason. The narrative curricula I have sorted through should not relinquish the expectation that what they are saying and hearing is believed by the speaker and listener to refer to something true and morally appropriate, and to be truthfully expressed. They may be mistaken, but they do not give up these assumptions when they listen to one another and try to understand one another's stories. These are Jürgen Habermas's (1984, 1987) requirements for a rational enterprise (Conle 2001) that aims at mutual understanding.

I close with a cautionary note: Propagandists of all sorts know that narratives can influence life and can become tools of indoctrination. Sixty years ago, the imagination of a whole nation was shaped by narratives and images of heroism and hate. Today the imagination of our youth is largely shaped by sitcoms, song lyrics, advertisements, TV news items and video stories. These have become tools for understanding and deliver imaginative repertoires. They may very well be regarded as informal narrative curricular delivered to our homes. The curricular processes described above are likely to apply here as well. Greater knowledge of locations for curricular gain, types of narrative engagement, differing functions of narrative and a variety of outcomes of narrative curricula become essential, if we do not want to let these informal curricula go undetected.

REFERENCES

Barone, T. 2001a. *Touching eternity: The enduring outcomes of teaching.* New York: Teachers College Press.

Barone, T. E. 1992. A narrative of enhanced professionalism: Educational researchers and popular storybooks about school people. *Educational Researcher 21* (8): 15-24.

Barone, T. and E. Eisner. 1997. Arts-based educational research. In R. Jaeger (ed.) *Complementary methods for research in education* (pp. 73-103). Washington, DC: American educational Research Association.

Beynon, C., Geddis, A. and B. Onslow. 2001. *Learning-to–teach. Cases and concepts for novice teachers and teacher educators.* Toronto: Pearson Education.

Booth, D. 1994. *Reading, writing and role-playing across the curriculum.* Markham, Ontario: Pembroke Publishers.

Booth, W. 1983 [1961]. *The rhetoric of fiction.* Chicago: The University of Chicago Press.

Booth, W. 1988. *The company we keep. An ethics of fiction.* Berkeley, CA: University of California Press.

Bullough, R. and S. Pinnegar. 2001. Guidelines for quality in autobiographical forms of self-study research. *Educational Researcher* 30(3): 13-21.

Carr, D. 1986. *Time, narrative, and history.* Bloomington, Indiana: Indiana University Press.

Clandinin, D. J. and F. M. Connelly. 1991. Narrative and story in practice and research. In *The reflective turn: Case studies in and on educational practice,* ed. D. A. Schön, 258-281. New York: Teachers College Press.

Clandinin, J., Davies, A., Hogan P., and B. Kennard. 1993. *Learning to teach, teaching to learn: Stories of Collaboration in Teacher Education.* New York: Teachers College Press.

Clandinin, J. and M. Connelly. 2000. *Narrative inquiry: Experience and story in qualitative research.* New York: Jossey-Bass.

Cole, A. and M. McIntyre. 2001. "Dance me to an understanding of teaching": A performance test. *Journal of Curriculum Theorizing* 17(2):43-60.

Conle, C. 1993. *Learning culture and embracing contraries: Narrative inquiry through stories of acculturation.* Unpublished doctoral dissertation, University of Toronto. Toronto.

Conle, C. 1996. Resonance in pre-service teacher inquiry. *American Educational Research Journal* 33(2): 297-325.

Conle, C. 1997a. Images of change in narrative inquiry. *Teachers and Teaching* 3 (2): 205 -219.

Conle, C. 1997b. Community, reflection and the shared governance of schools. *Teaching and Teacher Education* 13 (2): 137 - 152.

Conle, C. 1997c. Between fact and fiction: Dialogue within encounters of difference. *Educational Theory* 47(2): 181-201.

Conle, C. 1999. Why narrative? Which narrative? Our struggle with time and place in teacher education. *Curriculum Inquiry* 29(1): 7-33.

Conle, C. 2000a. Narrative inquiry: Research tool and medium for professional development. *European Journal of Teacher Education* 23 (1) : 49 -63.

Conle, C. 2001. The rationality of narrative inquiry in research and professional development. *European Journal of Teacher Education*. 24 (1): 21 - 33.

Conle C. and M. Sakamoto. 2002. "Is-when stories:" Practical repertoires and theories about the practical. *Journal of Curriculum Studies* 34(

Conle, C., Li, X. and J. Tan. 2002. Connecting vicarious experience to practice. *Curriculum Inquiry* 32 (4):

Conle, C., Louden, W. and D. Mildon. 1998. Tensions and intentions: Joint self-study in Higher Education. In Hamilton, M.-L. [ed.] *Reconceptualizing Teacher Research as Self-Study*. London and New York: Falmer Press.

Conle, C., with Blanchard, D., Burton, K., Higgins, A., Kelly, M., Sullivan, L. and J. Tan. 2000. The asset of cultural pluralism: An account of cross-cultural learning in teacher education. *Teaching and Teacher Education* 16 (3): 365 - 387.

Connelly, F. M. and D. J. Clandinin. 1986. On narrative method, personal philosophy and narrative unities in the study of teaching. *Journal of Research in Science Teaching* 23(3): 15-32.

Connelly, F. M. & D. J. Clandinin. 1988. *Teachers as curriculum planners: Narratives of experience.* New York: Teachers College Press.

Connelly, F. M. and D. J. Clandinin 1990. Stories of experience and narrative inquiry. *Educational Researcher 14* (5): 2-14.

Connelly, F. M., Clandinin, D. J. and Fullan, M. 1993. *Teacher education: Links between personal and professional knowledge.* Final report to the Social Sciences and Humanities Research Council. Toronto: Joint Centre for Teacher Development, OISE and University of Toronto.

Dewey, J. 1934. Art as experience. New York, NY: G. P. Putnam's Sons.

Dewey, J. 1938. *Experience and education.* New York: Collier Books.

Diamond, P. and C. Mullen. 1999. *The postmodern educator. Arts-based inquiries and teacher development.* New York: Peter Lang.

Doyle, W. 1997. Heard any really good stories lately? A critique of the critics of narrative in educational research. *Teaching and Teacher Education.* 13(1): 93-99.

Drake, S. 1992. *Developing an integrated curriculum using the story model.* Toronto: OISE Press.

Egan, K. 1986. *Teaching as story telling: An alternative approach to teaching and curriculum in the elementary school.* London, Ontario: Althouse Press.

Egan, K. 1997. *The educated mind. How cognitive tools shape our understanding.* Chicago and London: University of Chicago Press.

Elbaz, F. 1983. *Teacher thinking: A study of practical knowledge.* London: Croom Helm.

Elbaz, F. 1991. Research on teachers' knowledge: The evolution of a discourse. *Journal of Curriculum Studies,* 23, 1-19.

Fenstermacher, G. 1994. The knower and the known: The nature of knowledge in research on teaching. *Review of Research in Education* 20: 3 - 56.

Finley, S. 2001. Painting life histories. *Journal of Curriculum Theorizing* 17 (2): 11-26.

Frye, N. 1963. *The educated imagination.* Canadian Broadcasting Company Massey Lectures Series. Toronto, Ontario: Anansi.

Genette, G. 1980. *Narrative discourse.* Oxford: Basil Blackwell.

Gerrig, R. 1993. *Experiencing narrative worlds. On the psychological activities of teaching.* Newhaven and London: Yale University Press.

Goldstein, T. 2001. Hong Kong, Canada: A one-act ethnographic play for critical teacher education. *Journal of Curriculum Theorizing 17(2) : 97-110.*

Gudmundstrottir, S. 1991. Story-maker, story-teller: Narrative structures in curriculum. *Journal of Curriculum Studies* 23(3): 207 -218.

Grumet, M. R. 1988. *Bitter milk: Women and teaching.* Amherst, MA: University of Massachusetts Press.

Habermas, J. 1984 (German 1981). *The theory of communicative action. Volume One. Reason and the rationalization of society.* Boston, MA: Beacon Press.

Hare, W. and J. Portelli. 1993.*What to do? Case studies for teachers.* Halifax: Fairmount Books.

Hamilton, M.-L. [ed.] 1998. *Reconceptualizing Teacher Research as Self-Study.* London and New York: Falmer Press.

Hopkins, R. 1994. *Narrative schooling. Experiential learning and the transformation of American education.* New York: Teachers College Press.

Hutchinson, D. 1998. *Growing up green: Education for ecological renewal.* New York: Teachers College Press.

Hutchinson, D. 1999. The story of the universe: Ecology and narrative. *Orbit,* 30(3): 24-25.

Jackson, D. & J. E. Ormrod. 1998. *Case studies. Applying educational psychology.* Upper Saddle River, NJ: Prentice-Hall and Simon and Schuster.

Jackson, P. W. 1987. On the place of narration in teaching. In D. Berliner and B. Rosenshine (Eds.), *Talks to teachers* (pp. 307-328). New York: Random House.

Jackson, P. W. [Ed.] 1992. *Handbook of research in curriculum. A project of the American Educational Research Association.* New York: MacMillan Press.

Kagan, D. M. (1993) Contexts for the use of classroom cases. *American Educational Research Journal*, 30 (4), 703-723.

Kealy, W. and C. Mullen. 1999. "From the next scale up": using graphics arts as an opening to mentoring. In C. T. P. Diamond and C. Mullen (eds.), *The postmodern educator. Arts-based inquiries and teacher development.* New York: Peter Lang Publishing.

Kermode, F. 1967. *The sense of an ending: Studies in the theory of fiction.* London: Oxford University Press.

Kuhmerker, L. 1994. Curriculum review: Standing tall. Teaching guides for Kindergarten to Grade 12 from the Giraffe Project. *Moral Education Forum* 19 (4): 35 -37.

Lindsay, G. 2001. Nothing personal? Narrative reconstructions of registered nurses' experience in health care reform. Unpublished doctoral dissertation. Toronto: University of Toronto.

MacIntyre, A. 1984 [1984]. *After virtue: A study in moral theory.* Notre Dame, IN: University of Notre Dame Press.

Moll, L. 1990. *Vygotsky and education: Instructional implications and applications of sociohistorical psychology.* Cambridge: Cambridge University Press.

Mullen, C. 1994. A narrative exploration of the self I dream. *Journal of Curriculum Studies 26*(3): 253-263.

Mullen, C. 1997. Hispanic preservice teachers and professional development; stories of mentorship. *Latino Studies Journal* 8 (1): 3-35.

Nicholson, K. and C. Conle. 1991. Narrative reflection and curriculum. Paper presented at a meeting of the American Educational Research Association. Chicago, April 1991.

Ontario College of Teachers. 1999. *Standards of practice for the teaching profession.* Toronto: Ontario College of Teachers.

Ontario Principals Council. 2001. *Ontario teacher qualification test case study pilot.* Princeton, NJ: Educational Testing Service.

Oser, F. 1994. Moral perspective on teaching. *Review of Research in Education,* 20: 57-127.

Paley, V. G. 1979. *White teacher.* Cambridge, MA: Harvard University Press.

Paley, V. G. 1981. *Wally's stories: Conversations in the kindergarten.* Cambridge, MA: Harvard University Press.

Phillips, D. C. 1994. Telling it straight: Issues in assessing narrative research. *Educational Psychologist. 29* (1): 13-21.

Postman, N. 1995. *The end of education.* New York: Knopf.

Puka, B.1990. *Be your own hero. Careers in commitment.* Troy, NY: Rensselaer Polytechnic Institute.

Ricoeur, P. 1984, 1985, 1988. *Time and narrative,*Vols.1, 2, 3. Chicago: University of Chicago Press.

Sandlos, J. 1998. The storied curriculum: Oral narratives, ethics, and environmental education. *The Journal of Environmental Education.* 30(1): 5-9.

Sarbin, T. R. (Ed.). 1986. *Narrative psychology: The storied nature of human conduct.* New York: Praeger.

Scholes, R. & R. Kellogg. 1966. *The nature of narrative.* Oxford: Oxford University Press.

Schubert, W., and W. Ayers (Eds.). 1992. *Teacher lore: Learning from our own experience.* New York: Longman.

Shulman, L. S. 1992. Toward a pedagogy of cases. In J. Shulman (ed.), *Case Methods in Teacher Education*, pp. 1-30. New York, NY: Teachers College Press.

Silverman, R., Welty, W. and S. Lyon. 1992. *Case studies for teacher problem-solving.* New York: MacGraw-Hill, Inc.

Schwab, J. J. 1977. Structure of the disciplines: Meanings and significances. In A. A. Bellack & H. M. Kliebard (Eds.), *Curriculum and evaluation*, pp. 189-207. Berkeley, CA: McCutchan Publishing.

White, H. 1981. The value of narrativity in the representation of reality. In W. J. T. Mitchell (Ed.), *On narrative.* Chicago: University of Chicago Press.

ENDNOTES

---

[1] In graduate programs, narrative has become established in the professional development of teachers (Grumet 1988, Connelly and Clandinin 1988, Clandinin et al. 1993, Schubert and Ayers 1992, Paley 1979, Barone 1992, Mullen 1994, Conle 1997b). Narrative inquiry practices in preservice teacher education are beginning to be documented (Conle 1996, 1997b, 1997c; Conle et al. 2000). There have been classifications (Connelly and Clandinin 1990, Elbaz 1991),

critiques (Phillips 1994, Doyle 1997), defining statements (Conle 2001, Bullough and Pinnegar 2001) and reviews (Fenstermacher 1994).

[2] For the use of narrative in the primary classroom see Egan (1986), Paley (1981); in intermediate education, Egan (1997), Drake(1992), in art education, Booth (1994), in moral education, Puka (1990) and Kuhmerker (1994); and in environmental education, Sandlos (1998) or Hutchinson (1998). It has been discussed as a feature of teaching (Jackson 1987, Gudmundstrottir 1991).

[3] See Sykes and Bird (1992), Silverman et al. (1992), Hare and Portelli (1993), Jackson and Ormrod (1998), Beynon et al. (2001).

[4] Egan (1997) offers a radical reorientation of education, taking the notion of "understanding" to completely refocus our current aims of education.

[5] A specific discussion follows near the end of this article.

[6] These are the terms I will use throughout the article when I refer to Genette's categories.

[7] Conle, Li and Tan (2002) and Conle (1996) give examples of teaching candidates' intense involvement with each other's experiences.

[8] Although the connections were not explored by me at the time, a relationship likely exists between the repertoires referred to here and the "funds of knowledge" described by Moll (1990, chapt. 14).

[9] I italicize to remind the reader that I am using Schwab's terms here.

[10] These means range from folk art objects (Finley 2001), to metaphor (Mullen 1997) to fiction (Barone 2001a) to graphics (Kealy and Mullen 1999) to drama (Goldstein 2001) and dance (Cole and McIntyre 2001).

[11] Keeping in mind the narrative curricula reviewed here, I of course put aside enculturation into a literary canon, the development of capacities for literary criticism, and increased capacities for the appreciation of literary texts for their own sake.

[12] Habermas (1984) made it clear that the abandonment by philosophers of a philosophy of consciousness in favour of a philosophy of language discredits the Cartesian notion that we can indeed know the contents of our consciousness, a capacity already doubted since Freud's work in psychology. See also Conle (1999).

INDEX

R

S